I0471440

Torrey Holloway

Contact 727-851-1337

Fast Cash

A Novel

By

Torrey Holloway

Fast Cash

A POWERFUL MOVEMENT

TORREY HOLLOWAY

SELF PUBLISH: LULU.COM

EMAIL TORREY AT: torreyholloway50@yahoo.com

Contact Torrey at: 727-641-4940

Google Torrey T Holloway for comment: myspace, Facebook, createspace.com, and LuLu.com

Barnesandnobles.com, Amazon.com

Also, you can find Torrey in some games:

Final Fantasy XI online: world Asura Character Torrey

Dark ages of Camelot online: world Tristan Hibernia Character Torrey

Born and raised in St. Petersburg Florida R.I.P. Mable Brown who raise me and my brother Jermaine and sister Angela along with my step Grandad R.I.P Tom Harrell my mom Shirley Holloway and dad C.J. Holloway Through y'all created a light for the future Thank you all and love you. God Bless.

Thank you

First off, I would like to thank God, through him comes many blessings. I want to thank my mom for having me. Thank you: Teresa Patterson my editor, Olga and Dexter (Tony), Theresa Almost, Bosco Brown, Avis Rambue, Wendy, Ella, Linda & Tom, Melissa John, Marisol, Rika, Charise, Jermaine bro thank God you free, my grandma Mable R.I.P. who believed in me, Frank Gray a good man I mean a blessed man 4 real. If I didn't name you it's cool because these are the ones read my book so far and feels me…its cool just catch up, I promise your name will be on the next one.

Fast Cash

Torrey Holloway

PROLOGUE

So much time had passed. I couldn't believe those motherfuckers had finally caught me. I stood in the L.A.P.D. precinct caught like a motherfucker. This shit is surreal. After all this time, I am about to lose my freedom. Shit! Hell! Fuck! Damn!

I knew they'd soon be bombarding me with a lot of questions, but I'd be dam if they'd get any answers.

"Sit down," Mr. Dirty-Wannabe-Harry instructed. I immediately knew I would have to remain calm before I ended up in a worse situation.

I continued to stand. "Nah, I'd rather stand," I responded. "It makes me feel comfortable."

"Well, it makes me feel uncomfortable. So, fuck your feelings and sit your ass down!" he yelled as he kicked a chair toward me.

I wondered why when the police arrest people; they take them downtown for questioning. Why couldn't they either question them on the spot or just take them to jail and wait until their court date? Instead, they take them to their station and place them in an empty room with a long table surrounded with chairs. The room was set up like a courtroom; just like the set-up I was looking at. I was the defendant. They were the prosecutor, the judge and the jury. It's a losing battle.

I reluctantly took a seat, eyeing the officer suspiciously. I trusted him about as far as I could throw his ass.

"Okay, now look." He pointed a stubby index finger at me. "We can do this the easy way and get it over with, or we can do it the hard way and still get it over with. The choice is yours."

He was supposed to be putting fear in my heart. It wasn't working. I giggled as I looked at his fat, out-of-shape ass. You could tell he had eaten his share of donuts.

"What's so fucking funny? You think this is a joke?" he bellowed. A vein in his throat popped out as he yelled. "You think this is fun and games, boy? Are you having fun?" He was stressing. I mean, spit flew from his mouth and everything. I tried to control my laughter, but the shit was hilarious.

A black officer entered the room upon hearing the commotion. He stood in the doorway looking like he was Head of State or something. I almost gave him a salute but refrained.

The white officer slammed his fist on the table in front of me. The noise left a loud ringing sound in my ears.

"Okay, Mr. Player. It's time to start talking," he snarled. He glared at me as he and the black officer got ready to demolish my ass. I gave them both the silent treatment. Shit, if I told the truth, I might as well prepare to be locked up for a long time.

I folded my arms across my chest and leaned back in the chair. The only thing I could do was think about RonRon and how I got caught up in this bullshit in the first place.

In the beginning

CHAPTER 1

Nothing had ever been given to me while I was growing up. I had no father figure, and I didn't have any male guidance either. There was only me and my older brother, Jermaine. Mom did the best she could; she tried to raise boys into men, but you know how that goes. We were doing okay until our lives got thrown into a whirlwind when she died.

My brother and I is two years apart. Even though we are adults, we lived together. When mom passed away eight years ago, I was only eighteen and my brother twenty. She left us the house, but we had to figure out how to keep it. Like the saying goes, "Nothing in life comes for free."

My brother worked, but I've never had a job. Hustling was my thing. Every day I was on the block in my neighborhood making money. I was my own role model, but the rap industry guided me.

I had skills as a MC. Some of us free-styled and battled each other, mostly to kill time, but mainly to get paid.

It's said that money is the root of all evil, but without money you had basically nothing. It was hard to get money without a j-o-b. And jobs were hard to come by these days. Being unemployed could lead to multiple ways of trying to get money. You thought about robbing, stealing, conning others, and so on. You just had to have money in order to make it in this world.

Did I feel that money was the root of all evil? No, but the love of it was. I should know. Let me explain how I went from rags to riches.

September 13, 1996

My life was changing, and I hoped it was for the better. One of my homeys, Bosco, was getting out of prison after being incarcerated for seven years in Bushnell Florida. We sat on the block in front of my house waiting for Bosco to hit our street. Getting out of prison was a cause to be celebrated. My brother was already gone to go pick him up.

It wasn't long before they pulled up in our driveway.

"There's my homey!" I yell, jumping up to go see him. Everybody rushed pass me to get to him first. I just backed up and sat down, shaking my head. The neighborhood females hug and kiss all over him. They acting like they all want to be the first in line to get banged. He shook them off and heads my way. They should have known he was going to holla at me before he put his attention on anything else.

"What's up, 50ty?" he greeted. I glanced at him, seeing how much weight he'd gained since being locked up. I stood face-to-face with him, letting him know I wasn't scared to stand face-to-face with anyone. The rapper Bone Crusher said it best: "I am not never scared."

"What's up?"

He stepped back then slapped me on my chin. My reaction was dangerously swift. I caught him with a two-piece slap on his chin. We playfully grabbed each other. He may have gained weight in prison, but I still slammed him in the grass. We began wrestling while everybody stood around laughing and cheering us on. It wasn't long before we grew tired.

"So, how is life treating you in the business?" he asked as we brushed ourselves off.

"Shit, nothing's changed in this ghetto lifestyle, except the new generation is trying to take over," I said.

"We can stop that easily," he replied.

"They got to eat too, Bosco." I laughed. "Besides, there's enough money in the hood to be made for everybody. Anyway, welcome home," I said, passing him a blunt and a bag of weed.

"Damn 50ty, you must remember who's the best roller in the hood," he said, smiling.

"No doubt! That's why I gave it to you, homey," I responded, and he laughed uproariously. I joined in. "Man, let's go inside and smoke out."

"Bet it up," he said, following me inside.

Some of the girls standing around frowned in disappointment when Bosco headed inside. The women would just have to wait their turns. Bosco and I had to get our smoke on, an catch up on old times.

We stayed up all night getting wasted and tripping off the past.

"Yo, 50ty man, I'm glad to be back." He gazed at me. His eyes were red and slanted from the weed we'd been smoking all evening.

"We are connected again like an electric wire. It's going to be back on and popping," I said

"I know that's right, on like a chicken bone." We laughed. "Man, I got to dip, I still haven't made it around there to see my folks yet," he said.

"Nigga, it's too late to go 'round there now," I told him, bursting into giggles.

"Right. Right."

"Besides, I don't think you can make it, dawg. You fucked up."

"I guess I'll crash on ya couch, if it's okay."

"That's cool." I watched as he got up and wobbled from the room. That only elicited another fit of giggles from me. "Man, I got to stop smoking this stuff," I said and plopped back on the bed. It wasn't long before I was knocked out.

*** * *

Days passed in the Palmetto neighborhood. Everybody was on their daily schedule. They worked, went to school, or hustled. I hadn't heard from Bosco since the day he returned from prison. Jermaine told me that he was trying to get his life back on track. Shit, I felt him. My mom always told me and Jermaine to work in order to build up social security benefits. That way, we could have something to fall back on when we got older.

Mom had good intentions. It must have sunk into Jermaine's head, but it flew right over mine. I couldn't see myself working on anybody's job. With my lifestyle, I wasn't planning on living to become too old anyway.

CHAPTER 2

October 11, 1996

I decided to take it easy that particular day. I'd been hustling for a whole month, day in and day out. I hadn't even stopped to take a decent shower; I took a few quick ones. Showers weren't that important, it was my money that made me so fly.

Today, I took my time and lathered up really good. I touched up on the rough spots, letting the water hit me in all the sore places. There was no need to rush because I had all day.

As I got out the shower, I heard my cell phone ringing. I tied a towel around my waist and grabbed it. It was Bosco.

"What's up, pimping?" I answer.

"Dawg, I need to holla at you," he said, sounding kind of down.

"Alright. Just come on over," I told him.

I went back into the bathroom to shave. I was putting on my clothes when I heard a tap at my window.

Damn, he must really have something major to tell me, I said to myself.

I pulled up my Jordan's shorts, went to the window and gazed out. As I figured, it was Bosco. I signaled through the window for him to go to the front door and come inside. Minutes later, he was in my room.

"What's up, dawg?" I asked. I put on my jewelry as he sat down looking depressed.

"Nothing homey, it's just that I need a job and these motherfuckers won't hire me because I have a record."

"Bro, you don't need a job. There's money to be made out there, you just need to get out there and get it," I responded as I grabbed my keys off the dresser. "Let's bounce, dawg."

As we headed for the car, Bosco walked with his head down. He seemed defeated.

"Tell me something, homey." He had my full attention because of the strange way he acting.

"What's up?" I asked as I backed out the driveway.

"What are your future plans in life? I know I'm tired of Florida. I want to leave this place and never return- not even to visit." I just looked over at him, saying nothing. "I'm serious, 50ty. I can't deal with it no more. I don't know if it's because I was locked up for too long or what. I just can't see myself nickel and dime collecting, here in there. I can't see myself being here any longer."

"Damn, what's up with you?" I asked, because he was tripping hard.

"You aren't feeling me at all, homey. I need money, not change."

I pulled out an already rolled Blunt and passed it to him. He lit it up and took a drag as we rode up First Avenue North in St. Petersburg.

"I feel you," I told him. "But a million dollars is not going to be handed to you just because you asked for it. If you need it, you got to go get it, so I suggest you stop tripping' and get paid."

"Listen, 50ty, all you see out there is people hustling, working hard and shit, trying to make a living. I might as well have stayed in prison than to get out and be diss. I'm just trying to get a job in order to make it."

"I feel what you're saying, it's hard trying to come up, especially if you're not a rapper, lawyer, judge, or a porn star." We both laughed.

"Shit, even them porn stars be going broke." He passed me the Blunt and I hit it a few times.

"Man, pass me that Blunt. What you trying to do, make love to it?" He laughed. I handed it back.

"Shit, I don't see any other way out for me," I admit. "I can't work on no damn piss paying job, that little paycheck Jermaine brings home is a fucking joke. I just can't see myself settling for chunk change like that."

"We are men now 50ty, we don't need to stick our hands out to get them dirty. We need to stick our hands out and get that money. You know what I mean?" I looked at dude and fell out laughing. He was acting like he was tripping off X or molly's or some other shit.

"I'm serious, 50ty." He continued without cracking a smile. "I'm talking some serious shit, man, why get our hands dirty? Hey, pull over at this corner store," he said suddenly.

"Aiight." I pulled into a parking space, and we both got out the car. Bosco stopped me as I was closing my door.

"You can stay in the car, I'll grab you a soda and some chips," he said.

"Aiight." I responded getting back into the car to wait.

I thought about what Bosco was saying, it's true, but it would be impossible to find a way out the game. Besides, I didn't know any other way of living except for hustling.

*****

I got tired of thinking, tired of waiting, too. It been ten minutes. It shouldn't take Bosco that long to grab whatever he was going to grab from the gas station. It appeared to be empty of any other customers.

I got out the car, aiming to find out what was taking so long. All of a sudden, I heard three gunshots. My heart began pounding in my chest. I ran quickly inside the store and saw Bosco laid out on his back. His eyes were wide opened, looking toward me. His body shook. He had a bag of money in one hand and a gun in the other.

"Freeze motherfucker!" an Asian man yelled at me. "Are you with him?"

"No! No! I just got here," I said quickly. "What happened?"

"Man, here try and rob store," he explained in his accent. "I shoot him as he tries to run off with my money."

I looked at Bosco lying there in a pool of blood. His body stopped shaking. I was in shock. I could barely breathe and I felt numb inside. Why would Bosco do some dumb shit like try to rob a store? Damn, he fucked up. Damn! Damn! Damn! Had I known what he planned to do, I would have tried to talk him out of it. Shit!

The city streets soon filled with the sounds of sirens. First, a fire truck pulls up, then the police. They rushed inside the store. One officer came back out, opened up his trunk, and took out yellow tape. He began to rope off the front of the store.

I just continued to stare at Bosco still body until they placed a white sheet over him. People began to gather around the tape. I stood there speechless.

An officer came over and tried to talk to me.

"Did you know the perpetrator?" he questions.

I shook my head. "No, I never seen him before," I lied.

"Did you see what happened?"

"I didn't see anything, I had just pulled up when I heard gunshots," I said. "Man, I don't feel like talking, like I said, I didn't see anything." I refused to answer any more questions.

After one last look at Bosco sheet covered body, I climbed into my car and left the scene, eyes burning with unshed tears.

*** * *

I couldn't sleep for three days straight after Bosco death. Over and over, I kept replaying the last conversation we had in my head. Why hadn't I realized that something was going on inside of him? Maybe I could have saved him.

On the Saturday of his funeral, it felt like he'd just gotten killed. We were all in gloomy moods. I guess it was because it would be our last day seeing Bosco…forever.

I rented Versace suits for Jermaine and me to wear to the funeral. When we walked outside, I was not surprised to see everybody gathered on the block ready to go pay their last respects to Bosco.

Jermaine and I trailed the limo that Bosco mom and dad rode in. Pulling up at the church, I had a sick feeling in my stomach. I couldn't stop thinking about how much Bosco was stressing the day he got killed. I should have done something, tried to reach him. Now, his life was over, it is a damn shame.

It was tough sitting on the front view and watching everybody fill by his casket. Listening to his family members cry and watching his mom's reaction made my stomach flip-flop. I kept thinking about the day of my mama's funeral and burial.

Tears clouded my vision as I stood. I walked up to Bosco casket. I stared down at him for a long time. He seemed so at ease, peaceful. It was like he was sound asleep. I wondered where he was. Was he in heaven or hell? Was he there watching himself being mourned by his family and friends? "Wherever you're at, I know you're at peace now. We'll stay strong and carry on, playa," I whispered and looked at his face one last time before I walked out of the church.

*****

A week had passed since Bosco funeral and I still didn't have my mind and soul together. I kept hearing a voice in my head telling me: "Get paid and find a way out of the game." Not having any more cash was bringing me down. I was not in the mood for hustling. I just couldn't hustle hand-to-hand anymore. I was too old for that. But, I knew I needed money, and I still didn't plan to work on nobody's job. Something had to come my way.

I got out of the house, trying to clear my head. I ended up at a place called Child's Park. I sat on a bench by myself, deep in thought. I thought of all kinds of ways to get paid. I could try rapping, being a DJ, writing books. I needed to do something because I needed money fast. There was only one way I knew of that would work for me. Judging by what happened to Bosco, it was not a good idea.

I tried to switch my train of thoughts, but couldn't. Bosco actually was onto something, but he moved too quickly. He hadn't planned and strategized. Maybe I could do the same thing, just plan it out.

My brain was really churning because I was onto something. I looked around nervously. I was tripping. It wasn't like anyone could read my thoughts.

I knew exactly what I could do. Some of the drug dealers around the city had more money than they really needed. I saw them flashing the big rolls and fronting like they had the best lives. I could jack one of them. Hell, they had more than enough to share.

I laughed out loud and looked around again. I was still alone so I relaxed and kept thinking.

If I hit somebody, it would have to be worth it. I figured I'd have a 70/30 chance of getting away clean. If I did something so dangerous, it had to be for a lot of cash.

Who had that kind of bank?

I racked my brain until I came up with my first victim. It was this big-time drug dealer named G-Rod. I didn't know him personally, but I'd seen him around.

I will plan to find out all I needed to know about him before I made a move. But, for the time being I'd just chill and focus on a fine lady I saw approaching me. Did Janet Jackson have a twin?

CHAPTER 3

Tuesday, October, 31 1996.

Halloween Day.

For two weeks straight, I followed G-Rod enough to know all I needed to know. He rolled solo most of the time. He had his girlfriend driving when he conducted business. She would be a distraction if the police rode up and happened to look inside his car. He wouldn't appear too suspicious because he had a beautiful young lady pushing his ride.

He'd been riding on easy street for years. But, every dog had its day. I couldn't wait to creep up on that smug-ass nigga, G-Rod. His good luck was about to change.

After a couple more weeks of following him, I learned all of his whereabouts. I'd peeped out every move he made: from his mother's house, to his baby mama's house. It didn't take any planning, plotting, and strategizing to come up with the fact that most big-time drug dealers didn't have bank accounts. If they had no bank accounts that meant they had no credit cards. Not having credit cards meant they had straight cash.

My thoughts were on the money, where was the stash? Why would he keep it on him or at his house when he knew that would be a bad idea? If I was that strong in the game, I would keep my stash at my mama's house.

As bad as I wanted to have it all over and done with I knew it would be a mistake to rush. So, I just stayed low and scoped out his mama's house. I discovered that only his mama and daughter lived there. Not having to worry about a lot of people would make my evasion easier.

G-Rod's mama took his daughter to school every morning, and picked her up every evening. I'd planned it out in my mind. The morning would be the best. G-Rod arrived at his mama's house every morning around the same time.

I allowed myself three days to prepare for the event. The first day, I went over the plot again and again until I got a clear picture in my mind.

The second day, I was motivated. I stayed up all night thinking about what I was getting ready to do. I didn't try to talk myself out of it; it was too late for that. The next morning, I'd make my move.

The third day rushed up on me. Before dawn, I was already dressed and focused on handling business. I drove to a gas station that was close to G-Rod's mama's house. I popped my hood to make it look like my car had broken down. I casually walked up their block. I saw kids waiting on their school bus. I knew it arrived at seven o'clock. I glanced at my watch. I was two minutes early.

I walked past the house then circled the block. I spotted the school bus stopping. The kids got on and it pulled off. When I made it back around the block, G-Rod's mama and daughter were coming out the front door. They didn't notice me as they got in a car and left.

I exhaled. It was either now or never.

I rushed up then knocked on the door and looked around to see if any nosey people were outside. I made sure no one was peeking out their windows. All was clear.

I gave myself three minutes to unlock the dead bolt. I unlocked it in two, and hurried inside. Once inside, I peered out of the windows to check my surrounding. I planned to be in and out in no time.

I rushed inside the bedroom and searched for the stash. I went from dresser drawers to closets in every room. I couldn't find anything. I spotted two hundred dollars on top of the refrigerator, all twenties folded up. I shoved it in my pocket.

Damn, where is the safe or the money bag?

I knew he wouldn't keep it in his car. He couldn't have re-stocked, spending everything on products. He didn't have that type of traffic around him, only a few rich customers.

After searching everywhere with no results, I was getting frustrated. I heard a car pull up in the driveway.

"Shit. Shit. Shit," I swore in a low tone. I quickly hid under the bed as the car door slammed shut. I was glad the bed was high enough to fit under because the closet would have been a dead giveaway.

The front door opened, and then closed. The sound of two female voices drifted from the living room. There was another lady with G-Rod's mama. The two came into the room where I was hiding. My heart beat so loudly that I could feel it thumping in my chest.

Under the bed, I had a clear view of the ladies. I watched as guest lady gave G-Rod's mama a massage. The young lady has to be in her late twenties or early thirties. She was sexy as hell, dressed in a tight-fitting Baby Phat outfit. G-Rod's mama wasn't half-bad, either.

It didn't take long before they were both undressed.

Oh shit, I thought with excitement Something is about to pop off!

The guest sat on the dresser and opened her legs wide. Her diamond shaped vagina hair flashed my way. I instantly got a hard on as G-Rod's mama buried her face between the young ladies' thighs.

Without blinking, I watched the two ladies get down and dirty with each other. G-Rod's mama ate enough for breakfast, lunch, and dinner.

Damn!

"Okay, okay, okay," the young woman moaned and quivered. "That's it. That's it. I'm coming baby!"

"Give it to me." G-Rod's mama lapped up the woman's juices like a hungry cat. Finally, the woman stopped trembling.

"Okay, Sasha, it's my turn," she said, smiling naughtily. They switched positions.

So, G-Rod's mama's name is Sasha. Well, Sasha is a freak, and now she was up on the dresser sprawled eagle. I was enjoying every minute of the sexual display until I remembered where I was and why I was there. I snapped back to attention.

After they finished their sexual seduction, they quickly got dressed.

"Girl, my son will be here any minute," Sasha said. "You better go before he suspects something." They kissed passionately, feeling each other up. "Baby, I'll call you later." She walked the young lady out of the room.

Now that Sasha was out of my view it became silent, I couldn't make a move. All types of thoughts ran through my head. One thing was certain: I couldn't go anywhere without getting that stash. Basically, I'd already put my life on the line by being here. Since I'd made it this far, I had to get something out of the deal, two hundred fucking dollars was not cutting it!

After being under Sasha's bed for so long my legs and feet began to fall asleep. I didn't see or hear any signs of her inside the house. My guess was she'd fallen asleep in the living room or maybe she was in the kitchen. I didn't hear anything to let me know what she was doing. I heard no sounds from the T.V, no water running, nothing. I couldn't make a move until I knew the coast was clear again.

A car pulls up on the side of the house, Sasha walks past the room door, heading toward the back of the house. I hear G-Rod's voice. It wasn't long before the two enter the bedroom.

"Hey baby, what are you doing today?" Sasha asked. She was looking all innocent, like she didn't just get her cunt licked by another woman.

"I'm going to get my usual package from Keith. I need to grab seven grand real fast because I'm supposed to meet him at G-Joe's in a few," he told her.

G-Joe's was a corner store in the hood. Keith must be the big timer who kept G-Rod supplied. He went into the closet making me glad I made the under- the-bed move. He pulled out a coach bag which was hidden in the attic of the closet. He places the bag on the dresser and I watch as he looks inside.

He pulls out a stack of the money, when I saw solid hundred-dollar bills with rubber bands wrapped around them, I got excited.

Jackpot, I thought.

G-Rod counted out seven grands then placed the rest back into the bag, then returns it to the hiding place in the attic. The two walks out of the room.

"G-Rod, where is my money that I had on top of the refrigerator?" Sasha asked. He laughed and so did I. All that cash he has, why would he need her $200 bucks?

"What's so damn funny? It's the principle of the fact," she stated, thinking he took her money.

"Whatever, Mama," he said, laughing.

He was getting ready to leave and I couldn't let him make off with the money. I had to act fast. I slid from under the bed, knocking over a lamp, and slips into the closet. The sound of breaking glass got their attention.

"What the hell was that?" G-Rod ask. They both came back into the room.

"What happened to my lamp?" Sasha asked, looking at G-Rod.

"I don't know," he responded, unconcerned. The dude had so much money he didn't take time to even think about the little things.

"Well, help me get this up," Sasha told him. "That was one of my favorite lamps."

As he bent over to pick up the pieces of glass, I made my move busting out of the closet like I was Jason or Freddy Kruger, scaring the hell out of them both. I aimed my gun, and the Infer red beam shine on Sasha's forehead.

."Oh shit!" G-Rod yelled," Him and Sasha dropped to the floor.

"Alright motherfuckers, y'all know what to do,'" I instructed

"You," I said, pointing at Sasha with my gun. "Get up off the floor and lay on your stomach on the bed." I stood near the door. "It's like this here- whoever wants to get shot, might as well tell me to do it now, because my time is up." I pulled out my nine-millimeter. I aimed at each of them. "Who wants it first?" Sasha lifted her head up and faced me.

"No, please don't shoot," she begged.

"It's like I figured: nobody wants it. It's cools with me. Hell, bullets burn," I joked. "Turn over and get on your stomach," I told G-Rod because he was staring at me too hard. It was a good thing I thought to put on a ski-mask.

"What do you want?" he had the nerve to asked and in a loud voice. That nigga must not have known what I was capable of.

"Shut the hell up!" I said, angry because he thought he could just try me. I kicked the shit out of him. I planted my size ten all in his side and ribs.

"Argh! okay, okay," he pleaded, getting the message. They both decided to cooperate, "Good." I really hadn't wanted to kill anyone, just shake them up.

"If your bitch is out there, she'll have to wait until I'm finished with you," I told G-Rod. His face screwed up like he was thinking.

"Sasha, get up and lay on the floor with your son, I want you two to face opposite directions."

"How do you know us? Who are you?" she asked.

"Don't worry about that." I laughed.

Now both of them thought I knew them, and they were trying to figure out who I was. Let that fuck with their minds.

I'd come prepared. I quickly tied them up, pulling the rope so tight I could see the veins bulge in both of their wrists.

"Please don't kill us. We have a little girl to raise. Whatever he did, I'm sorry," Sasha apologized for what she thought her son did. He threw her an angry glare." Please, whatever he did, don't make me and an innocent child pay for it."

Reality kicked in as I listened to her pleading. I couldn't get all soft now, I had to finish business.

"Shut up and I won't hurt either one of you," I told her. "But, you better not say another word or I'll shoot." She just looked scared, but obeyed.

I grabbed the Coach bag out of the attic. I also got the seven grands from G-Rod's pocket and put it back in the bag. I placed the bag by the door. I duct tape their mouths and wrists over the ropes. They wouldn't be getting loose anytime soon.

I peered out of the window to see who was with G-Rod. I breathed a sigh of relief when I saw he came alone. Grabbing the bag, I left out the back door, I swiftly ran down the alley.

Moments later I discarded my clothes, giving them to a crack head I encountered as I left the alley. I kept my mask tucked in my pants, along with my guns. I made it back to my car which was still where I left it with the hood up. I fiddled under the hood like I was fixing a problem. I slammed the hood shut, got in, started the engine and drove off. Mission accomplished.

Back at my house I threw the bag on the bed. I locked my room door and pulled out a calculator. I counted the money, one bill at a time. When I finished counting there were eighty-six thousand dollars. I'd never seen that much cash before. But, it didn't excite me. I needed more and I was going to get it. I knew I couldn't be greedy, though. I'd just lay low for a while and think of something because with that much cash everything had to be planned out.

Quite a few days passed and all I did was stay home and read books to pass the time. Sometimes, I'd listen to music, but not often. For the first time in my life, I felt important. I had no feelings of guilt about what I'd done. Shit, I had to earn money somehow so I earned it the dangerous way.

The best kept secrets are the one that you keep in your mouth. I learned that lesson years ago. I knew not to tell anyone about what I'd done. I would take it with me to my grave.

*****

It was a few weeks before Thanksgiving and I was back on the block. I wasn't there to hustle, but to check out the ones who were. You could always tell who got the most sales from clientele because they attracted the most attention.

The most traffic headed toward a dude named RonRon. RonRon was in his early twenties, but that was cool. As long as he respected me and what I was about, it was all good.

I had so much on my mind that I didn't really have a clue as to what my next move would be. I'd already given up the hand-to-hand hustling. That was just not for me anymore. My main goal was to not let my brother into my business – at least not yet.

Another week passed and I felt a little claustrophobic. I'd been stuck in my room for weeks pondering what to do with the money. I wanted to flip the whole stash. If I could get at least ten people who knew how to act right on my team it would be all good. We could blow up and become rich in no time. But trusting some of the hustlers on the block would be testing the waters. Most of them were all for self. I didn't want to make the wrong choice and fuck up a lot of money. I'd see what RonRon was all about. Maybe he'd fit into my plan.

I was getting ready to go to the store, just to get out the house when I saw RonRon riding past on a bicycle. I grabbed the chance to find out if he'd be down for what I was about.

"RonRon," I yelled, calling him over to me.

"What's happing, 50ty? Where you been, playa?" he greeted.

"Working," I lied. We both laughed. I pulled out a cigar and a quarter of weed. "I see you have your hustling wide open now, and people in your spot. Why are you sharing your hole?" I asked as I rolled up a fat joint.

"They know I get my money first," he bragged.

"Oh, yeah?" I passed him the joint.

"Yeah." He pulled out his money and counted it in front of me. "I'm getting mine, 50ty." I laughed at him while he perpetrated.

"I feel you homey." I changed the subject. "The reason I called you over here is to tell you I'll have them bricks in a minute, so holla at me."

"Cool, 50ty, you know I'll holla at you on that tip."

"RonRon, player, I can make you rich lil homey, and get you off the block," I told him.

"I'm not a shorty anymore, 50ty, I'm getting paid so I'm straight," He passed me the blunt.

"See, that's where your ignorance ly's, right there," I said.

"What do you mean? I'm a hustler, 50ty, just like you. I'm making four to five hundred a day -even more at times. Shit, I think that's good enough, don't you?"

"Yeah, it's good when you're making it, but it's hard trying to maintain it, do you feel me?" He didn't answer. "RonRon, that's not enough to buy yourself something nice without being broke again."

"I buy what I want, when I want it," he stated with an attitude, picking up his bike.

"You hustle every day and buy big things. The next thing you know, you're back on the block getting nickels and dimes again," I told him while smoking on my blunt.

"So, what you saying, I'm a poor hustler? Cause right now you're not doing anything. How can you make me rich when you're not rich?" he insulted. It was useless to tell him to come to me for what he needed, I just shook my head.

"To hell with that shit you talking man. When you're ready to make some real money, holla at me. And for the record, when you label yourself a hustler, you're supposed to try to find a way out the game before it's too late." He had pissed me off just that fast, I walked off.

"So, have found your way out the game, 50ty?" he asked sarcastically.

I whirled around and faced him with a serious look on my face. "If my mouth is full of shit, then I'd be talking shit, nigga. I don't talk shit! When you're ready, holla at me," I repeated then I went back inside the house. I know it would only be a matter of time before he came knocking at my door.

The next morning, I was awakened by the sounds of sirens. I jumped up. Things happened in my neighborhood all the time. I peered out of my room window and saw an ambulance, three fire trucks, and eight or nine police cars. I quickly got dressed and went outside.

I spotted my brother so I walked over to him. As I looked through the crowd I saw a body on the side of the street covered with a white sheet. "Homicide," was the first thing that entered my mind.

My neighbor, Mrs. Wembley, sat in a chair about five feet from the body, crying hysterically. Her husband tried to comfort her, but he was crying too.

"Damn, bro, what happened?" I asked Jermaine.

"Mrs. Wembley's granddaughter got hit by a car," he said in a glum tone.

"People always come through here speeding. They know kids be out here playing and walking to their bus stops," I said angrily. "That's fucked up."

I'd seen people dead on the street before, but never a child. It really hit me hard and left a sharp pain in my chest.

I walked over to Mrs. and Mr. Wembley and gave them my condolences. I looked at their granddaughter and whispered "Rest in peace." Tears were in my eyes, I blinked them away and went back inside.

I felt so horrible that I didn't want to do anything. I went back to bed and ended up sleeping the whole day away. When I woke up again it was almost midnight.

I was starving. I looked in the refrigerator and my hunger got more potent. There was nothing in there but an empty jug of milk. I took it out and threw it in the garbage can.

"Shit, I need to go grocery shopping," I said aloud.

I got in my car and went through a drive-thru restaurant. After I left there I stopped at a gas station to buy a cigar and a pack of Black & Mild's. As I stood in line at the counter, G-Rod entered the store. He was with his fine ass girlfriend. He glanced my way, but didn't pay me any attention.

I breathed a sigh of relief because he hadn't recognized me. He had this calm look on his face, maybe that stash I made off with didn't mean anything to him. He'd just make more. I paid for my stuff and left the store.

As I pulled in my driveway and got out the car, I was approached by RonRon.

"What's up, 50ty? I came by earlier, but I didn't see your car so I didn't knock," he said, smiling. I knew it wasn't going to take long before he popped up.

"What's happening?" I asked, as if I've forgotten what we'd discussed.

"I want to know what you were talking about the other day," he said.

"Oh yeah? What made you change your mind?" I asked. "Come on in."

We went inside and sat on the front porch.

"You're right," he admitted. "All I'm dealing with is nickels and dimes. I've always looked up to you, 50ty. I know if you got a plan to get rich then it's all good," he said.

"How much cash do you have on you right now, RonRon?" I asked.

"Seven hundred and sixty-three dollar's to be exact," he answered. He knew how much he had without having to pull it out and count it. "Plus, I have some bricks. That's why I'm on the block now trying to get rid of them."

"What I'm going to do for you never happened for me. I'm going to change your whole life," I told him. "Follow me."

We headed to my room. In my room we chilled the rest of the night and talked. I just needed one person who knew a lot of people to conduct business with. RonRon was that person. He already networked the city. If I could trust him, he'd be my key to success.

"Can I trust you, RonRon?" I finally asked.

He looked at me with a serious expression. "You can trust me with your life, playa."

I pulled out my black bag and threw it on the bed. "I'm going to put you onto something, pimp," I said, unzipping the bag.

RonRon saw the stacks of hundred-dollar bills in rubber bands. "Damn, 50ty! Where did you get all that money?" he asked. I could tell he was getting nervous and paranoid.

"Doing business with me comes with no questions, homey," I told him as I zipped the bag closed. "Just know that we are aiming for a million dollars."

"Cool," he responded. After he calmed down he sat on the bed to get more relaxed.

I explained to RonRon how we wouldn't be selling anything hand-to-hand anymore.

"Breaking bread off other hustlers, they will be our clientele now." He nodded. "This will be our way to come up and get out of the game." I stared at him. "You have a connection for me?"

"I have just the dude," he said, his eyes shining. It was hard to hide the excitement when you know you're about to get rich.

CHAPTER 4

November 24

Thanksgiving Day

Me, Jermaine, RonRon, and a couple of females from the neighborhood sat at our table eating Thanksgiving dinner. I was deep in thought, thinking about my mom and grandma. I missed them so much. Neither Jermaine nor I said too much because it was a family day, and all we had left was each other.

The women cooked a traditional Thanksgiving feast. There was turkey, a honey-baked ham, baked macaroni and cheese, collard greens, corn bread, home-made dressing, and potato salad. Everything looked delicious. For dessert, there was red velvet cake, sweet potato pies, lemon cake and something I'd never touch with a ten-foot pole: fruit cake.

My appetite came as I stared at the food they'd dished out. I dug into the dressing and sighed in delight. It tasted almost like Mama's. The women had really put their feet into preparing the food.

"How is everything?" Sharon asked after we'd finished the first serving. I nodded because my mouth was still full.

"It couldn't have been better, Shay D," Jermaine said, smiling at her. "It's time for round two."

"Save some room for dessert now," she joked.

Thanksgiving turned out not to be such a bad holiday after all. I was thankful that I had my brother, and good friends like Shay D and RonRon to help me get through it.

RonRon got the word around to all the street hustlers that he was the man to contact when they needed something. The first stack I spent was five hundred dollars on a fifty-pack. When we flipped it, we'd make around fifteen hundred in return.

People contacted RonRon back-to-back because the word circulated quickly. He had to give up on the ghetto deals in order to break even on the fifteen hundred. Hustlers kept blowing up his cell phone, and pulling up to see him every thirty minutes. He was almost like a damn super star. I stayed with him in order to protect him and my investment.

Two weeks before Christmas RonRon made me fifteen grands. He'd proven to me that he could manage things with no problems. He was in better spirits, too - dressing clean every day. His new position had given him more confidence.

He bought a Chevy for twelve hundred dollars. The air conditioning, heat, and engine worked fine. He asked me if he should purchase it, first. I liked the fact that he always came to me for advice or to ask questions. I never had any bad feelings about RonRon because I knew he was on top of his game.

A few days before Christmas, I counted all of my money. I fell three grand short of having a hundred thousand dollars. Since it was just days before Christmas, it would be impossible to make that amount. Besides, I had to spend some of what I had because I wanted to get everybody something nice for Christmas.

I went to Best Buy and purchased Jermaine an entertainment system, because he loved music. I got RonRon a safe to keep his cash in. He kept it on him because he didn't trust banks. I visited a couple more places and got a few gifts for others. I put everything in storage until Christmas.

When I returned home, RonRon's car was parked in the driveway behind Jermaine's. As I got out, RonRon came outside.

"Yo, 50ty, I'm out of product, Pimp. We need to go see the man," he said, tossing me five thousand dollars.

"Damn, RonRon I might as well go all out on product. You are moving' and shaking'," I told him. He smiled proudly and we both got into his car.

RonRon grabbed a cigar off his dash board and split it open to roll up. "That will be a challenge. At least we'll have it though. Plus, we're doing good getting rid of it," he said.

While he sparked up the blunt I thought about how I needed more. To even think about another robbery was a crazy thought. I told myself to just leave that alone.

*****

December 25, 1996

Christmas Day

Just like excited kids, Jermaine and I woke up early. As Jermaine headed for the living room, I thought he was going to be surprised with his gifts. I was in for a surprise myself. There were two small gifts and another big one. They hadn't been under the Christmas tree the night before when I'd placed his stuff under it.

"What is this?" I asked.

He looked at me with a smile and shrugged.

"I don't know. Santa must have paid us a visit?" The gifts had my name on them. Jermaine spotted his name on the ones from me and opened them fast. His eyes lit up when he saw the entertainment system.

"Sweet!" he exclaimed.

I slowly opened my gifts. Of course, I opened the big one first. It was a top of the line Compaq computer. A card was attached. I opened it up and found it was from RonRon. The note said, "I didn't know what to get, but I know I had to get something that cost a lot of money." I chuckled.

"Damn, I hope that $450 dollar safe somewhat matches the price of this pc!

Jermaine new all was all about expensive things so he went out and brought me a platinum bracelet with a necklace to match. I wouldn't dare ask the price of it because it's the thought that count. He must have saved up for this gift.

For the rest of the year RonRon and I did really well. He still kept it real with his partner. I had to slow him down on spending his money left and right. I wasn't spending much cash myself. I just bought food, gas, and more products.

It saddened me that Bosco couldn't be there to join our empire. Thinking about Bosco made me sick at heart. Hell, I waited seven years for him to get out of prison. Now he was free but gone forever. Jermaine was still affected by it too even though he didn't bring it up. I hardly saw him anymore because he is always working.

** * *

As I dozed off for the night my cell phone rang. It was RonRon.

"Hello. What's going on? Why are you up late, bro?" I asked, getting out of bed and going to sit on the corner of my dresser.

"Oh, it's nothing wrong, Pimp. Just letting you know that I'm almost out of things. That's all," he told me.

"Cool. You can come over or you can wait until tomorrow. It's totally up to you. I got something for you, though." I told him quickly.

"I'm on the way," he said.

I unlocked my door so RonRon could just walk in. I flipped on the television and sat in the Lazy Boy waiting on him. I felt tired as hell. He came to my window instead of knocking.

"Come in man. It's open."

We sat at the kitchen table to negotiate. I gave RonRon the whole bird, which would make me around twenty grands. When he left, I sat there thinking. I wouldn't rush anything. I'd just sit back, take it easy, and stay focused. It was a damn shame that I hadn't found my way out of the game yet. At least I could say I was doing fairly well since me and RonRon became partners in crime.

I bought two cell phones so that RonRon and I could stay in touch more often. Whenever someone needed anything, they'd holla at him and he came to get me so I could ride with him. I missed the hand-to-hand dealer shit, but we had to make a change.

"50ty, when we get this million can we sit our ass down somewhere on an island? Somewhere near the Keys?" RonRon stated while he rolled a blunt. We both laughed.

"Yeah man. We should go out of town somewhere we never been before and relax," I responded.

In St. Petersburg, Florida, from Child's Park, Jordan Park, Palmetto, 18th Ave, 9th Street, and Bartlett Park, RonRon had every big timer buying from him. The only thing I had to do was have it ready to be shipped out. No doubt, we had the city on lock! We even had the neighborhood police on our team.

"Yo, it's this cat I want you to meet, 50ty," RonRon said.

"Who?" I asked.

"I don't know him, but I've seen him around. He's one of the JP boys. He wants to buy a brick from us."

"Oh yeah? I asked while I popped open a big bag of Lays barbeque chips. I felt a buzz.

"I got his phone number. He told me to call him whenever I'm ready to meet him at a convenient location," RonRon said.

I put the chips on the bed and RonRon rushed them like a hungry pelican attacking a fish.

"Call him up and have him meet us at a place around people, like at a grocery store downtown somewhere," I advised.

"Cool. Good looking out, 50ty," RonRon said. He put the chips down in order to dial the dude's number. I snatched my Lays back and saw that he'd devoured them like an Ethiopian.

Our plan was to conduct our business in the Winn Dixie parking lot. It was out of view and in the mix, too.

We waited in the parking lot for five minutes before a black Acura pulled up. It circled the lot twice. We watched suspiciously. RonRon called to see if it was the guy. It was, so he started to get out.

"Wait RonRon," I cautioned, stopping him. "Tell him to park, get out of his car, and get into ours," I said. RonRon relayed the message.

The Acura pulled beside us and parked. I grabbed both of my glock nine's and placed them under each of my thighs- just in case somebody wanted to act stupid.

The dude got out of his car and got into RonRon's vehicle. I had jumped into the back seat before he pulled up into Winn Dixie. I was peaking dude out and. I'd be damned. It was G-Rod.

He looked at me and nodded his head. I nodded back. RonRon should have driven around the block, but he made the transaction swiftly. I had his back, plus my eyes were secretly posted on G-Rod the whole time. Dude must have had money everywhere.

We watched G-Rod get back into his car and drive off. When he left, he took the chills I felt along with him.

"Man, RonRon you got the city on lock for real bro," I told him as we pulled out of the Winn Dixie parking lot.

"Yeah thanks to you, 50ty, it's going to stay like that," he replied, throwing a grand into my lap.

I pulled a cigar from my top pocket. "RonRon, homey, I'm thinking of relocating further north, bro," I said.

He gave me a look like it was Judgment Day or something.

"What do you mean, further north?" he asked.

"I have a cousin name Derrick in Georgia. He's on the same level as we are down here. I'm going to go up there and change his environment, just like I did for you, Pimp."

"Oh, okay. I understand," RonRon said as we pulled up in front of my house.

"With you as my right-hand man here in St. Pete, I ain't got nothing' to worry about. You'll always keep your head above water. Just stay connected to the big timers and focus on the small timers."

"I understand, Pimp. I will keep it moving down here," RonRon replied with pride and confidence.

"We just need to be smart now so in the future we won't have to touch this shit anymore. We can just check our mail, and there it is: a fat ass special delivery, baby," I said, smoking on a Black & Mild.

CHAPTER 5

My next move was Bainbridge, Georgia. In preparation, I talked to my cousin Derrick for a while on the phone. Before our conversation ended, I let him know that I was coming his way soon.

"It's time for better days," I said, thinking it would sink into his head.

"True dat. True dat," he agreed, not even knowing what I had in store for him.

I gave myself a week to get everything situated in order to make that move. I put up a hundred grand and gave RonRon a key. He'd make from twenty to thirty grand off that. I told him I'd call him when I arrived at my destination.

I aimed to hook Georgia up. My cousin Derrick was probably buying his stuff from half-able folks. Shit, he wouldn't need them anymore. The police were probably watching their asses anyway.

*****

Jan. 22. 1997

7:30 AM

I was up, dressed, packed, and ready to go to the airport. I gave RonRon a copy of my house key so that he could have access to my room. Jermaine was on top of things now, because I'd filled him in on everything. Both of them rode with me to the airport.

"Look ah here, bro, I'm going up Georgia to peek out the area. I don't know yet, but we might have to bring stuff up there."

We parked inside the airport garage and chilled for a minute.

"If so then the best way to do that is by bus," Jermaine said.

"Yeah, out of view from the cops," RonRon agreed.

Both of them got out and walked into the lobby with me to wait until my plane arrived.

"I feel that we'll rise strong now, 50ty, because I got St. Pete on lock and I know you'll have Georgia the same way in no time," RonRon said.

"Yeah, then we'll be able to rotate from the bottom of Florida to the top of Georgia," I responded.

"No need to rush things though. Y'all don't want to run into a dead end," Jermaine cautioned. We all agreed.

"No doubt we'll have to take this step by step," RonRon said as he answered his phone. Minutes later he ended the conversation.

"We got to bounce, Playa. Got to handle some biz," he told me.

We all did the man-hug thing and wished each other the best. My plane arrived shortly after they left.

Even though that was my first time ever riding on a plane, I wasn't nervous. I was glad the flight was short, though. I never thought about the plane crashing or nothing like that. I had my mind on making money.

We arrived in Tallahassee in an hour and a half. I got off the plane and headed for the lobby. I looked around for my cousin. I saw Derrick and some lady waiting for me.

"Cuz, what's up"? Derrick greeted, giving me a one-armed hug. His friend gave me a hug as well as if she'd known me for a while.

"Oh, 50ty, this is Cara," he introduced. She was a fine redbone, and she was thick as hell. "She's a good friend of mine," he added.

We walked outside to his car. I was surprised to see him pushing a candy apple red, four- door Cadillac on twenties. Inside, there were leather covered seats, an Oakwood dashboard and steering wheel. He had a built-in DVD player in the back of each seat, and two in the car's visors.

"Damn, cuz! Nice ride, Playa," I complimented.

"Thank you. I put a lot in this girl," he responded and blasted the music. I'm sure it was to show me that he had an impressive system. I wasn't even mad at him.

The ride was smooth and comfortable. We took our time getting to Bainbridge. It was about an hour's drive. On the way, Derrick rode slowly through every neighborhood possible with his music blasting. No doubt all eyes were on him. People had respect for him, but he would gain more than that soon.

Derrick pulled up in front of an all-white wooden house. A fence, with a gate, surrounded the yard. Cara got out.

"I'll call y'all later tonight," she said, looking directly at me. We watched as she walked through the gate.

"Derrick, why you not trying to get at her?" I asked, getting into the front with him.

"I went with her mom for about two years," he told me, laughing.

"You still banging the mom, ain't you?" I joked as he drove off. He just laughed.

"I know you're hungry, so let's make a stop at Whataburger."

"Cool," I said. He pulled in to Whataburger off the Havana exit. Derrick felt comfortable so that made me relax a bit. Even so, I still thought about my hundred grands.

"Let's get it to go, Cuz. I'm tired and want to relax," I told him so he went through the drive-thru.

"I feel you. We can go after this. Get whatever you want, Cuz. It's on me," he said, pulling out a stack of twenties. After we ordered we headed straight for Derrick's crib.

Bainbridge, Georgia is straight up country. There's sets of houses like in neighborhoods, but only in certain areas. Woods surrounded the entire town. Stores were miles apart from each other. They had to ride all the way to Tallahassee just to go to the mall.

My main concern was that I kept my bag with me. I trusted my cousin and the love was there, but for the time being I had to stay focus.

I called RonRon and Jermaine to let them know I was in Bainbridge and that everything was cool. RonRon told me that business was good as usual, which relaxed my mind. I just needed to concentrate on running things in Bainbridge. I decided to stay low key and peek Derrick's way of hustling.

So far, I could tell that Derrick never rushed into anything. I liked that about him. I rode around with him checking out his way of living, which was somewhat different from ours, but it was all in the game.

The next day came faster than I realized. My short nap turned into a deep ten-hour sleep. I got up and took a shower. I peered out the bathroom window and saw Derrick outside washing his car. Once I finished dressing, I joined him.

"Got to keep this baby clean," he said with pride.

"I feel ya on that."

"So, what you getting into today, Cuz?" he asked and I told him my plans.

First, I had him take me to the pawn shop. I needed to buy some artillery. We had to drive all the way to Tallahassee to hit up a Cash America Pawn. I searched through the selections of guns from the biggest to the smallest.

Shit, I was out in the country surrounded by woods. They only had two or three police officers. That spelled danger to me. I selected a 3030, and an AR15. I had to fill out a gun permit. It would take three days to get approved because they had to do a background check. That wouldn't be an issue because I didn't have a criminal record. I'd never been caught for anything. Once finished there, we headed back to Derrick's place.

Back at the house, Derrick and I finally got a chance to talk.

"So, what's happening, cuz?" I asked to spark up a conversation. He turned on his PlayStation and put in Madden '96.

"Eight-minute quarter," he said as he threw me one joy stick and he grabbed the other. We began to play the first quarter of the game. I picked the New Orleans Saints and he chose the Atlanta Falcons. I believed he picked the Falcons because they were a Georgia team. We both said to hell with the Tampa Bay Bucs.

"So how much money are you making up here?" I inquired casually. His phone rang.

"Shit, it depends on how long I be out there trying to get it. Sometimes six to seven hundred, when it's on and popping. But on a regular day, I pull about three to four hundred." He showed me a sample of what he was working with. He hadn't touched it yet.

Damn! Their stuff was bigger than the stuff in St Pete. The dudes who he got his stuff from must have the capital connection.

As we played into half time I had him by ten points. The score was 38 to 28.

"Damn 50ty! I got to go and make this money. Do you want to roll with me?" he asked. That was right up my alley.

"Yeah, I'll roll with you." I was already on my feet and ready to go. We headed out and got into his ride.

It wasn't long before we pulled up in a wooded area and Derrick got out. I watched him vanish into the woods. He was in and out real fast.

"Yeah, cuz, that is a quick fifty bucks I had to collect. I'm out of product so I need to holla at my homey, Reco, tomorrow sometime," he told me.

"Reco?" I asked.

"Yeah, 50ty. He sells them stones and green or whatever you need. I'll holla at him tomorrow."

"That's cool." I didn't ask any more questions, just leaned back in the seat and enjoyed the ride.

Early the next morning I was the first one up. Derrick came into the kitchen where I sat, talking to Jermaine on my cell.

"Tell G, I said what's going on with him," Derrick said sleepy, leaning in the doorway wiping crust out his eyes. I relayed the message.

"He said 'Hey,' I relayed back.

"So, what are your plans for today?" I asked after ending my phone conversation.

"I need to holla at Reco. If you want to meet him you can roll with me," he said.

"Aiight."

Before we headed to Reco's house, we stopped at the store to get a cigar. They didn't sell El Productos so I grabbed the next best thing: a Swisher Sweet. Once we left the store, we headed to Reco's place. I was impressed when Derrick pulled up.

"That's a big ass house," I said, admiring the nicely cut grass, trimmed trees and new driveway. "Sweet," I whistled. "He must not be hurting for nothing."

"This is Reco's house, 50ty. I called him and he said to come on over. Usually he meets me somewhere. Don't anybody usually come over here like this. This dude is real low key," he said.

"Who does he live with?" I asked, not really trying to get personal.

"This is his crib, but his chick, Tera, stays with him," he answered, hitting the blunt.

I should have known he had a woman. A man had to have a backbone to hold him down in this type of business.

"Hold on, 50ty. Let me go tell him you want to unite with him," he instructed, getting out the car.

"Cool." While he went inside the house, I continued to smoke.

"This just might be the key to my success," I said aloud.

After five minutes passed, Derrick came to the door and signaled for me to come inside. I got out the car and walked up the huge driveway.

When I entered Reco's crib I was immediately impressed. The living room had a zebra statue looking up toward the ceiling, and there was a waterfall flowing through the branches of a tree. The entire living room was black and white. There was no carpet, just a polar bear rug that met company at the door. The house was so nice I automatically took off my shoes. It was a good thing I did too because when I looked up I saw a big ass sign that read, "Take Shoes Off." I could respect that.

His furniture was also lavish. There were two eight-ball lamps. We sat down on a leather couch to wait. After a few minutes, Reco came downstairs to meet us. He was still in his pajamas. Shit, money talked, bullshit walked.

"What's up Reco? This is my cousin, 50ty. 50ty, this is Reco." They slapped hands in greeting which let me know they were tight. That was a good sign.

"What's up, playa?" he said shaking my hand.

"Nice crib you got here man. I like your setup," I told him.

"Yeah, it took me some time to get it together," he said, walking around checking out his own shit. "What up Derrick? What you need?" he asked, leaning against the zebra statue.

"I need a 50ty pack for now, "Derrick said with confidence.

"Cool. What you need, 50ty?" he asked. It was as if he knew everything about me, as I did with G-rod.

"I need a whole key," I replied, as if everything was simple and easy to get. Derrick and Reco paused for a second then they looked at each other and laughed. "What?" I asked them. "I'm dead serious," I said sitting down on the couch. "How much is it for a whole key?"

"Are you serious?" Reco asked looking at Derrick as if it could be a set up.

"I have the cash right here. I just don't let my left hand know what my right hand's doing," I explained. That was to let him know that I hadn't told Derrick everything.

"I feel you," Reco said, calming down.

"See, my whole reason of coming up here to Georgia is to put my cousin on his feet by showing him the finer things in life. You and I are basically in the same boat. Why not share it when there's plenty of room in it?" It felt good saying that. Derrick was silent, not quite figuring out what was going on. "See, I got it made back home in St. Petersburg like you probably have it here. I can easily get what I need. I'm just placing my cousin on the right track so he can stop nickel-and-dime pushing."

"Damn, cuz, when you got it like that?' Derrick asked.

I just gave him a mysterious look and responded, "I hit the jackpot."

"Where? In Las Vegas?" Reco asked.

"Nah, at the Hard Rock Cafe in Tampa," I lied.

"I see," Reco replied.

If only they knew. It was rough out there in them streets. I might as well get it while the getting was good. If I couldn't get it from him then we all might as well bond and get it from whoever he got his stuff from. I didn't even have to mention that. He automatically volunteered the fact that he went to Atlanta to cop his product.

"Hold up. Let me get your number, 50ty," he said as he ran upstairs.

"Cuz, you're serious, aren't you?" Derrick asked in surprise.

"We'll talk later," I told him as Reco came back downstairs with a Coach bag.

"I really don't conduct business this way, but since you're Derrick's cousin and you seem to be good people, we can talk. Talk about money always makes sense to me," Reco said, laughing. He opened the bag. I spotted all types of stuff in it from drugs to money.

"Damn, Reco," Derrick whispered as if we were at Reco's parent's house or something.

I got Derrick's attention, caught his eye, and shook my head, indicating that he should chill out. He understood.

I pulled out my pouch from around my waist which was hidden under my Sean Jean shirt. I took out a stack of solid hundred-dollar bills.

"I know you probably wondering if this counter fit because of how people are these days. But it's real," I stated. Smiling, I tossed a stack at him.

"I know it's real, bro. I'm not tripping. Here you go," he replied. I could tell he was nervous. We made a fair exchange quickly then Derrick and I left.

Back at Derrick's house it was like a repeat with RonRon. I explained the ropes on how there would be no more hand-to-hand drug dealing out in the streets. We were on top now and I planned for us to stay there. It was time to get rich or die trying. I hoped they were ready.

"I know you know other hustlers out there such as yourself, right?" I asked Derrick.

"Yeah," he said.

"Well, they will be your clientele now. In due time, Reco will holla at you for some product. He'll be spending seventy to eighty grands at a time. I'm trying to get you ready for that, cuz."

Derrick's eyes began to shine just like RonRon's had. I knew he was on my level of thinking.

"That's what's up!" he said, laughing joyfully.

Trip to Atlanta

CHAPTER 6

March 18th, 1997

A month later.

With everybody that Derrick knew and the people his peeps knew, he was set on making close to two grand a day. It was early and I waited for him to come home. I needed him to take me to the pawn shop so I could buy artillery. I was about to starve waiting on him to pull up. My cell phone rang. I thought it was either him or Reco, but it was RonRon.

"Yo, what's happening, playa?" I asked.

"Nothing much. Doing business as always. Haven't heard from you in a while so I decided to call. What's up nigga?" he greeted.

"I'm up here working with my cousin. He's straight. We found a connection up here and all, but I'm cool. How are things down there?" I asked.

"Man, I already made ten grands, plus I'm holding fifteen. I just want to know where you want me to wire it," RonRon said.

"I'll call to let you know sometime later today or tonight, aiight?"

"Aiight."

I quickly got off the phone. You couldn't be too trustful in this business. You never knew if someone was listening in.

Derrick finally pulled up in the driveway and I met him at the door. He handed me seven grand up fronts.

"Cuz, you don't have to give me nothing until you straight," I told him as we headed to his room.

"Nah, 50ty, I'll get your money up first then work on mine. I'm loyal to my peoples."

"But you still need cash in your pocket to put your mind at ease while you're out there." I threw two grands at him and told him to just keep it for spending money. "You want to ride with me to the pawn shop?" I asked.

"Nah, I'm just chill, dawg." He tossed me his key.

"See you when I get back," I said and headed out.

"Peace."

I drove to the pawn shop in Tallahassee by myself. When I arrived, I got my previous order, which was the 3030 and AR-15. After I left the pawn shop, I stopped at Wal-Mart off of Jefferson near the Capital and bought a couple cases of ammunition. I called RonRon from the phone booth inside Wal-Mart. I instructed him to just put my money up until I came back down there because I was straight for the time being. I had well over a hundred and forty grands with me, and forty G's circulating around. It was a lot, but I wanted more. I needed to figure out another way to get it.

It was dark when I returned to Derrick's house. I found him in the kitchen talking on the phone. I just placed his keys on the table and walked into the room with my boxes.

"What you got, 50ty?" he asked after hanging up.

"I got my 3030 and the AR-15 out of the pawn shop and a lot of ammo." I placed both guns and the boxes of hollow tip bullets on the bed.

"Damn, cuz, you must think we're going to war with fools up here or something!" He laughed as he went back into the kitchen and grabbed his keys off the table. "I got to make a run," he said.

I stayed at the house while he was out because I was tired. I called and talk to my brother for a while then I passed out. I must have fallen into a deep sleep because the next day was upon me before I realized it.

Derrick heard me go into the restroom to wash up and met me as I was going back into the room to get dressed.

"Here, cuz," he said handing me two stacks of hundred-dollar bills. "That's eight grands, playa. It's on and it's going to stay on," he stated, sitting on the edge of the bed.

"I can relate to that, cuz," I told him as I grabbed a Swisher King out the pocket of my bag and some herb I had tucked into my socks. "With well over a half of key, you'll be straight until I return."

He gave me a strange look. "Where are you going?'

I just laughed and told him. "With Reco." I grabbed his .45 Magnum off the dresser and checked the clip to see if it was loaded. It was. I placed the loaded gun in the holster and put it inside my duffel bag. I called Reco to tell him that I would be ready whenever he was ready.

I chilled in the house that whole week, only going out to get something to eat. Derrick continued to make his rounds and get paid. I called RonRon to check on him. He was doing great on his end. Patience was all we needed for our million-dollar come up.

Friday came too fast. Reco called me early that morning, which was cool because I was already dressed and ready to go. Derrick came into the room as I was getting ready to walk outside and handed me eighty-six hundred dollars. Now, I sat on one hundred and sixty thousand dollars flat.

Reco pulled up in the front with two ladies with him. I peeked that as soon as he let his window down to show the view. One of the ladies got out of the passenger's seat and got in the back. When I opened the passenger door to hop in I noticed one of the chicks in the back seat was Cara. She was the one that was with Derrick when he picked me up from the airport.

We took Interstate 10 toward Jacksonville. It was the long route, but I just sat back and let them drive as long as business was being handled.

I noticed Cara staring at me through the review mirror. She was probably thinking that I hit the jackpot or something. I bet she was picturing us in Las Vegas together or out on Long Beach relaxing.

I just smirked at her. She was fine as hell but I couldn't waste time with her right now.

"So how is St. Petersburg treating you?" she asked, to spark up a conversation.

"Cool. I lived there all of my life," I responded.

I guessed Derrick told Reco everything he knew about me and it was passed down to Cara.

"By the way my name is Tera," the other lady in the back seat said. She playfully slapped Reco in the back of his head.

"Oh, my bad. 50ty, this is Cara, and that's my lady, Tera," Reco said laughing.

Those two chicks were the finest I'd seen since I'd been in Georgia. I thought they were related based on their style and their names, but they were just best friends.

It took us about eight and a half hours to get to Atlanta, only stopping twice for gas and using the restroom on the same spot. We stopped and got a room at the Holiday Inn in downtown Atlanta near the Atlanta Falcon Dome.

"50ty, me and Tera going to go take a swim for a bit. You and Cara can scroll through the city or whatever," Reco said. He and Tera headed off.

Cara was about to get a separate room when I stopped her.

"It's just for the night. Why can't we just shack up?" I asked.

"No problem with me," she responded with a smile.

I wasn't sleepy so I took a walk around the motel just to be alone for a while. I walked and thought about my life. The beginning of last year I was broke, selling hand-to-hand throughout the year. In the beginning of the New Year I planned to become rich. I felt myself getting greedy. I wanted it all. I had a hundred and something grand and I was still feigning for more.

"Excuse me," A man whispered from behind, scaring the hell out of me. "Do you have any spare change on you so I can put it on a room?" he asked.

I looked him up and down, examining him. He was dressed in a raggedy pair of Files, cut up jeans, and had a dirty white shirt thrown across his shoulder. I knew he was a crack head.

"I'm broke," I said and turned to walk off. Only taking a couple steps I suddenly felt two sharp pains in my side. I quickly turned around. He was stabbing me! I dropped to the ground before he got a chance to stab me for a third time. As he went to step over me and stab me again, I kicked him off of me. I rushed to my feet, defending myself.

I'd left my gun back at the room so I had to stay focused on trying to take the knife away from him. He was bigger than I was. As I faced him, he charged at me, swinging the knife left and right. I jumped to the opposite side as he misses. He had a wild look in his eyes; a dangerous look. I knew he planned to kill me. I continued to dodge his jabs as best as I could. He was getting tired. I waited for the right moment to stick him with a right cross and take him down.

I heard Cara screaming for help. The crack head looked in her direction dropped the knife and take off into the darkness. Cara ran over to me.

"50ty, are you okay? Oh my God!" Seeing all the blood she started crying. "You're bleeding. I'm calling 911." She took out her cell phone and made the call. "Lay down. The ambulance is on the way," Cara said. She helped me lie down on the concrete then grabbed my hand. "It's going to be alright. You'll be fine."

Hearing all the commotion caused Reco and Tera to come running toward us. They were still wet from the pool. People gathered around me like I was dead. I heard the sirens through the night air. By the amount of blood dripping from my wound, I figured I was cut pretty deep. I felt dizziness then everything went black.

I kept hearing BEEP! BEEP! BEEP! I rubbed my arms because they felt itchy. I felt tubes on both of my wrists. As I tried to open my eyes, I quickly closed them again. The bright lights from the ceiling hurt. I slowly opened them and saw doctors and nurses walking past the doorway. I realized that I was in the hospital. Everything that happened at the hotel came back. I sat up and looked around the room. Cara was asleep in a chair beside me.

"Oh shit!" I groaned and it was loud enough to awaken Cara.

"Hey," she said. She stood up, rubbing the sleep from her eyes.

"Hey Cara, sorry to wake you," I replied. My mind was on my money. I hoped Reco was who he really said he was because he had my belongings.

A nurse walked into the room to check on me. "Hello Mr. Terrill. How are you feeling?" she asked with a smile. I told her that I was in serious pain and she gave me some medicine that made me weak and sleepy. "Okay, Terrill just rest and relax," she said before everything went black again.

"Excuse me Sir, are you a relative of this young man?" a feminine voice asked.

"Yes, I'm his older brother. I just came in from Florida to see how he is doing," a male's voice answered. I opened my eyes slowly and focused through the bright ceiling lights. As my vision cleared I saw that my visitors were Jermaine and RonRon. If anything could make a patient in the hospital happy, it was seeing real friends and family there by their side.

Seeing that I was awake, RonRon stuck his face close to mine.

"Damn, it's only been a couple of months and look at you all up here in Atlanta in the hospital," RonRon said.

"You feel me? I got caught with my guard down," I managed to reply and laughed a bit.

"Are you alright?" Jermaine asked in concern.

"I'm a soldier, bro, for as long as I live. It will take more than a scar to hold me down." I sat up in bed to show them that I was alright.

Derrick had told them his version of everything that went down. While we talked, Tera and Cara entered the room carrying flowers, balloons, and candy.

"Oh, I'm sorry. I didn't know you had company, 50ty," Tera said. She walked over to give me the candy and balloons. Cara placed the flowers in a vase on the counter.

"It's cool," I told her. "That's my brother, Jermaine and my partner, RonRon. And that's Tera and Cara." I introduced everybody.

"Damn, 50ty, it's like that, pimp? I at least want to wear one of your shoes," RonRon joked.

Derrick and Reco entered the room. Jermaine and Derrick hugged and people were introduced again.

While we talked and got to know each other, two female nurses came to check on me. I asked them how long I was going to be there.

"It's up to the doctor, sweetheart," one of the nurses said. "Your stab wound is pretty deep. It has to heal and we don't want you to relapse."

After the nurses left I told RonRon and Jermaine that everything was cool with me until I got out of the hospital. They could go back home if everything was worth going back home to.

"I'm going to chill up here for a while with, 50ty," RonRon told Jermaine.

"Yea okay, but I got to go and catch that flight. I have to be at work tomorrow," Jermaine replied. He gave me and Derrick a hug, told everybody goodbye and left.

"Tera and I are going back to the room, 50ty. We'll come back later," Reco stated as the two headed out. Cara walked them downstairs.

"Damn, RonRon, the only thing on my mind, bro, is my money," I said. "I'm not going to say anything about it yet. I'm just going to see how it returns." I reclined in the bed.

"Damn 50ty, I wish I was here when that shit went down." He started flipping through the channels on the T.V.

"I got caught with my guard down, RonRon. I just have to learn from my mistakes," I responded.

"What gets me, bro, is for a person to ask you for some change then try to kill you because you don't give it to him. It doesn't make sense at all," he said.

I looked at him, thinking. It was hard to believe that it could have been a set up. But all that time that RonRon and I were on the streets selling, it never got that serious. Now that I had it, they were trying to kill me for it. I decided to just stop thinking about what had happened.

Derrick came in carrying my duffel bag. It made me a happy camper. I grabbed it and peeked inside to look at my money. I couldn't count it in the hospital so I told Derrick to keep it with him. I let him and RonRon know how much I had. They went downstairs to his car to count it. I was glad to have Derrick and RonRon on my team. I trusted them and I felt more comfortable with them in Atlanta with me.

RonRon called up to my room and told me how much cash I had in my bag. The amount was correct: one hundred and sixty-seven thousand dollars. RonRon also had sixteen grands for me that he put in the bag and Derrick put in ten grands.

Derrick finally got Tallahassee and Quincy down pact, alone with Bainbridge, Georgia. It was just a matter of time before we'd be set with the mills.

They left to get a room at the same Holiday Inn where I'd gotten stabbed. Cara was still downstairs. The doctor finally came in the room with two police officers. I frowned because I hated cops-worldwide.

"Hello, Mr. Terrill. My name is Officer Lonnie. I came to get a statement on what happened to you at hotel yesterday. How are you feeling?" the black officer asked.

"I don't really know what happened, Sir. It happened so fast. I just walked out of my hotel room and got stabbed twice," I told him.

"Do you know anything about the guy who stabbed you?" The other officer who didn't give his name asked.

"No, I don't really know anything about nothing up here," I answered truthfully. "I'm from Florida. It's all good. I guess he thought I had money and tried to rob me for it." I shrugged. The officer squinted at me, nodded and wrote something down on a notepad.

"That'll be all, Mr. Terrill," Officer Lonnie said. "You have a good evening."

After the officers left the doctor examined me. As I got ready to take a nap the phone rang. It was Derrick telling me he made thirty grands just that fast. "You're straight, playa," he said.

"We're straight," I corrected him. We talked a bit then I hung up.

Derrick and RonRon were well off. Both of them were sitting on a few grand. It was only a matter of time before the hood in St. Pete got hot. RonRon had Tampa, Sarasota, Clearwater, Largo and Tarpon Springs on lock. Now, he was the man. It was probably best if he kept his business going, but relocated in order to stay low-key.

The third day that I was in the hospital, the doctor examined me again. From his expression, I got the feeling that he didn't want me there any longer.

"You're doing better." He lifted my robe to check the wounds on my back. "Your cut is still bleeding a little through the stitches, but not much." I didn't say anything, just watched his facial expressions. "After your stitches dissolve, come back to see me. You can also visit your doctor in Florida or any hospital."

"No problem. How long will it take for me to be released?" I asked.

"As soon as the nurse finishes your paperwork and writes the prescriptions you'll need, she will come in to release you." He answered abruptly and left. He must have been having a bad day or something because his bed-side manner sucked.

Four hours passed before the nurse finally came into the room to release me. She gave me a fake smile.

Bitch, I thought, giving her a phony smile back.

"You are all set and ready to go, Mr. Terrill. You be careful and be sure to have those prescriptions filled right away. It will help with the pain." She said.

I thanked her and went to the lobby to wait for RonRon and Derrick. It wasn't long before they pulled up in a rental car. We went back to the hotel. As I walked toward my room, I looked up the hallway and had a flashback of that guy stabbing me. It pissed me off. I quickly shook it off and went into the room.

Everybody was there at the hotel, like it was a welcome back party. I told RonRon and Derrick that I had unfinished business with Reco and the dude up here regarding our product.

"Fuck that, 50ty. I'm rolling with y'all, cuz. You just got out of the hospital," RonRon said. He got up and grabbed his pouch and fitted cap.

"No problem. It's cool," Reco replied. We walked out the door. Derrick remained in the room with Tera and Cara.

While on our way to the guy's house, my whole right side was aching. I didn't say anything. It was something I just had to deal with. I wanted everything to fall into place.

"This guy is low-key and smooth with his shit. So just be cool with him and straight up." Reco said.

We pulled up to a huge white house with two garages. Three Benz's were parked in the driveway. No doubt this dude's house was lavish.

"Get out. You guys are straight as long as you're with me," Reco stated. He acted as if he was the vice president of this guy's operation.

A big black dude met us at the double front doors of the house. I looked up and spotted the cameras on the roof. When we entered the house, I saw two big muscular dudes taking two Rottweiler's into another room and close the door.

"Them are my guardians," a man said as he came around the corner.

"Hey Los. This is one of my homey's in Bainbridge's cousin. 50ty, and his people's, RonRon," Reco introduced us all politely.

"What's happening?" he asked while shaking our hands with a tight grip. "I usually don't conduct business like this, but Reco know me and I have whatever you guys need. So, what's the word?"

"No doubt. What do you need, 50ty?" Reco asked. I looked at him with a smile.

"Let me get seven keys of that soft."

"Damn. You're spending over seventy grands today?' Los asked in surprise. I looked him straight in the eye.

"Man, I'm all the way up here hurt and scared. I'm on a mission. I might as well get enough to last me for a while because this may be the connect I need." I responded.

"Cool, cool, my type of guy. Let me see the money." he stated with a smile.

RonRon took out the seventy grand and placed it on the table. Los and two of his men examined it.

"Why do you carry all this cash around on you?" Los asked. I thought it was a dumb ass question, but I answered anyway.

"In order to buy my product. That's why I'm up here now," I said.

"I'm going to spend twenty grands with you Los, as usual," Reco said. He handed him his money. Los placed the money in the bag with my cash. He didn't even count it. Damn, he trusted him like that?

Los handled his business on the down low. He didn't keep shit in his house. He had it taken from an undisclosed location to somewhere different every time. We had to go to a supermarket somewhere near Atlanta. With over a hundred grand on me, we traveled in the direction Los gave us. After the run I planned on heading back to Florida to rest and heal.

We parked at the supermarket and I sent RonRon inside so we wouldn't appear suspicious. Plus, I needed some pain killers anyway.

Reco got out of the car to help some ladies put groceries in their car. I noticed them give Reco one of the grocery bags. It was smooth and fast. I could relate to that. Reco talked to them for a minute. RonRon came back to the car and gave me some pain relievers and a bottle of water. I immediately took two of the pills.

The two ladies pulled off and Reco got into the car with the bag.

"We straight, 50ty. Those are Los's connections," he said.

"Whoa, that was a slick move. You even fooled me on that," RonRon said. He laughed and began rolling up a blunt.

"Yeah, man Los is a police officer," Reco said.

"What the fuck you mean?" RonRon asked in disbelief.

"I've been dealing with him for years. He never touches shit. His workers take care of things," Reco said.

"I see. That's understandable, shit. We have crooked cops in St. Pete.," I said as we pulled up to the hotel.

The product was already spilt for us. Reco placed his portion in a bag that he had in the back seat and gave me the grocery bag. We all went to our separate rooms.

We picked up Derrick and the girls and headed back to Bainbridge. When we got to Derrick's house, I called Reco and told him that Derrick would probably be contacting him because I was going back home until I recovered.

After hanging up with Reco I felt dizzy from the medication I'd taken and I was still in pain. I went to lie down while Derrick and RonRon cooked up a miracle. Their phones rang back-to-back. I just closed the room door and passed out.

After a couple of hours of sleep RonRon came in the room and woke me up. He showed me what they had. All and all we had more than three hundred grand and three big blocks. Now it was time we turned heads. I split one hundred and fifty among Derrick and RonRon. I told Derrick that I was going back home to recover. He had everything in order so that was the least of my worries.

The next morning RonRon was already ready when I woke up. I showered and got dressed and told Derrick that I would probably be back before he sold out. We were heading outside to get in the car when Cara pulled up.

"Hey," she greeted as she approaches over to our car.

"Hey there, how are you doing?" I asked

"Fine, I just stopped by to see how you are. That's all," she said. She looked sexy as ever.

"Thank you for being there for me back in Atlanta," I told her. She smiled and blushed.

"Your cousin told me you're going back home. I thought maybe I'd catch you before you left to say bye." I got out of the car and we walked to the back of it.

"Yea that's what I'm going to do. I'll be back once I heal up."

She reached in her purse. "Let me give you my phone number." I put her number in my phone and gave her mine. She hugged me, waved at RonRon, and walked into Derrick's house.

"Damn, 50ty, she is fine as hell," RonRon said when I got back in the car.

"Hell yea bro. I'm going to get at her one day. The time is just not right. Besides, business before pleasure," I replied.

"Yo 50ty, it would be my business to get that pleasure," RonRon said. We both laughed. My back started hurting from my wound, but I just ignored it.

On our way to Tallahassee we stopped at a restaurant and got dinners-to-go. We also stopped at a gas station, grabbed some cigars and purchased gas then we were off to St. Petersburg.

My back started hurting more and more until I had to pullover and let RonRon drive the rest of the way. I damn near overdosed on the pain pills. I fell asleep and slept the whole way home and missed out on smoking the Blunts that RonRon rolled up.

RonRon woke me up after we pulled in the driveway. I got out the car and went inside. Jermaine wasn't home. RonRon left to drop my prescription off at Walgreens. Since I was home alone I just put my bags up and went to my room to lay down for a bit.

As soon as I got comfortable, my house phone rang. It was RonRon.

"50ty, I'm going to pick up your medicine in a couple hours. I'm headed to this chick's crib to knock her off for a few then I'll be there." he told me.

"Cool. I'm going to just lay down for a bit and relax." I said.

A couple of hours into my nap I heard the front door open and close. I quickly grabbed my gun that I always left under my pillow. I peered into the hallway and saw that it was my brother.

"You scared me, bro. I can't get caught with my guard down anymore," I told him. I stood in the doorway with my gun in my hand.

"You don't have to be paranoid, bro." He chuckled. "Where's RonRon?"

"Off in some chick's private places, where else?" I responded, laughing. I went back into my room to get some sleep.

A couple hours later RonRon returned with a medical kit from Red Cross and a Walgreen's bag. "50ty, you got to take that bandage off and put another one on." He opened the Red Cross box and handed me a bandage wrap. I took two of the pills before placing the new bandage on my wound.

"That's more like it." RonRon said, inspecting my handiwork. "Now, get some rest." he advised.

"I'll be back in one piece in no time," I said. Pretty soon, the medicine had knocked me out again. I slept like a newborn baby wrapped in a warm blanket.

On and poppin

CHAPTER 7

I felt seventy-five percent better just from resting for almost a week. I talked to Derrick most of the time and he kept me posted. It was good to know he was holding it down up there.

When I finally got up, I felt like a brand-new man. I called RonRon and told him to come over whenever he got the chance. Bored out of my mind I decided to call Cara to see what was up with her.

"Hello?" She answered the phone sounding sexy.

"What's up, baby? Do you know who this is calling you from an unknown number?" I teased.

"It would be fun if I called out names. But if I called out the wrong name then that wouldn't be too fun now would it?" She laughed.

"Well this is a guy who really digs your style and wouldn't mind having a beautiful lady like you on his team," I said.

"Oh really?"

"Do you have company?" I asked.

"No. Do you have a name and do you know mine?" she asked.

"Well my name is Terrill, and your name is Cara. They call me 50ty," I said. I laughed while I fired up a blunt.

She screamed out loud as if she had an orgasm when she realized exactly who I was. "Hey! How are you doing?" she asked, excitedly.

"I'm fine and a whole lot better now. How have you been?"

"I'm doing good- just relaxing on my day off," she said.

We talked for a while and really got to know each other over the phone. She made me want to catch a flight back to Bainbridge just to hit.

Not long after my conversation with Cara, RonRon arrived.

"50ty, I sold everything that I had except five hundred dollars' worth, and I'm still pushing them for chunks. Derrick did the same thing," he told me. He grabbed my blunt off the ash tray and hit it.

"Nice. All together that's a million bucks. I only want two hundred and fifty a piece. We will all have our heads above water," I said.

As we talked about our come up, Derrick called. He let me know that had my cash stacked in hundreds, ready to deliver to me. I told him to just put it up until I returned.

*****

Another month passed. RonRon sold out of everything, which put five hundred and sixty grands in my possession. RonRon got more respect than all the little dudes out there hustling just to go broke. As long as they got what they needed from him, it was all good.

I called Derrick to see what was up with him since we hadn't talked in a while. Our conversation wasn't all that long because he had to make that money. I knew he was handling his business so I wasn't worried.

I went to Bayfront Hospital later that day to get my wound checked. They removed the stitches, leaving me with a battle wound. I called Derrick again from the hospital to update him.

"What's up, cousin?"

"Chilling. I'm leaving Bayfront. I got my stitches removed. What's good on your end?"

"Word, well that's good news. Now you can bring your ass up here and get your money before I put it with mine and run the whole state," he joked.

"Go ahead, cuz. Do what you need to do to run that shit," I replied.

"Nah, on the real, I got it put up until whenever. There's three hundred thousand wrapped up in rubber bands in your Coach bag."

"Cool man. I'll be there soon."

"Aiight, cuz."

"Peace."

July 17th 1997 - Three days later.

It was RonRon birthday. He turned twenty-years old and had more money than all the twenty to thirty-year olds in the Palmetto neighborhood combined. Jermaine threw him a birthday block party. People gathered on the block early. Three Chevys blocked the left end of the street off so traffic could come in but not go out. The thing about the party was that everybody knew RonRon since he was the man with the product. I felt I had to keep a close eye on him.

People brought coolers of beer and alcohol and other drinks. Jermaine had chairs all over the yard. From the front porch of my house, I kept my eye on RonRon. I called his cell phone.

"50ty, what's up? Where are you, cuz?"

"I'm inside the crib, on the porch. I want to holla at you for a second. Come here."

He hurried inside.

"What's up, bro?" he asked, concerned.

"Oh, nothing's wrong. I just wanted to tell you that everybody is expecting to chill while you get fucked up and ball out of control. It's on you. But them Kats that be buying from you, don't trust them tonight, RonRon. Keep your eyes open."

"Shit 50ty, I'm going to stay out in the open and around my homeboys. Besides, I put up my cash and my stash. It's not happening tonight. Believe that," RonRon said.

"Just be careful. I got ya back. Go 'head and enjoy ya self," I told him and he went back outside.

The later it got, the more crowded it got. I kept my eye on RonRon and the people that kept passing him blunts. I spotted Jermaine across the street, sitting at a card table, gambling. People parked their rides a block down the street and walked up the strip.

I left the porch and went outside to where RonRon was. As the music blasted from the different cars, I knew the neighborhood was wide awake. Somebody would complain because they wouldn't be able to get any sleep. It would only be a matter of time before the police came and shut it down.

"Look. Look," one of RonRon friend shouted as he pointed at my brother. He was standing face-to-face with a couple of men. We just chilled. Everybody watched them and looked over at us. One of the dudes pushed Jermaine into the crowd. They caught him before he fell.

Jermaine was twisted. I knew he was down for whatever, but the crowd held him and wouldn't let him go. I got up and walked toward them. RonRon and his boys were right behind me.

"What's up, bro?" I asked.

"Them fools stepped all over Mrs. Wembley's granddaughters' flowers, where she got killed at," he yelled.

"Let that drunk ass man go so I can beat him down," one of the men said.

"Hold up, playa, this is my brother and it's not hard to see he's fucked up, so step," I told him.

"I don't care. That fool disrespected me, so what you want to do about it?"

"Terry, dawg, chill with that shit man," RonRon said angrily.

"RonRon, your boy's trying' me, nigga," Terry said.

"Everybody just chills out," RonRon told them.

Jermaine calmed down, grabbed his drink, and sat back down to continue playing cards. I watched as people picked the flowers up and placed them back around the cross. The party continued. Everybody went back to doing whatever they were doing. I returned to the steps where RonRon and his boys chilled.

I watched as the dudes faded off up the strip, keeping my eye on them. It wasn't long before they returned with more people. I sensed there was going to be some shit started.

"RonRon." I got his attention and pointed at the dudes as they made their way up to us. "Act like you don't see them."

I went back over to where Jermaine was before the other dudes got close. They walked by us not even looking in our direction. But Terry kicked the flowers everywhere. RonRon jumped up and I signaled for him to back off.

They just stood there. I got up and walked toward them with the whole hood behind me.

"What's up, punk? What y'all want to do?" Terry asked.

"Did you guys come here to start shit or to get into shit?" I asked.

Terry and his homeboys took off their shirts, ready to fight us. "Y'all trying' us like we're soft. What's up?"

"Can y'all just pick up those flowers? Y'all disrespecting the dead right now," I said as I stood face-to-face with Terry.

"Make me, punk," Terry said and pushed me backward into RonRon.

"What?" I walked back toward him. One of his homeboys hit me on the side of my head with the handle of his gun, knocking me to the ground. Jermaine rushed the dude and knocked the gun out of his hands. They both scrambled for it.

Everybody started fighting. I went in and out of consciousness, while two females picked me up from the ground. When I regained my focus, I saw RonRon stab Terry. I jumped over RonRon's shoulder. With a powerful swing, I hit Terry in the temple, knocking him to the ground. I grabbed RonRon, pulling him out the way as Terry rolled on his back and started shooting at us.

Everybody ran in different directions. Jermaine grabbed the dude's gun and shot at Terry and his homeboys. He let off six shots then ran up the block. I jumped over the steps and rushed into the crib. RonRon and Jermaine split up. I grabbed my 30/30 and rushed out the back door. I ran up the alley. I spotted Terry getting into his car. Before I could let off, Jermaine ran up on the side of the car and fired inside. One of Terry's homeboys let off a round and hit Jermaine in the leg. He fell to the ground, yelling in pain. I rushed into the street and started shooting at Terry's partner. I fired thirty rounds, clearing the whole area. Terry sped off, driving wildly. He lost control of the car and ran into my neighbor's yard, coming to a halt.

RonRon and I grabbed Jermaine and carried him to the backyard to where my car is park. Blood was everywhere. RonRon applied pressure to Jermaine's leg. I had to think things out. I looked at Jermaine.

"You alright, man?"

"Yeah," he responded. Then he laughed and said, "Hell nah, I'm not alright. I'm shot." We all laughed. I knew he'd hold up while I rushed to St. Joseph's Hospital in Tampa. I wanted to be out of St. Pete.

While I drove, wetness flowed down the side of my face. Thinking it was sweat, I smeared it across my face.

"You're bleeding," RonRon told me. I ignored it until we got close to the hospital. I pulled over to a gas station located on the opposite corner of the hospital. I sent RonRon inside to buy Tee-shirts and a wash cloth.

61

Jermaine was in serious pain, but he stayed strong. We quickly changed shirts and cleaned most of the blood out of the seat. I parked inside the garage, out of view. We helped Jermaine inside the hospital. The doctors and nurses quickly grabbed him and took him into the back.

After Jermaine was admitted, one of the doctors came to question us. He noticed the cut on the side of my head.

"What happened?"

"We got robbed," I told him. Jermaine was already hip to the lie.

They bandaged my head and gave me some pain relievers. I immediately took two of them.

Hours later while we sat in the room with Jermaine, two police officers walked in. We remained calm. Sticking to the lie, we explained how Jermaine was at the gas station pumping gas when some dudes rushed us. We couldn't describe them, but knew there were three of them- all black guys.

After the police left, we decided to head for Bainbridge that night. I instructed RonRon to get out of the hood and lay low in a motel until I called him.

We got the word that Terry died at Bayfront hospital. We dropped RonRon off at a Days Inn and headed out of St. Petersburg. We left everything behind but our money and guns.

Jermaine was nervous as hell. I was calm, but it wasn't wearing off on him.

"Damn, now what am I going to do?" he asked, rocking back and forth in the seat.

"Bro, you're straight. Just chill out man. You're messing with my nerves. Don't flip out. We're good. They don't know anything."

I called RonRon at the hotel and told him to get everything out of my house before the police rushed in and confiscated it.

We made it to Bainbridge in five hours. When we got to my cousin's crib, Derrick pulled up behind us.

"What happened to y'all?" he asked.

"Stupid people do stupid things," I replied, walking into the house.

Jermaine went into the bedroom to lie down. He was still all nerves.

"Derrick I need you to do me a favor." We headed to the kitchen.

"What's up?" He gave me the Coach bag with three hundred and fifty grands in it.

"Split whatever you make with my brother until he gets back on his feet. I'm going to fly back to St. Pete to check on RonRon," I said.

"You sure about flying?" he asked.

"I'm going to the airport in Tallahassee. I'll park my car there until I return."

"Alright, man. Handle things," he said. I wasted no time heading to Tallahassee.

On my way to the airport I called Cara.

"Hey, 50ty," she greeted.

"Hey, Cara. I'm in Bainbridge, but I'm heading back to St. Pete. I'll return in two to three days."

"Well, give me a call when you get back and I'll come see you."

"Cool," I said. Since I didn't have too much to say, we hung up.

I'd left my bag of money at Derrick's house, only bringing a grand with me, plus the hundred and fifty dollars for the ticket. As I sat in the airport I couldn't stop thinking about Jermaine. He was all shaken up. But this was the part of life that most people didn't understand. Respect was powerful and it was really taking over. In the process of gaining respect, tragedy and pain came along with it.

I call Jermaine and talked to him before my plane arrived. I assured him that everything would be alright because nobody knew he was there but me, RonRon and Derrick. We would all ride or die for each other.

I slept the entire trip because I hadn't slept in a day in a half. I arrived at the St. Petersburg/ Clearwater airport in two hours. I called RonRon to pick me up. After he arrived, we headed for the hotel.

"Man, 50ty the hood is hot," he said.

"Yeah, it's time to relocate for a while. Where do you want to move?" I asked.

"I'm going to look around," he responded.

RonRon told me about everything that went on after we left. The police surrounded the whole neighborhood looking for Jermaine. The detectives were asking people questions about both me and Jermaine. I wasn't going to tell Jermaine any news until things calmed down.

"Just stay on point homey," I told RonRon. "Take these two hundred and fifty grand and work wonders. This will be my million-dollar ticket. Then you can go on and pump up, nonstop."

RonRon gave me a crazy look like he was addicted to hustling for me or something. "So, after your million-dollar come up what do you plan to do?"

Damn, what is my next step?

"I really don't know," I finally said. "I haven't thought of that yet." We drove the rest of the way to the hotel in silence.

At the hotel room we just sat and smoked a blunt. Both of us were lost in our own thoughts.

How did everything that was going so good end up turning so bad? I thought. Jermaine had to stay low key for a while, at least until the shit settled down.

Terry's homeboys, along with the police were most likely looking for me and Jermaine. RonRon would probably have to leave the city for a bit, too. But Terry's dudes were the least of my worries. The law, on the other hand, was a problem. I plan to head back to Bainbridge the next evening.

Later that night I talked to my brother for a while. I lied to him and told him everything was cool and that the police didn't know shit. RonRon stayed at his grandma's house that night. At least he had somewhere to stay that was away from the hood.

The next day I grabbed some things that Jermaine and I needed. It was three hours before check-out time. I walked to the Citco gas station to buy a blunt and a soda. I'd get something to eat when RonRon arrived.

As I split the cigar open and stuffed it we have some of the best green in St. Pete, RonRon pulled up like he sensed something good was about to go down. Two heads were better than one. We blazed up the hotel room before we headed out.

"50ty, I'm almost out of product. I need to go re-up. You might as well ride with me," RonRon said.

"Nah, RonRon. I'm going to catch flight to Atlanta to meet up with Reco to re-up. I got you. I'll bring you some back down."

"If you're going to Atlanta 50ty, I'm going too," RonRon said.

"Alright, I just got to call him to see what's up with that mission."

After smoking damn near a quarter ounce, I was lit. RonRon could smoke up a whole tree if he had it. He was laughing at me while I coughed and talked to Reco on the phone. Reco was waiting in Bainbridge for me to return to go with them to Atlanta. I told them to go ahead, and we would catch a flight there. They could pick us up from the airport.

They were leaving early in the morning around 6am, arriving in Atlanta between two and three o'clock in the afternoon. We would catch an 11am flight so that we'd get there around the same time the next day. I passed RonRon the blunt and lay down with my head spinning. Soon, I was fast asleep.

CHAPTER 8

The next morning the ringing of RonRon's cell phone woke me up. I heard him talking, so if I wanted to go back to sleep, that was not an option, I groaned.

"Damn 50ty, I didn't mean to wake you up. I got to go catch this money. This my last batch too so that's straight," he told me.

"Handle your business," I said as he walked out the door. I looked at the time and saw that it was still early. I debated on whether or not to get up. Fuck it. I turned over and went back to sleep.

An hour and a half passed and my side was hurting. My phone rang as I rubbed my scar, looking at it in the mirror.

"What's going on?" It was Cara. My heart did silly things just hearing her voice.

"We're headed to Atlanta. Reco said you and RonRon are catching flight there, right?" she asked.

"We'll be leaving in an hour so we should be there around the same time y'all get there," I said. Cara was really digging me. I could tell by the conversations we'd had. After hanging up, I looked forward to seeing her again.

I went to the lobby of the hotel to get breakfast and milk and took it back to my room. After I ate, I took some aspirin. RonRon returned. I was packed and ready to go. We headed to Tampa International Airport. We didn't have long to wait for the plane to arrive.

The flight was terrible. I was scared the entire time because the wind shook the whole damn plane. RonRon slept the entire trip or maybe he fainted, shit. I would rather die in my sleep than to see my death coming, too.

As soon as the plane touched down, you could hear the relieved sighs from everyone on the plane. I hadn't been the only one nervous and worried about that motherfucker crashing.

"Atlanta bound, where a fool stabbed me in the side. I will never forget this place in a million years," I told RonRon as we headed for the lobby.

Reco spotted us from a distance.

"Damn 50ty, what happened to your face?" he asked, grabbing my bag.

"People around my way acted a fool at RonRon's birthday party. A nigga hit me in the face with the handle of a gun, but I'm straight."

He gave me a weird look. I guess he wanted to know what happened next, but I didn't say anything else. The less I said the better.

"Sorry, homey. I would have had to kill me somebody," he stated. RonRon and I gave each other a secretive look. We walked outside the airport into the parking lot where Cara and Tera stood by their rental.

"Hey guys. How was your trip?" Tera asked, giving us a hug.

"Stressful," I said as I hugged Cara. We hugged for a second longer than me and Tera. We behaved like we'd had sex every day and night and were sprung. I told them what happened to my face before they had a chance to ask. The swelling had gone down, but it left an ugly black mark under my eye. Cara just looked at me and shook her head.

"The flight was terrible the whole way here for four hours." RonRon changed the subject.

"Sorry to hear that," Tera said.

"Man, how do you know? You were slobbing on that lil pillow the whole time," I joked as we pulled out of the parking lot.

Atlanta was huge. I just stared out the window as we rolled under the turnpike to downtown Atlanta. We checked into a room at the Comfort Inn.

"How long have you guys been here?" I asked Reco as we walked into the office to reserve three more rooms.

"Well, a little before you guys arrived. We left at 7, an hour past our planned departure."

"I see." The clerk behind the desk handed us our hotel keys then we went back out to the car to grab our belongings.

"Now that we're here 50ty, Los wants us to holla at him tomorrow, just me and you," Reco said as he and Tera headed for their room.

"Cool," I told him. "I'm going to go to the pool and catch a swim, see if it'll refresh me."

"Okay me and Tera might come join you," Cara said as she followed Reco and Tera.

"50ty, I'm tired. I need to get some rest, at least an hour, then I'll be straight," RonRon said after grabbing our bags.

"That's cool."

I headed for the pool. The water looked cold. I knew I couldn't just step in slowly or I'd change my mind. I ran and dove in before I lost my nerve. It felt good to my body. I needed that relief. I swam around for a while, clearing my head of everything. I turned over on my back and floated. I saw Cara and Tera coming down the stairs.

"Hey, 50ty, mind if two chicks join you?"

"Sure, the water is fine." I laughed, then backstroked toward the deep part of the pool. I watched as they removed their robes. They had big butts and nice tits, perfect bodies. Sweet! They got into the pool where the water was three feet deep then swam over to me.

"You always getting into trouble, but you look so innocent, why?" Cara asked.

"Soljas come in different forms. People should get enough of underestimating me," I said mysteriously. I walked around them in a circle, splashing water on them. They laughed and splashed me back.

"So, what are you saying? Did people in your life take you for a joke or something?" Tera asked.

"Well, you have to understand the game I'm playing. I'm wide open. Shit always bound to happen."

"What's the worst thing that ever happened?" Cara asked. I had a flashback of everything bad that had ever happened to me. I saw my mom being buried, Bosco lying dead in front of the store with his eyes open staring at me, Mrs. and Mr. Wembley's granddaughter dead in the streets.

"I can't really say. A lot of terrible things happened. But seeing a grandmother sit and watch helplessly as her granddaughter lay dead in the street because of a hit and run driver is probably the worst I've seen so far."

They placed their hands over their mouths. I saw the tears gather in their eyes as I told them what happened. I didn't know why people set themselves up just to break down. They wanted to know. Well I told them, it was too much to handle. Now they got quiet.

The last story I told them was about two brothers riding on motorcycles. They were speeding down 5th Avenue north in St. Petersburg. They crossed a yellow light and a truck that was coming in the opposite direction didn't see them when it turned. It struck one of them, knocking him backward through the air. He landed on his brother, killing him instantly. The strange thing is, the brother who got hit, didn't die.

We stayed in the pool for a while after I finished telling them war stories.

"Where is Reco?" I asked Tera.

"He said he was going to the store for something. I really don't know," she replied.

Tera got out of the pool to go back to the room because she was tired. I couldn't help but to look at her ass as she walked off.

"So, behind that charming innocent face and body lies a bad boy," Cara said teasingly. "I should have known because of your hustling." She started splashing water on me.

"What are you trying to say? Because I'm profiting in an illegal way, I'm a bad person?" I asked grabbing her and dunking her underwater. Damn her ass was soft! She knew what I was trying to do. She just laughed and played along.

After the good time we shared in the pool Cara was tired and wanted to head in for the night. I walked her to her room.

"I had fun tonight, 50ty. Thanks." She searched in her bra for the key to the room.

"No problem. I enjoyed every minute with you."

"Do you want to come in for a bit? I'm not going to sleep just yet," she said, standing in the doorway.

"I can chill for a minute, if you're up for it."

Having sex for the first time in a hotel room was not happening- bad business. I sat down on the bed while Cara went to take a shower. My phone rang while I flipped channels on the T.V. It was RonRon.

"What's up, player?"

"50ty, what's happening? Where are you?" he asked. I laughed and told him that I was in the room with Cara.

"Oh damn! Handle your business." He laughed and hung up.

When Cara came out of the bathroom wearing lingerie and smelling all good, my shit stood up like the Empire State Building. She knew it too. It was hard trying to hide it when my pants stuck up like a tent. I laughed as I wondered what she could be thinking about.

"What's wrong with you and why are you sitting straight up like that?" she asked, smiling. She sat beside me on the bed.

"You are a beautiful lady and to see you come out of the bathroom with what you got on turns me on. Sorry," I explained.

"Thank you," she responded.

"Don't thank me, baby, thank God and your momma for what they gave ya."

She smiled and blushed, grabbing a wine cooler out of the little ice cooler.

"Do you want one?" she offered.

"Nah, I only drink Hennessy, baby."

"So, what do you actually do besides hustle?" she asked. She looked sexy as hell and it was getting to me, seriously.

"Well, I have never had a job," I admitted. "I know that's something I would hate to do. But I would love to hurry up and get my hands on a million dollars."

"Damn are you really trying to get a million dollars?" she asked.

"Yeah. Can't you picture yourself lying in a pool full of cash?" I asked, teasingly. "I'll have it before Thanksgiving. I have two more months to go." I was most definitely getting to her.

"Whoa 50ty, did you hustle to make a million dollars or did you already have money from the start, but flipped it?"

"Well you can say I hustled, basically," I replied.

I began to rub her feet and legs. We stayed up talking the whole night until she fell asleep in my arms. Before I knew it, I dozed off still fully dressed.

The next morning, I got up early. Cara was still asleep. I didn't wake her up as I eased out of the room. I walked down the hallway to RonRon's room. He was still asleep too. I went straight to my bag to count the money I needed for the trip to Los's crib. I left the money that I wasn't going to spend with RonRon.

Reco called to tell me to meet him in the parking lot in twenty minutes. I didn't know why Los just wanted to meet with just me and Reco. But, business was business. I just wanted to get it and go.

Pulling up in front of Los's mansion always amazed me. I could picture myself in a big ass house like that one day. The same three cars from before were in the parking lot. We walked up to the double doors and the same big dude met us at the door.

"Sit down," the big dude said in an angry tone, giving me a mean look. I wondered what that was about.

"Sit down, 50ty," Reco said as the big dude walked around the corner.

"Nah, I'd rather stand Reco. It makes me feel more comfortable."

Fifth-teen to twenty minutes passed, I really started to get frustrated. I said "fuck it" a couple times to Reco and suggested we leave, but he didn't want to. A couple minutes later, Los came from around the corner with the big dude and three more guys with him.

"Thanks, Reco. Good looking out. I'll holla at you later," Los told him. I gave Reco a puzzled look. What the hell did he look out for?

Carlos stared at me as if I'd done something wrong.

"50ty. That's your alias, right? What's your real name, playa?" Los asked with a smirk on his face. Reco quickly exited the house.

"Terrill. Why? What's up?" I didn't have a clue as to what was going on.

"Come in my office. I want to holla at you," he said turning around and walking back around the corner.

"Get up," the big dude ordered with authority. As I followed them around the corner I reached in my pocket and pressed send on my phone because RonRon was the last person I talked to. I prayed he answered.

As I entered Los's office I could hear RonRon asking, "50ty, what's wrong?"

"Los, what's going on?" I said loud enough for RonRon to hear so he'd shut the hell up and listen.

"You remember the last time you were here and made that purchase from me?" he asked.

"Yeah. That's why I'm here now. I wanted to spend another three hundred grands with you today." He narrowed his eyes at me.

"Cool, well we are going to go together and get that there," he stated angrily.

I know something was up. "We?" I responded, clueless.

"Yeah that's right, partner." He replied with a smile. Since I didn't know what was going on I remained quiet hoping he'd tell me. We walked out of his office side-by-side with the four dudes behind us.

"Well 50ty, I told Reco last night when he was here that two of my chicks that transacted with you got robbed that same day."

Damn Reco was here last night?

"Damn Los. I didn't know nothing about that," I said.

"Of course, that's what you're supposed to say," he snapped, giving an evil chuckle.

As we headed out the back door I looked around the corner for Reco's car and saw he was gone. I realized then that he'd set me up. I got into one of the porches with Los and another guy. When we pulled out of the drive way, I spotted RonRon in the rental.

"Los, think about it for a second man." I tried to reason with him. "Why would I want to come in your city, your town, by myself and set you up when I don't know you? Plus, I don't know my way around here in Atlanta. Besides I gave you mad props on how you conducted business. Why would I want to destroy that? I can't get that much stuff from nowhere else for the amount I spend with you." He remained silent and just listened. "If anything, Reco was acting funny the whole way up here for some reason, like he wanted me here bad. From his reaction, it looks like he had something to do with that robbery. I don't know."

"Hold up," he interrupted. "I've known Reco for years."

"That's where the problem is. He knows too much about you and I don't know nothing. So, I'm bait, for the most part. What he discussed about you should have been a warning to me that he was a snake, but I had my guard down thinking I could trust him to."

Los gave me a weird look. I looked back at him dead serious. "Do you want me to just call it out?"

"Tommy, pull over to that store and get out for a second," he ordered. Tommy did as instruct, leaving me and Los in the car alone. I was ready to fight for my life and I felt comfortable knowing RonRon was behind us listening to everything. This was the third time I'd gotten caught up without my gun.

"So, what do you know about me, 50ty?" he asked.

"Look Los I'm in the same business you're in. I'm not a snitch, aiight? I'm someone who recognizes another person who is trying to get money."

"Okay, what did Reco tell you?" he asked again.

"He told me that you're a police officer." Prepared for his next move, I just stared at him.

"That bastard," he said angrily, getting ready to call Reco's number. I stopped him.

"Wait. Let me do you a favor and bring his ass to you now. Then we can all settle this shit." There was anger and tension in the car. It radiated off both of us. "I hate a snitch, a rat ass nigga. And not just that, he set me up," I said angrily.

"Well, what's up?" Los asked.

"That punk ass motherfucker," I exploded, letting my anger get the best of me.

"What's up?" Los repeated.

I must have been too loud because Tommy looked in the car to see if everything was okay. Los put his thumb up indicating that everything was straight.

"Los, call the chicks that got laid down that day," I told him.

"Why?" he asked.

"Because the night before I met you, I got stabbed twice, and that's why we got held up for them couple days before seeing you."

"What? Reco told me that y'all had car problems."

"Bullshit! I got stabbed twice at the Holiday Inn in downtown Atlanta by a crack head. He tried to rob me with a pocket knife." I showed him the wounds on my side. His expression changed, like he was beginning to believe my side. He nodded.

"I'm going to get him. How in the hell do he think he's going to turn tables on me like that and destroy my organization?" Los was fuming.

"What I'm going to do is bring that fool to you. I promise you that," I said.

Los let down the back window and signaled for Tommy to get back in the car.

"You can let me out here, Los, I'm straight. I'm going to hurry and catch a flight to Bainbridge to be there when Reco arrives. Call him and tell him that I'm history or something so he'll be comfortable going back home."

"I'll take you back to the hotel and to the airport. We're quite a way off from there," he pointed out.

"Thanks Los, but I have a rental. My homeboy RonRon is behind us so I'm straight." I replied. He looked back at RonRon, surprised. "I wasn't aware of what was going on, so I had to call for back up," I explained. "Now that I know what's up, we are going to handle this."

"I like you 50ty. You're a brave man," Los said.

Tommy would have been the first to get it. Luckily, we settled things because RonRon be itching to get into some shit.

"I still need the stuff when I return with Reco. Business is always running. Feel me?" I said as I got out the car.

"Bring me Reco then we will get down to business, son," he replied.

"Cool." I watched as they drove off.

I called Derrick and told him what happened. I instructed him to meet us at Reco's house, and told him to bring my AR-15 and his 9mm.

We rushed to the airport to catch a flight to Tallahassee to retrieve my car.

"Call up Reco and see where he's at and ask what's taking us so long. Act like you don't know what's going down," I told RonRon while we waited on our plane to arrive.

He did and Reco answered on the first ring.

"Yo Reco what's up? Where you and 50ty at? I called his phone he didn't answer," he lied.

"Oh, I left and ran up to the store, RonRon. Where are you now?" Reco asked just to see if he had a head start back to Bainbridge.

"I'm at Burger King grabbing some food. Is 50ty with you?"

"No, he's still at Los's crib handling his business. But, hey while you're there grab me a Whopper. I'll pay you back when I return to the hotel."

After RonRon hung up our plane pulled in. Good timing.

On the plane, I rocked backward and forward because I was so angry and disgusted. I never thought about the flight as we headed to Tallahassee. It took us an hour and a half to arrive. We hurried out of the airport and jumped into my car, rushing to Bainbridge. An hour later, we pulled up on Reco's block.

"Call him again to see where he's at," I told RonRon. He did and got no answer.

Derrick and Jermaine pulled up behind us driving a black S.U.V. I got out and gave Jermaine and Derrick a one-armed hug. Derrick introduced me to the two big dudes, Eric and Rodney. They were brothers.

I explained everything to them and told them how we'd go about getting Reco. Everybody spread out on the block. The neighbors weren't paying us any attention because they knew Eric, Rodney and Derrick.

After waiting for damn near six hours, I finally saw Reco coming up the block. From the way he parked in front of his house it was clear he planned to be in and out. But I had to stop him in his tracks. When they got out of the car, Eric and Rodney pulled up in the S.U.V. like they were going to holla at Reco for some product. Reco walked over to see what they needed. Tera went into the house. It was time to act.

I knocked on the back door and saw Tera through the blinds coming to answer. I hid on the side of the door so she wouldn't see me. She peered out and saw Derrick who waved and smiled. When she opened the door, I snatched her outside, putting my hands over her mouth so she wouldn't scream. RonRon put the 30/30 to her head.

"You'll live to remember this day if you keep your mouth shut. Understand?" I whispered.

RonRon and I entered the house first. Derrick and Jermaine took Tera upstairs. RonRon went in the kitchen and I headed to the living room. I kneeled behind the white bowling ball couch.

Reco entered the house, quickly locking the door behind him. He called out for Tera. When she didn't answer, he ran upstairs to search for her. First, he looked in the bathroom then the room next to it. When he opened his bedroom door a bit, he saw Derrick holding a 9mm pointed at Tera's head. He whirled around and tried to run, but he encountered me. We stood face-to-face. He screamed like he'd seen a ghost.

I swung my AR-15 with all my might, hitting him in the temple. It knocked him back into the room. He fell out, unconscious, on the floor. Tera jumped up, screaming.

"Oh my God! You killed him!"

"Bitch shut up," RonRon snarled, striking her in the back of the neck with the 30/30, knocking her out, too.

"Damn RonRon! You didn't have to do that," Jermaine said.

I picked her up and put her on the bed. We tied Reco up like an alligator and placed him on the floor of the SUV. Eric parked in the backyard. They put Tera in the back seat of my car, between Derrick and Jermaine. I let RonRon drive my car while I rode in the back seat of the SUV with Eric and Rodney. When we were ready to leave, I called Los and told him it was a done deal and instructed him to meet us at the Days Inn.

"Oh, shit wait, wait," I said. Eric stopped. I got out and ran back into the house. I grabbed all of Reco's stuff: the drug money, jewelry and guns. I put it all into a Coach bag that he had. Then it was off to Atlanta.

RonRon called to inform me that Tera was straight tripping. I told them to pull over at a Wal-Mart off the next exit. Reco was quiet, just lying there.

I gave Rodney Derrick's 9mm. "If Reco starts tripping, shoot him in the head. Don't even waste time with that nigga," I said. I walked over to the other car and looked in the back window at Tera.

"Fuck you, 50ty!" she mumbled through the handkerchief they used to gag her.

"Look, if it's fuck me, then it's fuck you. Your boyfriend set me up. He tried to get me killed. And I know he's the reason why that basier stabbed me. He had some peeps rob Los and blamed it on me then brought me to Los so he would kill me. The good thing about it though, Tera, is I'm not going to touch him or you. I'm going to let Los handle this matter."

"You should have knocked his ass off, 50ty," RonRon interrupted.

"Fuck you," Tera mumbled again.

"Tera please. I don't care nothing about you, either," I said, irritated. "But can you let me know something? Did you and Cara have something to do with this, because she will be the next one dealt with?" Tera shook her head no. She started crying again. "See, you thought you had a winner. But that nigga is a liar, murderer and a thief. The only reason we got you with us now is because I didn't want you to run to the police. If you stop tripping, we'll let you go in Atlanta, because Los wants you too. The choice is yours, aiight?" I went back to Eric's vehicle and got in. We continued on.

After seven hours of driving, we pulled up at the Days Inn in Atlanta. I called Los and told him we've arrived. Jermaine received one room. I tried to convince Tera that Reco was no good. He'd left her to die. He was all for self. She was still crying and scared.

"Will you scream if we take the rag off?" She shook her head. Derrick removed it and RonRon stared, cracking his knuckles, hoping she tripped out. She remained quiet. We kept her tied up though. Rodney and Eric were still in the SUV with Reco.

I contacted Cara and told her what happened. She seemed surprised.

"I knew something was wrong. Reco was acting strange when we were driving home from Atlanta. Tera and I didn't know what were up. We were confused," she said. That let me know that they didn't have anything to do with the set up. It was all Reco's doing.

"What are you going to do to Reco?" Tera asked as I headed out of the room.

"I don't know what's going to happen, Tera. But I'm not going to touch him. Once Los get him, it's out of my hands. They've known each other for years so Los will handle him."

As I closed the room door Tera spoke. "Be careful," she said softly.

I stood at the door for a second and thought Damn, I'm turning into a monster.

Los called to tell me to follow the Monte Carlo that was parked by the office. I walked to the SUV and told everybody to stay at the room until RonRon and I returned. I jumped into the back with Reco while RonRon drove. Reco was trying to say something. I tried to ignore him. I just stared at him and wondered why he'd go and mess up people's business like that, and set people up to get killed.

We followed the Monte Carlo as it traveled down a dirt road in the middle of the woods on the outskirts of Atlanta. As we drove up a hill, I saw lights from a fire or something. The Monte Carlo stopped and my phone rang.

"Go around the Monte Carlo and drive up to the fire that's burning," Los instructed. I pulled up close to the barn. We saw Los heading toward us with two dudes with him. RonRon clicked the 30/30 back putting a bullet in the chamber. I let the window down. I had the AR-15 in my lap.

"Where is Reco?" he asked.

"Right here," I told them, opening the door. The two dudes' drug Reco out of the SUV. He was helpless as they snatched him into the air and dropped him flat on his back to the ground.

"Bring him to the barn," Los demanded. "50ty, you got to stay and watch this. It will make you feel better." Just when I was about to say no, RonRon yelled 'hell yeah.'

As the two guys drug Reco over to the bonfire, Los gave him an evil satanic look. I looked at RonRon and saw that he was enjoying every minute of it. Los took out a chrome 45 Magnum as they untied Reco. I pulled out my 9mm. RonRon was already standing by a tree with his 30/30.

"Hold up, Carlos. Hold up, please listen," Reco cried.

"Spit it out," Los snarled.

"What did I do?" he asked, as if he didn't know what was going on.

"You know what you did fool!" RonRon said, laughing.

"I didn't do shit!" Reco denied. "Carlos, you got to be-" I interrupted him.

"You think that putting the blame on somebody else will set you free? You fucked up by getting me involved in this here, playa."

"What you need to do is admit to your actions, fool," RonRon said.

"I didn't do shit," he insisted. "What are you guys talking about?"

Los waited in silence for a while until Reco finally shut up.

"Why did you give out information on me that is confidential?" Los asked. Reco was speechless.

"Why did you tell Los that the reason we were late is because your car broke down, when it was because I got stabbed?" I asked. He didn't answer. "Sense you didn't succeed, you moved to the next target, Los's connection. You must be in debt or something? You seem desperate for money," I said, but he still didn't respond.

"I'll let you set it off with this nigga," Los told me, looking at Reco.

Reco glared at me as if he was ready to defend himself. That made me angrier.

"Y'all I got this," I said. "Don't interfere 'because this nigga is tripping'." I dropped my gun near Carlos and approached Reco.

"What you going do, nigga?" I challenged.

He swung at me, barely missing the tip of my mouth. I kicked him in the stomach as hard as I could. It knocked him to his knees. I then swung and caught him under the eye with a bawled fist. The blow knocked him on his back. He began gagging, trying to catch his breath.

"Pick 'em 50ty!" RonRon yelled. He and Carlos picked him up. I removed my shirt, handing it to Los.

"You ready?" I asked Reco. Instead of answering, he charged at me. I grabbed him by the collar, while he grabbed my pants. I slung him to the ground. As he was getting back up, Los caught him with a powerful right, knocking him back down again. Immediately, the other two dudes started stumping a mud hole in his ass.

"Stop!" Los yelled at them and they complied. "Let him get up." Everyone backed away and watched as Reco struggled to his feet. "50ty, handle your player. I just had to get that off my chest. I'm straight."

I walked up to Reco and whispered, "Payback is a motherfucker, ain't it?" Then I turned to walk away, thinking about all the things that happened in my life. It might be karma on my behalf. "Los, I'll let you finish him off." I got my shirt and gun from him. "I'm done." As I walked past RonRon, he pulled out his knife and rushed Reco.

"This is my nigga's payback, bitch!" He stabbed him repeatedly. Reco fell to his knees. I grabbed RonRon after the fourth or fifth stab. He was crying and coughing up blood. "Pussy!" RonRon said, feeling no remorse.

We got back in the SUV and pulled off. Before we passed the Monte Carlo, three shots sounded off. "Damn," I said. It hit me that someone had been murdered.

"Fuck him, 50ty! He got what he deserved," RonRon said. He had a calm look on his face.

"I wouldn't have done anything if he hadn't tried to blame that shit on me, RonRon," I said, feeling guilty.

"Karma is a bitch!" RonRon said. "Just get it out ya head." We headed back to the hotel. I just sat in silence. When we got to the room everybody was still there watching TV. Tera was curled up like a baby, sleeping.

"She cried herself to sleep," Derrick told us. I shook my head sadly. RonRon shrugged his shoulders nonchalantly.

"We got to figure out what she wants to do," I said.

"Wake her ass up," RonRon said.

I gently shook her shoulder. "Tera, wake up."

"Huh?" she mumbled.

"Wake up." She finally opened her eyes and managed to sit up. "Do you want us to take you back to Bainbridge?" I asked.

"Where is Reco?" she asked, ignoring my question.

I thought that RonRon would blurt it out, but he didn't. He let me handle it by walking out the room. Everybody followed him.

"I'm sorry, Tera. He's dead," I told her.

She jumped up. "Motherfucker, why?" She started swinging on me. She caught me with the first slap, but I grabbed her hands before she could hit me again. RonRon burst through the door and grabbed her off of me, slinging her to the floor rather hard.

"RonRon stop. Don't hurt her. She's just confused and upset, man. I got this under control," I told him. "Go back outside."

"You sure? I'll knock her ass out again if you want me to," he said, giving her a fierce look. "She needs to stop tripping'."

"No. You can go. I got this," I assured him. He gives me a look, shook his head and left again.

I helped Tera up. I let her cry while I just looked down at my feet.

"Why did you kill him? Why? You and Los aren't dead. He didn't kill anybody," she said angrily.

"Listen Tera, I could have died behind what he did. He didn't tell you nothing about his plans on destroying me and Los. He didn't even know me like that. Los was going to have me knocked off because of Reco's lies. He set me up. He had to be dealt with."

"Fuck you," she yelled. She started acting a fool again, going wild for about two minutes, then she calmed down and the tears dropped from her eyes again. I didn't touch her because it was my fault that Reco was gone, in a way.

"Can I call Cara?" she asked. I gave her my cell phone. She started crying more after hearing Cara's voice on the other line. She told her Reco was dead and surprisingly said she wasn't going back to Bainbridge.

"What do you mean?" I asked.

"I'm going with y'all," she said, giving me the phone.

"Hello? What's up Cara?" I asked in a calm voice.

"I don't know and don't want to know what happened, 50ty. I just knew he was up to something. I'm just glad you guys are okay. Just come and get me. I'm leaving with y'all and I'm ready now," she said excitedly.

CHAPTER 9

"What happened wasn't your fault 50ty," Tera told me. "I'm sorry for accusing you," she said crying. "He fucked up. Reco fucked up and you did what you had to do. I'm sorry," she said again and gave me a hug. Everybody chose that moment to come back into the room.

"Derrick, you guys can head home in the morning or whenever. My time here is up," I told them.

"What are you going to do now?" Jermaine asked.

"First, I'm going to holla at Los and grab a load of stuff from him. Then I'll take RonRon home after everybody gets their cut." I gave Rodney and Eric twenty-five grand a piece and they got excited. "But right now, I'm going to go wash my ass."

"Good cause I smell ya," RonRon joked causing everyone to laugh, breaking up the tension in the room. I headed for the shower.

Los called me right after I got out of the shower and told me to come over to his crib. I hadn't felt comfortable sense I'd been in Georgia. I knew it was time to hurry up and make that transaction and leave Atlanta for good. I got RonRon to ride with me over to Los's house while Jermaine and Derrick remained in the room with Tera.

Pulling up to the mansion, I really took the time to examine Los's crib on the outside. It was very nice. From the pure green cut lawn, to the trim trees, very few men could take care of a house without a woman being involved. We walked up to the double doors and, as always, the big dude met us and escorted us inside.

"Sit down. He'll be with you in a moment," he said in a calm voice this time. He walked around the corner toward the kitchen. RonRon and I continued to stand. Los entered the room carrying three big bags and wearing a smile.

"I don't give money away, but I can give you three bags of different types of good stuff to choose from." I grabbed what would make the most money which was that white stuff. It could be whipped up into miracles.

"Good choice, 50ty. I just want you guys to know that this game is real, man. And the only credit you get while playing this game is no credit. If you don't play by the rules then you will get dealt with one way or another," Los said.

"I feel you," I replied. He shook our hands

"I'm not a bad guy 50ty, so you don't have to be afraid of me. Holla at me anytime. My home is your home," he told me, smiling again.

There's something up with a man that smiles too much. I thought.

"How much do you want for that big bag of weed?" I asked. He looked at the bag then looked back at me.

"You a soldier in the field, 50ty, and I don't want you to think once that I never done any favors for you okay? So, here." He tossed me the bag of weed. "It's on me." That gesture showed me that Los wasn't so bad after all. He just wanted his respect as any man would. Shit, you step on me then I step on you. That's life. I gave Los a one-armed hug then me and RonRon were out.

We left for Bainbridge that night and damn near blazed the whole trip. That bag of weed I got from Carlos was on point. Everybody was feeling calm and mellow, even Tera.

Back in Bainbridge we went to Derrick's house. I cooked up the coke with baking soda and made five hundred grand worth of bricks. I let Derrick and RonRon split the rest. After we finished the settlement I packed up my bags to head back to St. Pete. RonRon was already set to go.

As me, Tera and RonRon walked outside, Cara pulled up in a cab. I was happy to see her. She paid the cab driver then gave me a hug first. She and Tera started crying then they hugged for a minute. They were two strong women that understand the situation we were all in.

RonRon pulled up in front driving my car, ready to go home. I told Derrick and Jermaine to holla at me on a regular basis because I really didn't know when I'd be back. They understood. Jermaine going to stay with Derrick for a while, which was all good.

RonRon, Tera, Cara and I headed for "Da Burg." Tera had been to St. Petersburg a couple of times while passing through on Interstate 275 heading to Miami, but Cara never had.

"Tera, I just want to apologize for my actions back there in Bainbridge and Atlanta," RonRon said with a sad expression on his face. We could tell he was really upset about it.

"It's okay, RonRon. I forgave you a long time ago and you too, 50ty. So, don't think about it anymore. We just have to stay focused on what lies ahead," she said.

What she'd said was true, because thoughts of the past can lead us in the wrong direction. On the road that we travel, we couldn't afford to be led in the wrong direction.

In Bushnell, we stopped to fill up with gas so we wouldn't have to make any more stops. Then we went to a fast food restaurant and went inside to eat.

"Bosco was in prison here in Bushnell, RonRon," I said as we sat at a table.

"Oh yeah? Man, I miss Bosco. It's crazy what happened to him," he said.

"He is the main reason why we have all this cash and are on top of things now," I told him. Cara brought our food to us while Tera got the drinks.

"How is that?" he asked.

"It's like he brain-washed me right before he died. He was talking about how tired he was of being broke and told me I shouldn't still be out there selling hand-to-hand drugs. Basically, he was telling me to stack and build then get out of the game. Then he got out of the car and told me to stay in. Said he would grab me a soda and some chips. He went in the store and that was the last time I saw him alive."

I had RonRon's full attention and I was in a zone, thinking about that day.

"So, damn, why he wanted to go in there and lay the place down by his self?" RonRon asked.

"I don't understand why he just flew off the edge like that without letting me in on it." I had everybody's attention, no one is eating. "All I can see now is him lying there with his eyes open, staring right at me—dead."

"Let's get off of that 50ty and let's eat. Shit, I'm buzzed as hell and don't need to get blowed out off that there," RonRon said. We all began to eat in silence.

Back on the road traffic was thick on the interstate. Everybody was full and they all fell asleep. It didn't take long to get home from Bushnell. Pulling up on my block, we rolled by my crib and saw bullet holes all over my house.

"Damn," RonRon said. We both laughed.

"Damn, is that your house, 50ty? What happened?" Tera asked.

"That's the reason for my bruised face when y'all saw me at the airport in Atlanta."

"Yo 50ty, it's this dude name Pepper Singletary. He sells and rents houses. You can call him and see what's up with that," RonRon said.

"No doubt," I replied.

We grabbed two rooms at the Ramada Inn. RonRon and I went into one room and Tera and Cara shared another. We really didn't trust them after what happened with Reco. RonRon kept peering out of the window at their room.

"RonRon go holla at your grandma and your homeys. I'm straight playa. You don't have to stick around just holla at me later," I told him, while we both peered out the window at their room.

"I don't trust them as of yet, 50ty," he said, reading my mind.

"They're cool. Just go get paid and holla at me later."

RonRon finally left and I jumped into the shower. I heard someone knocking at my room door. I quickly got out and grab my clothes, putting them on. I looked through the curtains without touching them and saw that it was Cara. I examined her then looked around for signs of the police or anything out of the ordinary. I didn't see anything. Feeling slightly fearful, I grabbed my 9mm and tucked it in the back of my pants. I was ready for whatever. I unlocked and opened the door.

She came in looking around curiously.

"Where's RonRon?" she asked, sitting on the foot of the bed.

"Oh, he went to holla at his people and to let them know he's back home. Why?"

"I'm just asking. Tera wanted him, not me," she said, smiling.

"So, Tera is feeling RonRon?" I asked, smiling back at her.

"I guess so. She told me to tell him to come see her." She fired up a blunt that was in her cigar pack. "Anyway, let's get off them and talk about your plans. What are you going to do?"

"I really don't know," I told her as she passed the blunt and I hit it.

We smoked and listen to 95.7 FM the Beat. An old song by The Isley Brothers came on.

"Oh! That's my song right there!" Cara said. She starts singing it and hitting the blunt.

"Damn Cara I didn't know you listened to oldies but goodies."

"Yeah that's all my parents used to listen to as I was growing up."

As we chilled, Cara called for Tera to come over and smoke with us. I called RonRon to see what he was up to. Tera arrived quickly.

Tera and I were up for a while because Cara fell asleep on my bed. It was quiet and peaceful because we were both lit. Then she fucked up the mood.

"You think they found Reco's body yet?" She asked, blowing my high clean off the cliff.

"I can't answer that question, Tera."

"I just can't put it together for nothing," she said, taking a long puff from the blunt.

"The picture is really clear. It's just unbelievable to you right now," I told her. She kept taking strong pulls on the joint.

"But why did he set you and Los up like that?" she asked.

I just shook my head. "I don't know. He never said why. But the picture was clear. He was greedy and wanted more."

"Well if he did have y'all hit like that, what did he do with Los's cash?" she asked.

"You should know that answer better than me. He usually keeps his stash in his room closet, in an Atlanta Falcon's coach bag. I already got that. It wasn't much."

"Did you see his GA Tech bag?" she asked.

"No, I never saw that in his room."

"Bet he got it in the cabinet in the kitchen. That's where he kept all his most important products and cash," she revealed.

I called Derrick immediately and relayed the information Tera had given me. I told him to handle that and call me back. From the look in Tera's eyes she was tired.

"Go to sleep Tera, before you faint," I told her, jokingly. She smiled then went to her room.

RonRon came to the room and knocked on the door shortly after Tera left. I quickly let him in before he woke Cara up.

"Tera wants to see you homey," I told him.

"For real?" He asked, looking excited. I nodded and he left again.

I was exhausted and tired myself. I got in the bed with Cara. As I got comfortable, she turned over and faced me. She placed her hand on my side.

"I'm hungry, Terrill," she said in a sleepy voice.

"Me too. I'll go grab us some chicken from KFC." I got back up and put on my shoes.

"Can I come with you?"

"Sure. Let's roll."

KFC was a block up the road. We got a box of chicken to go. We stopped at a corner store to get more blunts then we went back to the hotel to drop some chicken off to Tera and RonRon.

"I'll be right back Cara. I want to take you somewhere." I got out the car and went to Tera's room with their food. I knocked three times before Tera peered out the curtains.

"Hey," she said, opening the door. I acted as if I wasn't aware of what was going on.

"Tera, I got y'all some chicken. We'll see y'all tomorrow." Before I turned to leave, I noticed RonRon sitting on the foot of the bed with his shirt off.

"What they in there doing?" Cara asked, noticing the smile on my face.

"From the looks of it, it's mighty damn good," I answered.

We cruised around the city from St. Pete Beach on up to the pier. We got out and took a walk up to the pier and went inside the stores. Cara was enjoying every minute of our time together.

"Do you like fishing? I asked.

"Well the sport yes, but I don't like eating fish," she answered.

"I like fishing and I like to eat certain fish."

We walked outside of the pier and up to the water. We ate on the edge of the bank and watched the waves and gazed at the stars in the sky. The view was beautiful. Cara was amazed at the view because in Bainbridge they didn't have beaches or salt water. She had a calm look that showed so much love toward life.

"Terrill, I have an idea," she said, placing her hand on mine.

"What's that?"

"I have family in L.A. My Aunt Laurie, she wants me to come there to visit."

"That's a great idea, Cara. You should do that. I'll get you a flight whenever you want to go."

We started eating our chicken which I'd brought with us. "You should come with me and check it out," she said.

Los Angeles. Every time I thought of it, I envisioned the rap game and the music industry. Gangbangers were there. I would probably make a couple millions there easily. Plus, I heard they had the best weed. I'd just have to check out the dress code. I knew the basics. Bloods wore red. Crips wore blue. All the other gangs, I had no idea what their colors were. I'd just check out the environment when I got there.

"When you want to go up there, shit? I'll go," I told her.

"For real?" She asked, excited.

"Yeah. I'll check it out."

We went back to the hotel, but we didn't have sex. RonRon's car was still in the parking lot so we knew he'd stayed with Tera. I didn't mind waiting. I was cool with giving things some time and just getting to know each other.

I fell asleep hugging Cara. She was fully dressed, and so was I. It was hard to maintain control because Cara was fine, but I knew she'd be well worth the wait.

CHAPTER 10

November 20, 1997

A week later we were still at the same hotel. Cara called her aunt to tell her that we would be up there by the end of the month. RonRon and I had solo time throughout the week. I found out he and Tera hasn't had sex, he'd just been comforting her that night.

Derrick will have over eight hundred grands for me once he sold everything and got the cash from Reco's GA Tech bag. I told him to be sure to break Jermaine off nicely.

I spent the whole day with Cara while Tera and RonRon went on their runs. It was weird that I was home, but hadn't seen any of my friends since I got back. Maybe there was a good reason not to.

Cara read a book while I watched TV. Basically, we were bored.

"Cara, let's get out of here and go to the movies or somewhere." She agreed and jumped up to get dressed. I went to the office and grabbed a newspaper to see what movies were playing.

We decided to see a scary movie showing at Baywalk. I called RonRon and told them to meet us there.

Baywalk was a place where all ages hung out. They had restaurants, video game stores, clothing stores, plus the movie theater. While we waited for RonRon and Tera, we walked into the game store just to kill time. I also wanted to see if they had any new R.P.G. games or if any were coming out soon. That's all I play when I'm bored.

Cara stood by the door smiling at me while I looked through the games. The police were out like mad. I was paranoid, but I ignored it. Cara spotted RonRon and Tera in the line at the ticket office, we went to join them.

Once inside, Tera and Cara headed to the concession stand to get popcorn and drinks while RonRon and I went to find seats. We sat at the top of the row and watched the movie. Tera and I jumped on every scary part. Cara laughed at us every time. After the movies ended, we went to Denny's to eat.

"That was a good movie," I said as we sat down at a table.

"Yeah, you and Tera jumped on every scary part," Cara laughed.

"RonRon slept through the whole movie," Tera said.

"I don't do scary movies," RonRon said. "Y'all can have that."

We left Denny's, went back to the hotel, and turned in for the night.

I slept late the next day. Cara was with Tera and RonRon out handling business. Derrick's call woke me up. He told me that he was almost sold out of everything. Once he was done, he will call me back so I could come get the money.

RonRon returned wearing a big smile. "I sold out, playa!" he said and fired up a blunt. "It's time to smoke out."

We'd been smoking our asses off since we got back in St. Pete. My chest hurt every time I inhaled. I knew that was an indication that it was probably time to stop smoking.

I wait patiently until Derrick called and told me he was out of everything. I was happy as hell and screamed out loud. "I'm Rich Bitch!" I called RonRon and told him he was on his own. It was the day Cara and I were heading to the west coast.

"I feel you, pimp. You only got one life to live so take advantage of it," he said.

"Thanks for everything you did for me, RonRon. I trust you with my life," I told him.

We didn't know what Tera planned to do so I asked.

"Tera, are you going with us?" She looked at RonRon and shook her head.

"Are you staying with me, baby?" he asked, giving her a hug.

"Yes. When are you guys leaving?" she asked.

"Tomorrow," I said.

"So soon," she said, sounding disappointed. Cara and Tera started crying and hugging. RonRon and I walked outside.

"Did you and Tera have sex yet?" I asked.

"Hell yes. Plenty of times now," he answered.

"Nice, but I didn't hit Cara yet. It's B.B.P. with me, business before pleasure.

"True, true," RonRon said.

Later that night, we ordered pizza. Everybody decided to stay in our room because that would be our last night together for a while. Of course, they had to smoke. My lungs were still hurting so I only hit the blunt a few times.

I got up super early the next morning. Our flight would leave at 12 noon. It was only 7 AM. Cara woke up too.

"Good morning," she greeted. She looked finer than she did when she went to sleep.

"Good morning," I replied.

Our voices caused the rest of them to wake up.

"Hey y'all," Tera said, sitting up in the bed.

RonRon yawned and stretched. "What time y'all leaving?" he asked.

"Around eleven o'clock. The plane takes off for Tallahassee at noon."

Everybody got up; showered and dressed then we headed to kiss in' Cozzens to eat breakfast.

"50ty, how are you going to get your car up to Cali? That's across state?" RonRon asked.

"I guess you will have to keep it or sell it. It's up to you," I answered.

We chilled at the table after we'd finished eating.

"I'm going to miss you guys," Tera said. Tears started forming in her eyes.

"Here we go with this shit," RonRon said sarcastically and we laughed. "On a serious tip, take care of Cara, playa. I'm going to miss you dawg."

"I'm not with all this gay talk, shit," I said. " Y'all stop all this damn whining." Everybody laughed again. We got up and left after leaving a hefty tip for the waitress.

10:30 arrived quickly. We rode around the city one last time, going through our neighborhood. I saw most of my friends, but didn't stop to talk to them. I just honked the horn and kept rolling.

We stopped at RonRon's grandma's house. I got out and talked to her for a while. I told her that I was leaving for California and might not return. We stayed there until it was time for us to go to the airport. I sat on the steps alone while everybody was inside talking. I reminisced about my life in the Palmetto neighborhood. I thought about murder, death, selling drugs to basiers, burglary, and all the problems.

So, is this a place that I will miss?

"Nope," I said aloud and went inside to join the others.

We blazed on our way to Tampa/International Airport. We said goodbye in the lobby.

"RonRon homey, take care of Tera as if she is another part of you," I said.

"No doubt, pimp. I know where the love's at," he said, giving Tera a kiss.

We got on the plane and found our seats in first class. Cara took a deep breath.

"Well, it's onward to a new life in California."

"I feel you," I said. California was a place that I'd always wanted to visit. I was glad we were making the trip.

The plane took off. I looked out the window as we got high in the sky. I told Florida goodbye forever, then I leaned back in my seat and got comfortable. I gazed at Cara and she smiled at me.

I thought, I'm higher than a motherfucker.

I left RonRon and Tera the whole package of weed. I hoped I'll be able to find some of L. A's finest when we arrived.

We made it to Tallahassee in two hours. I checked for the next flight to California and saw it arrived in two and a half hours. We met up with Derrick and Jermaine in the lobby so that I could get my money from Derrick.

"I'm free from Florida and Georgia now. Cuz, you and Jermaine need to be careful out there," I said. We all sat at a table inside the restaurant.

"Damn 50ty. All this time you haven't bought anything. You've been wearing the same old clothes and shoes," Jermaine said. I laughed because he was right.

"Shit, I'm sitting on a million-five hundred and fifty grand. When I get to L.A. Cara and I will buy out the mall, since you put it like that," I said. They all laughed.

An hour before our plane arrived, Aunt Laurie called to let Cara know she'd be waiting for us to arrive. "When you get to L.A. bro, what kind of car do you want?" I asked Jermaine.

"Surprise me," he said.

I'd do just that because I owed him. Jermaine took me in, but he always knew I was a hustler. When our mom passed we had to find a way to survive. Jermaine chose to work; I took another route. I would never tell anybody, not even my brother, how I hit up G-Rod. The best secrets are kept in the mouth.

Once I found a connection in L.A. it might be on and popping again, but nothing heavy. I'd hustle just enough to keep a mill in my pocket.

The last thirty minutes passed quickly. I started to feel a little nervous. My first move would be to stop at a gun shop. Derrick and Jermaine left. It wasn't long before we were on the plane.

"Los Angeles bound baby!" Cara said. She gave me an excited hug.

"For real. I can't believe it to tell you the truth."

"Believe it, baby. This is a reality check. I haven't been in California since 1991, six years ago," she said.

We made one stop in Texas then we were back in the air. It took about seven hours to make it to L.A. I must have dozed off because Cara had to shake me awake.

"Yeah baby. What's up?"

"Look, isn't L.A. pretty at night?" I gazed out the window. The building's lights and car lights made Los Angeles look well lit up at night. It looked similar to Tampa and St. Pete., but bigger. It wasn't much longer before the plane landed and we onboarded.

"Cuz, cuz, over here," yelled a tall dude standing near the telephone booths.

"Hey Anthony," Cara greeted, giving him a hug.

"This is my man, Terrill, but they call him 50ty," she told him. "Baby, this is my cousin, Anthony."

"Welcome to L.A." He said, shaking my hand.

"Glad to be here, thank you."

A fat kid walked up to us. "Hey Cara," he said, smiling.

"Hakeem boy, damn you done got big." Cara gave him a hug and a kiss on his fat cheeks.

"Let me get ya bags." Anthony grabbed mine and Hakeem got Cara's. I kept my eyes on all the bags because they were full of money. I planned to hit the mall and let Cara get us some of L. A's finest gear. I was glad she knew her way around.

We got a rental car at the airport. Anthony and Hakeem put our bags in the trunk.

"Dang, them bags were heavy," Hakeem said.

"For real," Anthony replied.

"We'll meet you guys at Auntie's house after we leave the mall," Cara told them. I gave them a hundred dollars apiece for helping with our luggage.

"Whoa 50ty, I like you already." Hakeem smiled and put his money in his pocket.

"Cara, marry him," Anthony joked and we all laughed.

We got in the rental and I started the ignition. "Let's go get something to eat first, baby. I'm hungry. Then let's go to the mall," Cara suggested.

"I want to make a good impression on your aunt, baby. I hate that she thinks I'm doing bad."

"My aunt doesn't care anything about that. She's going to love you," Cara said, but I had my doubts. No aunt wanted her niece to be dating a broke ass Negro. I had to come correct and I intended to do just that.

We rolled through L.A. Cara showed me where her mom and dad used to live when she was younger. It was an all-black neighborhood. People wore blue dickies and T-shirts. We stopped at a Burger King and ordered to go.

"Do you want to ride around a bit, or do you want to just go to the mall then go to my aunt house?" Cara asked.

"This is my dream, to just ride around California," I said. "Let's roll a bit then head to a mall."

"I have family from Oakland all the way down to Compton," she said as we rolled through every neighborhood in Los Angeles.

In L.A. the females had less to worry about than the men. We had to play by the rules. As Cara drove, we went through different sets with no problem. I checked out all the dress codes, just to know what colors not to wear. I'd never join a gang…that wasn't me at all, but I had much respect for their way of living.

Low riders were everywhere, sitting on low lows. Six-fours with hydraulics', clean material parked in a three-wheel motion. The view was sweet.

I called RonRon and Derrick to tell them I'd made it to California safely. Cara talked to Tera for a while. We coasted the blocks for about an hour and a half then went to a huge mall.

"Hey, you take this." I gave Cara fifteen grand to spend. "I'm going to stay here with my cash. Don't buy me nothing but expensive clothes and shoes. I don't need any jewelry." I had Reco's stuff in my pouch with the cash.

"Alright baby. I'll be back in a few." She kissed me and headed into the shopping mall.

My next move would be to check out the gun shop. I would look into buying a house and a nice car, but until then we would check into a motel.

I had one million five hundred and thirty thousand on me. I couldn't fall asleep while waiting on Cara so I turned the radio on to listen to some West Coast stuff. I was going to be smart and take full control of my movements since I didn't have a gun.

After I'd waited for almost thirty minutes, I got a call from Tera.

"Hey there, Tera. What's going on?"

"Hey, 50ty. I'm just calling to see what y'all up to up in California."

"I'm just sitting in the car waiting on your slow ass girl to come out of the mall."

"50ty, you should know better than to send us in a place like that alone. You think we can just walk in and out of a clothing store? That's not happening," she joked.

"Well, it shouldn't take her much longer cause her aunt is waiting on us. We haven't seen her yet."

"I hope you're right," she said.

"How is RonRon treating you?" I changed the subject.

Her voice changed to reflect the excitement. "That's my baby. He is so sweet and we have a house in the making. We're just waiting on them to finish the paperwork then we'll get settled in."

"That's what's up!" I said. "I'm happy for y'all. I'll tell Cara to call you when she gets back."

Even though I didn't mean to fall asleep, I must have nodded off. Cara knocked on the window, scaring the hell out of me. I tried to play it off as I opened the door.

"Oh baby, I didn't mean to scare you. I'm sorry," she apologized. She placed three Big Boy bags in the backseat.

"I just got off the phone with Tera not too long ago. She called to tell us that she and RonRon have a place in the making."

"Oh, that's good. Now they can get out of that damn hotel." She got in the car and we pulled out of the mall's parking lot.

On the way to her aunt's, we stopped at a gas station to get something to drink. There were a lot of young men standing around the gas station. I noticed all of them wore red bandanas on their heads or hanging out of their back pockets.

"This is Blood territory," Cara told me before she got out. As she walked into the store the guys tried to holla at her right in front of me. I just watched in silence.

"That's you there?" One of them asked and I just nodded, letting them know it was cool. As she exited the store and headed back to the car she looked at them with a sexy smile.

"Sorry sweeties, but I'm taken," she said. I could tell she liked the attention, but what chick wouldn't?

I peek what was going on. They were hustling on the side of the store.

"No respect at all," Cara said to me, still smiling while getting into the car.

"That's life Cara. Men are going be men."

"Doesn't mean they have to be jerks, though," she said, pulling off. I didn't respond.

"Baby, before we go to your aunt's could you stop at a firearm place?"

"Okay. I know this place right around the way," she said.

"Cool."

Inside Knights of Round there were all types of guns, knives and other weapons. I grabbed a 45 Magnum, two cases of bullets and an extra clip. I also grabbed a Mac 10 with an extra clip and ammo and walked to the counter.

I guess the clerk could tell that I was about money. "On the down low," he said lowly. "We have bulletproof vests for sell if you're interested." I was shocked to hear that since we couldn't get that in St. Pete.

"What kind do you have?" I asked.

"All kinds. What kind are you looking for?"

"Let me get a couple of Teflon vests," I told him.

"Whoa! Those are big vests. That's going cost you."

"How much will it cost for everything?" I asked.

"Since you bought guns and ammo as well, I'll sell you everything for ten grands," he said. I didn't even flinch as I paid him.

"We're going to have to keep the guns for three days pending a background check," he told me. I already had that covered. They would be registered in Cara's name. I got the vests upfront.

After leaving the range, we went straight to Aunt Laurie's house. There was a mixed race of people, Mexican and blacks, standing on the corners. From the looks of it, they were Crips. They wore white T-shirts and blue Dickies.

We pulled up to a brown house with a fence around it. Older people sat on the porch. I noticed that the palm trees were taller than the ones in Florida. We walked up to the porch where two elder men were. A lady stood by the door.

"Hi Aunt Laurie." Cara ran up to give her a hug.

"Hey baby. How you doing?" she asked, looking her up and down.

"Fine."

"You aren't lying about that sugar," one of the elder's said and the two men laughed.

"Y'all shut up," Cara's aunt said. She held the door open for us. I hit the switch on the key chain to lock the doors on the rental car. I smiled at the two old men and spoke.

Cara introduced me to everybody in the family. There were others there, but she doesn't know them. She went into the kitchen with her aunt and the other women. I walked back outside to get to know the two elders on the porch.

They started asking questions as soon as I sat down on the steps.

"So where are you from, son?"

"St. Petersburg Florida, born and raised," I answered with pride.

"Is this your first time in Los Angeles?" the other elder asked.

"Yes, first time here. I always wanted to come to California so I wasn't going to miss this chance for nothing." They laughed.

"Welcome to L.A.," they both told me.

"Thank you. My name is Terrill, but they call me 50ty."

"We are Tom and Frank." We shook hands.

"All that gang banging stuff you see on T.V. and hear about on the streets about California is true, but hell life is how you make it. If you can survive in any ghetto, you can survive here in L.A.," Tom stated. I totally agreed with him.

"Terrill come here," Cara called from inside.

"Excuse me," I told them and went inside to see what she wanted.

"I want you to meet someone else, baby," she said, leading me to a bedroom where a young man rested in the bed.

"Terrill, this is my cousin, Ronnie. Ronnie, this is my man, Terrill." I shook his hand. It dawned on me that both of his legs were missing. I didn't say anything or show any indication that I noticed.

"How tall are you, baby?" Aunt Laurie asked.

"I'm 6 feet 4, ma'am."

"Gracious," both she and another lady in the room said at the same time.

I let them have their family moment and went back outside on the porch. I asked Tom and Frank about what happened to Ronnie.

"Some of them damn fools from Crenshaw was messing with him and some more people at the corner store one night and trouble started. They open fire with some type of machine gun," Tom explained.

"Yeah, and Ronnie got caught with nowhere to run and they shot him in the thigh a couple times. Anthony was up there that night it happened," he added.

Damn, I said to myself. People are sicker up here than they are in Florida.

I talked to Tom and Frank for about an hour and a half. You could always learn from older people because they'd been around longer and saw stuff that happened back in the day. I listened to them more than I talked.

Cara checked to see if I was ready to leave and I told her no. Since we just got to L.A. she should spend some time with her aunt. I could tell her aunt was really happy to see her.

I wanted to get a room, but Ms. Laurie insisted that we stay with her until we decided what we are going to do. It was 2 AM when I looked at my watch. It had gotten late before I even knew it. Tom and Frank finally got up and walked off the porch, going separate ways.

I grabbed my bags and brought them into the house. Cara showed me to the room that her aunt wanted me to sleep in. I placed my bags beside of the bed.

"Baby, you can go ahead and take a shower after you get organized," Cara told me. I took her up on that then got in the bed and went to sleep.

I woke up early, as usual. Looking over at my bags, I saw they were in the same position that I'd left them. My money bag was under my clothes bag. Cara was out cold. I didn't even remember when she'd gone to bed. She had to be tired as hell because it was my first time hearing her snore. I laughed as I went into the bathroom.

As I washed my face and brushed my teeth, I heard a terrible coughing from the room next to the bathroom. I returned to the room and turned on the T.V. to watch the early morning news. After about five minutes of hearing about murders, missing kids, and bad accidents, I turned it back off. It was too depressing.

I got my bag of clothes that Cara brought, matched them up to hang in the closet. She brought seven different pairs of shoes: Lugz,

Nikes, G-Units and L.A.'s finest Converse. I pulled out a G-Unit outfit with matching shoes and socks.

"Damn baby, you are fine," Cara said, sitting up on the end of the bed watching me.

"Good morning baby. I didn't mean to wake you up."

"You didn't wake me up. I was getting up anyway." She gave me a kiss and went into the bathroom. Once she'd finished getting dressed, we headed downstairs. Her aunt had prepared a big breakfast. I hadn't eaten so heartedly since my grandmother passed a couple years back. Everybody was at the table except for Ronnie.

"I talked to a real good friend who sells and rent houses about you two. She has a two-bedroom house for rent right now if you want to go and check it out," Aunt Laurie said, looking at me with a smile. "I know every man needs his privacy." She gave me the number.

After we finished eating, Cara went back to the room while I helped her aunt put the dishes away.

"You have all that money in those bags. Son, why won't you open up you a bank account?" she asked. I almost dropped the dish that I held. "Don't panic, son." She took the dish from me. "I didn't go through your belongings, just peeked inside. You are with my niece. I know she told you all about me. I'm very concerned about my family. I wanted to know what was in those bags so I looked inside. I'm just glad it wasn't any drugs, son."

I relaxed and turned back to the dishes. My phone rang.

"Excuse me," I said politely and left out of the kitchen.

"What's up, 50ty?" RonRon greeted.

"Chillin', pimp. I'm going to go check out this landlord Aunt Laurie hooked us up with about a crib. What's going on with you?"

"Dawg, G-Rod got killed last night, him and his lady," he said.

"What the fuck?" I yelled, unable to help myself. Cara gave me a look for swearing so loud. I apologized quickly, not wanting to offend her aunt. "What happened?"

"They were at Snow Peak's last night and a dude pulled up and open fired on them. They counted forty bullet holes in his Acura."

"Damn," I repeated, thinking about his mom and daughter.

I went and sat down on the porch after hearing the distressing news from RonRon. I thought about everything that happened to me. I remembered how I'd become rich and the trouble I went through to do it.

Cara came outside to comfort me. "What happened, baby?" she asked, placing her arms around my neck.

"Someone I knew got killed last night during a drive-by."

"Oh my God."

I tried to shake the bad feelings so I wouldn't mess up the day. "It's cool. I didn't know him like that. He was someone from around the way." I kissed her on the forehead. We got up and went back into the house.

I called the lady who was renting the house and she told us we could check out the house that morning. As we drove to meet the woman, Cara was talking excitedly. I could tell she was very happy to be home.

We arrived at an all-white house, with a black Honda parked in the driveway.

"It looks nice from the outside, baby," Cara said. A well-dressed lady came out the door and approached us.

"Hi. Are you Cara, Laurie's niece?" she asked.

"Yes ma'am."

"My name is Oriel. Laurie and I are good friends," she chatted. "I've known her for years. Come on inside and look the place over," she said, showing us in.

I immediately noticed the huge fireplace in the living room. There were shiny hardwood floors. In the bedrooms the carpet was nice and plush. The kitchen was very spacious with plenty of counter space and lots of cabinets. The master bedroom had its own bathroom. There was even a utility room where a washer and dryer rested in the corner.

Cara and I looked at each other and agreed that we liked the place.

"We'll take it," we said in unison and laughed.

"Since you're Laurie's niece, just fill out the paperwork and you can move in whenever you are ready," she said.

"I'm curious. How much would you sell this place for?" I asked.

"First and last month will be two thousand dollars," she answered, missing my question.

"I know you want that for renting, but how much are you willing to sell it for?" I repeated. "I don't want to rent because that will be a waste of money. I'm thinking about planting my foot down on the West Coast. I might as well start early."

"Oh, you'd like to buy it?" She got an excited look on her face. "I'll sell it to you for eighty thousand, even though its market value is more," she said.

It was a very nice house inside and out. It was well worth a hundred grand. We agreed on the amount that she wanted. Since I planned to pay her in cash, I had to go back to Aunt Laurie's house. I left the two women inside the house and drove back.

"Aunt Laurie, we like the house and we're going to buy it today," I told her.

"Well, I am so happy to hear that. I'm glad y'all are staying so I can be close to my niece," she said happily.

"Thank you for watching our stuff. I have to get back over there with this money," I said and left again.

I returned to the place and gave Ms. Oriel the bag with eighty-grand inside. She looked surprised, as if she was scared to take the bag of money.

"I do take cash, but this amount- I'll need a money machine to count all this," she exclaimed causing us to laugh.

"It's all there Ms. Oriel. You just take your time and count it," Cara said.

The lights were already on in Oriel's name but only for a few days. We had time to transfer everything. I placed my money in the attic of a small closet located in the hallway. I planned to buy a safe to put it in later.

We went to L.A. furniture, located on the West side of Los Angeles, and bought furniture for the entire house. Cara decided to purchase everything in black: black leather couch, love seat, and dining set. After leaving the furniture store, we went to R&J's Carpet and Sheets. We picked out an all-white, Stain Master carpet. After getting that taken care of we went to Publix to shop for groceries.

Everything was in place within two days. It looked like we'd been living there for a month.

"Baby, you got taste," I said as we sat at the split-end table. I was at one end and she at the other. There were roses in the middle of the table for a centerpiece.

"Thank you for making me feel special and for letting me chose everything for the house," Cara said.

We fell asleep in the living on the floor after being overwhelmed from arranging the house all day. I woke up in the middle of the night and looked at the time. It was two in the morning. I called my brother to tell him that I was straight and ready for him to come up whenever he could.

Before going back to sleep next to Cara on the floor, I added up what I'd spent in my head. I still had well over a million dollars. I'd paid two hundred grands on everything for the house and twenty-five hundred on a big screen T.V. We were set for a while because I wouldn't have to spend that much on anything else.

When I woke up at eleven the next morning, Cara was already up. She'd decorated the bedroom and put black sheets on the bed with a Zebra print comforter. It looked nice. She gave me a smile when she noticed me watching her from the doorway.

"Hey baby," she said, giving me a kiss.

"What's up, ma?"

"Nothing. I want to go over my aunt's house to see what they're up to."

"Cool, I'll drive because I want to check out a couple places."

After dropping Cara off at her aunt's house, I drove off and spotted Anthony and Hakeem rolling up the street. They stopped next to me.

"What's up, 50ty? "Anthony greeted.

"What's going on with y'all?" I asked.

"Nothing much, just heading to my aunt's house to chill," Anthony said.

"I'm going by a couple places. Do y'all want to ride along?"

"Yeah, follow us to the house and we will jump in with you," Hakeem replied.

They parked in the front of their aunt's yard and got in the car with me.

The first place we visited was a place that sold statues and mirrors. I bought a panther climbing up a tree. Water ran from its mouth and traveled down its body. Then I bought two baby panthers to put on each side of the statue. I gave the delivery guys the tip money for delivery upfront, so they followed us to the crib. I had them place the fountain in the middle of the living room.

Anthony and Hakeem were amazed at how Cara had the inside of the crib set up. As soon as I opened the front door, the fresh brand-new scent rushed our noses.

I didn't know Anthony smoked weed until he pulled out a blunt from his top pocket. I hadn't smoked in a while. I was anxious for the delivery guys to leave so I could get to it.

"50ty, don't tell Cara I smoke, okay," Hakeem said, smiling.

"How old are you, Keem?"

"Fourteen," Anthony replied

"Shit, I smoked around your age. It's cool. I won't say anything, homey." I passed him the blunt. "Hey, do you guys know where I can get a nice ride?"

"What kind of ride are you looking for?" Anthony asked.

"Like a Hummer or something nicer."

"Go to Hummer City," he said.

"Let's go." I hit the blunt one last time before putting it out in the ashtray.

The neighborhood was quiet so I really didn't have to worry about being burglarized. I learned never to trust the streets at all so I turned on the alarm every time I left or went to sleep at night.

We went to a car lot that had a lot of Hummers to choose from on the lot. One in particular caught my attention when I got out of the car. A salesman came up to us and asked if he could help.

"How much are you selling the red and black Hummer for?" I asked.

"Oh, that's going for a couple hundred thousand and if you are planning on renting one that will cost you eleven grand a month," he stated with a look that seemed to say it was too much for us to even look at.

"How many miles does it have?" I asked.

"Well it's only been driven twice, and that's only around the lot," he replied.

"I want it."

That bald to the top of his head, high-water wearing ass man gawked at me.

"Are you serious?"

I looked at Anthony and Hakeem, giving them a smirk.

"What the hell do you mean, am I serious?" I said, aggravated as I glared back at him.

"I'm sorry. I didn't mean anything about that but-"

"Fuck the explanation," I cut him off. "I want the red and black Hummer, man."

I paid for the Hummer upfront and drove it off the lot. Anthony followed me and Keem rode with me to their aunt's house.

When we pulled up in front of their house Cara came to the door. She got a surprised look on her face and placed her hands over her mouth. She began screaming and came running up to us.

"What's this, baby?" she asked excitedly.

"This is our family car," I told her.

"Wow, that's a nice way to start out in L.A." Aunt Laurie said from the porch as she stared at the Hummer from the door.

"'You think you can handle this truck, baby?" I asked Cara.

"Yeah, I can drive it. Stop playing," she said laughing. I gave her the keys and jumped into the rental. "You can drive it home then, baby. I'll see you when you get there."

She bent over and gave me a kiss through the window.

"Thank you, baby." Her eyes twinkled naughtily. "I'll thank you properly later." She winked and walked back to the house. I just shook my head and drove off.

I called RonRon when I arrived home. "What's up, playa?"

"Yo 50ty, what's happing?" he greeted.

"I'm chilling. I'm settled in now. You and Tera can come up whenever you're ready. "

"Nice! We can decide. We're doing well down here. Tera wants to get married," he said.

"Damn bro, y'all really are making moves. When and where do y'all want to get married?" My ear was glued to the phone.

"Like next month on the 17th which will be on the weekend. Probably up there in L.A," he said.

"That will be straight, RonRon. I'll decide here. Just don't tell Cara or Tera anything yet. Let's surprised them," I said.

Cara came home shortly after I hung up with RonRon. She was upset and crying.

"What's wrong, baby?" I asked, getting up from the floor and meeting her at the door.

"Ronnie got gangrene in both of his thighs. They rushed him to the hospital because he's in a lot of pain."

"I'm sorry to hear that," I consoled, giving her a hug.

We both sat quietly while the television played. Cara placed her head on my lap. I really didn't have anything to say. The bad news about Ronnie left a melancholy mood in the air.

Visiting Ronnie

CHAPTER 11

November 25, 1998. Thanksgiving Day.

We went to the hospital to visit Ronnie. While Cara was in his room with their family, I waited in the lobby for over an hour, before Cara and her aunt came out, they were both in tears as a doctor spoke to them.

Cara came over to me, while her aunt remained talking to the doctor.

"I'm sorry to have you waiting here so long, baby. You can go home and I'll see you later tonight," she said. She gave me a hug and a kiss.

"No problem, baby. I'll see you later then." I waved goodbye to her aunt. Cara walked me to the elevator. "Baby, stay with your aunt as long as you need, okay? I know things are really twisted right now and you just got here. She needs you by her side." Cara started to cry. I gave her a comforting hug then kissed her on the forehead.

"Thank you for understanding," she said, getting on the elevator. As the elevator door closed she waved goodbye and mouthed, "I love you."

Back at the house I paced around the living room deep in thought. I thought about how I was living and if I'd be able to change things. I promised myself that I would only spend money if necessary and only after careful consideration.

I called my brother to see how he was doing and told him about the wedding on the 17th of next month. He and Derrick would catch flight to L.A. that weekend. When he arrived, I hoped he'd stay because I felt it was for the best. We talked for a while. He told me about how Derrick was doing his thing and that they were keeping low key. I couldn't remember hanging up, but I guess I did since I fell asleep.

I was in a deep sleep when my phone rang. It was still on my ear and it scared the crap out of me. I saw that it was an unknown number. I didn't want to answer, but so much was going on in my life, it could be anybody.

"Hello?"

"Hey baby. It's me," Cara said. "I'm going to stay at the hospital tonight because Ronnie isn't doing so well."

"I understand, Cara. Do whatever you need to do to support him, baby. If you need me just call."

"Okay. I'll call you a lil later tonight," she said and hung up.

It was boring and I had nothing to do. I placed a microwave dinner in the microwave then decided to count all my money that was in the attic. I trusted Cara to the fullest, but I just had a habit of constantly counting my money. I went to take it down.

It took me over an hour to count it all. I had 1.3 million dollars. The house and the Hummer had cost 2.3 grand. I would have never thought in a million years that I'd be counting that much cash. I couldn't get over G-Rod and his girlfriend dying. If it hadn't been for G-Rod, I wouldn't be where I was. I felt bad for his mom and daughter, but thought, hey life is twisted. What happened to them isn't my fault.

After counting my money and eating dinner I went to take a shower. It cooled me off and relaxed my mind. Since there was nothing to do, I turned in for the night.

Later, I heard the alarm sound off and jumped up. Not having a gun, I just stood by the bedroom door waiting to see who was there. Rushing to the alarm system was Cara. She quickly put the code in, disarming it. I quietly jumped back into the bed so she wouldn't know she'd scared the shit out of me. I pretended to be asleep.

She came into the room and got her night clothes out of the drawer then went to take a shower. It took so long for her to come out that I fell asleep from boredom.

The radio came on low playing a slow jam. I opened my eyes and saw Cara standing by the dresser with a towel wrapped around her head and body. She smiled and walked over to the bed.

"I'm ready for you now," she said in a sexy voice, dropping her towel.

I stared at her body in silence. My dick jumped, poking the blanket up. She pulled the blanket back, looked at it and smiled

"I can see you missed me," she said.

She dimmed the lights and got in the bed. She climbed over me and grabbed my dick with both of her hands. Giving me a sexy smile while biting her bottom lip, she licked around it then placed it in her mouth. She started sucking it up and down, as if it was her favorite lollipop. After that, she eased up to my neck and started working on my upper body. No lie, she had skills. As my hands palmed her as she eased her warm pussy over my dick. She gave a soft moan as she mounted it. I felt really superior when I kept my dick on hard for a long time, until she came twice. I flipped her over on her back. I kissed her legs and thighs, making it around to her warm pussy. I had to skip the eating because I'd never done that before. I kissed her belly button and around her stomach. She kept trying to push my head down to her pussy, but I eased it back up to her chest. I kissed her nipples instead.

"Go down baby. Go down," she whispered.

I never did that before but it was what she wanted so I kissed her body until I was near her vagina. A porn flick I'd watched ran through my head as I performed. By the sounds she made, I must have been doing it the correct way. I placed my fingers on her clit rubbing it up and down as I slurped her juices. When she was soaking wet, I eased my dick in slowly. She moaned and wrapped her legs around my waist, splash!

Days came and went and nothing changed but the time. One day we were at Aunt Laurie's house for the whole day. I decided to chill with the two elders, Tom and Frank, on the porch.

"So, how do you like L.A., son?" Frank asked.

"Just like you guys said before: life is how you make it. And I'm just living my life," I said, not really answering the question. They both laughed.

I'd been sitting on the porch for over an hour. Anthony pulled in the drive way.

"What s up, 50ty?" he greeted. He looked high as hell.

"Nothing much, just chilling out here with these two funny guys," I said jokingly. Hakeem got out of the car and sat beside me on the steps. Anthony went into the house where Cara and her aunt were, in the room with Ronnie.

For some reason little niggas that hung around me, respected me like I was a king. I guess it was because of my style and ways with connecting to them. I have much respect for their bad asses, too.

"What's up Keem? What are you guys up to?" I asked. I saw the glazed look in his eyes as well. "Nothing. Anthony wanted to see Ronnie."

"Oh, I see."

"Hakeem, boy your Auntie baked some cookies in there. You better go get some before they disappear," Tom said.

"For real?" Hakeem asked, excited. He jumped up and ran in the house.

119

"That boy is well over a hundred and fifty pounds," Frank said. "If he keeps smoking and eating, he is going to get bigger than an ice box." I couldn't stop laughing. Those guys tripped me out every time I came over. That was cool because it kept the day moving.

Cara came outside a couple of minutes later. She was hungry and ready to go home. I went inside to say bye to her aunt, Keem, Anthony and Ronnie then went back outside to say bye to the elders.

We grabbed some Chinese food to go then went to the crib to grub out. After the meal, Cara went into the living room and called Tera. I went to take a shower and called it a day early.

The week passed fast. I got my guns and ammo from Knights of Round, and prepared for Tera and RonRon's visit to California. When we went to the airport to pick them up, I let Cara drive all the way to San Diego.

We were going to surprise them because they didn't know anything about the marriage taking place at the court house. I called Jermaine and Derrick to see where they were. They said they were getting ready to go to the airport as we spoke.

While I shot the breeze with RonRon, Tera and Cara caught up. I noticed that Cara was happy. She was laughing and talking a mile a minute as we walked outside the airport to the garage.

"Damn 50ty, is that you're Hummer?" RonRon exclaimed when I popped the lock on it.

"Yeah homey, that's us."

He jumped into the driver's seat. Cara and Tera hopped in the back.

"You think you can handle this, RonRon?" I asked.

"50ty, I can drive anything, homey," he bragged. "Just put your seatbelts on," he warned. He didn't have to tell me twice.

We rode around the city for a while. We went to San Francisco and stopped at the mall to do some shopping. We bought everything from clothes, shoes, to video games for the PlayStation 2. We left with four big shopping bags.

Since it was early, we drove out of town to Compton. We wanted to see if any of their hoods were similar to Da Burg. RonRon was mean-mugging niggas in Compton and niggas were mean mugging him back. Cara and Tera laughed and talked, not paying us or Compton any attention.

We headed back to Los Angeles to Aunt Laurie's house so she could meet Tera. Cara always talked about her so much.

While we were at Aunt Laurie's I tried to call Derrick and Jermaine, but didn't get through. I figured they were already on the plane.

RonRon and I sat on the porch. The two elders weren't there since it was kind of late. They had probably come over earlier.

"Damn 50ty. I'm here with you in L.A. Now everything's on me, playa," RonRon said.

"Yeah, I got about a mil G's," I said.

I saw Anthony and Hakeem making their way up the block. Hakeem was the first to get out of the car. He gave me a smile. Anthony got out and walked up to us. He smelled like weed and I could tell that they were both high.

"Anthony and Hakeem, this is my partner from Florida, RonRon. Ron these are Cara's people, Anthony and Keem." They exchanged greetings and slapped hands.

"Anthony, lil homey, you smell like you smoked some good ass green. Where it's at?" RonRon asked acting as though he was feining to smoke.

I wouldn't mind smoking my damn self. I'd left all my green in Georgia with Derrick. Thinking about the big day the next day had me convinced we might as well go grab a couple ounces.

"Anthony, how about taking us to get some of that good stuff, pimp," I said.

That was right up their alley. They couldn't wait to hop in the Hummer.

"Okay. Let's go," he said. We all piled into the Hummer and rode out.

When we got to the weed trap, Anthony and I got out. As soon as they opened the door for Anthony their first words were, "Who is he, Ant?"

"Oh, this is my cousin from St. Petersburg, FL. He just moved up here. I want y'all to get to know him because he will be copping from y'all too."

We walked inside and I looked around. It was no different from any other place you went to. Niggas were going to be niggas. They were playing cards and gambling with dice, smoking and talking cash shit while the big screen T.V. played and nobody watched it.

They all gave me strange looks until the dude that let us in told them that I was straight. After that, they continued doing their thing. The dude walked into another room then came back out with a Nike shoebox that had some weight in it.

"How much are you trying to buy?" he asked.

Since I didn't know how long everyone was going to be in town, I went ahead and grabbed a half a pound. If it wasn't enough I could always come back for more.

He placed the weed on a digital scale on the table then grabbed eight single Fold-Top Glad bags and weighed it in front of me.

"It's good green homey, and I need seven hundred."

I didn't question him or think about it twice. He didn't know me and vice versa. I paid the seven hundred then Ant and I left. I gave Anthony a whole ounce to smoke with Keem then dropped them back off at their place.

At eleven o'clock I hadn't heard from either Derrick or Jermaine. They both knew about the wedding the next day. RonRon tried calling them too. Tera and Cara came outside ready to go home. I talked to Aunt Laurie for about ten minutes then we flexed to the crib.

Pulling up to the crib I noticed the look on Tera's face. "What were you expecting Tera, a mansion or something?" I asked laughing. I knew our place impressed her.

"The mansion is on the inside, Tera," Cara said.

"This is a beautiful house, Cara girl. It's very nice," Tera commented.

We sat up most of the night waiting on Jermaine or Derrick to call us. We had to pick them up from the airport, but they never called. Everybody passed out on the floor. I woke up and looked at my watch. I walked into the kitchen and called both Derrick and Jermaine's phones constantly, back to back, leaving messages.

No plane took that long to get to California from Florida. I called the airline in Tallahassee to see if they had any listing of them. They didn't have any of their names on their list for yesterday's flight. I got worried.

"What's wrong, Terrill?" Tera asked entering the kitchen.

"I'm sorry if I woke you, Tera."

She sat at the table. "It's okay. What's wrong?"

"Something is wrong with my brother and cousin. I can feel it," I said.

"It is strange," she said. "He didn't answer my call either." RonRon joined us in the kitchen, trying unsuccessfully to get either Derrick or Jermaine on their phone.

I grabbed a cigar that Cara had on the sink, split it open and rolled up a blunt to ease my mind. I sparked it up and hit it a couple times then let RonRon and Tera have it.

I woke Cara up and we went into the room to let them have privacy.

"Baby, I haven't heard from Derrick or Jermaine. They would have been contacted us. Not hearing from them tells me something is wrong. I don't know what's going on." I sat at the foot of the bed.

"They're probably alright. They're just running behind. They might be here later tonight or early in the morning, honey. Just get some rest," she replied. She gave me a kiss then turned over to go back to sleep.

*****

The next morning, Anthony and I went back to the Hummer dealership. I brought RonRon and Tera an all-black Hummer with rims. We parked it in the back of the court building until everybody went inside. While everyone was gathered together for the ceremony, I eased outside and moved the Hummer to the front of the building. It had a ribbon around it and a banner that read "We just got married" on it.

It was a simple court house wedding. Everything happened quickly. I was the Best Man. I congratulated both of them, and gave RonRon the ring to place on Tera's finger. Tera and Cara looked so damn good, like celebrities. RonRon and I were dressed in all white tuxes that Aunt Laurie ordered for us.

Cara gave Tera a ring to put on RonRon's finger. They were pronounced husband and wife. We cheered as they kissed. When we finally walked outside, they immediately saw the black Hummer with the ribbon and banner.

"What's this"? Tera asked. She and RonRon both looked my way. Cara and I smiled while Hakeem gave them the keys. "Oh my God," Tera screamed, giving me a hug.

Cara's phone rang. She was smiling when she answered. All of a sudden, she gasped. "Okay. Okay. I'm on my way right now. They rushed Ronnie to the hospital. We've got to go," she told us.

I drove while RonRon and Tera followed us. Luckily, we were able to rush through all green lights. Cara rocked back and forth. I placed my hand on hers. She started squeezing it.

"Don't stress yourself out, Cara. You have to remain calm."

"I'm trying to be calm," she said.

We arrived at the hospital within 15 to 20 minutes. RonRon and I sat in the lobby for over half an hour. Anthony rushed out of the room in a hurry heading towards the double doors, Cara runs out the room behind him trying to get him to stop.

RonRon and I stood up as Tera hurried over to us looking glum.

"Ronnie just died from gangrene in his blood. The doctor said it was too late. It had circulated from his thighs into his blood system before they knew it," she said.

We went outside to find Cara and Anthony, but didn't see them anywhere. We stood by RonRon Hummer and waited.

"Damn, I don't know what the deal with us, RonRon," I said solemnly. "When we try to find happiness in our lives stuff always happens to fuck it up."

"Yeah, but when you can't control it don't let it get to you. There's nothing you can do about that, playa," RonRon said.

We waited for almost an hour and Cara hadn't returned. I called her cell phone and found out she was back inside the hospital. I went inside to give her the keys.

"I'm going home with RonRon. Stay with your aunt and take care of her," I said. We gave each other a hug. I also gave her aunt a hug. "I'm sorry for your loss," I told Aunt Laurie.

RonRon and I spent the whole day smoking and drinking Hennessy.

"Damn! What a day to get married, bro," I said, thinking about Ronnie.

"Yeah tell me about it," he said, exhaling loudly. "But it's cool 50ty. I tried calling Derrick and Jermaine and still didn't get an answer."

"I still don't know what's up with them," I said.

He stretched out on the couch. I left him sleeping while I went outside just to get some fresh air.

I fired up another blunt while I thought about Jermaine and Derrick. I tried both of their cells again and waited for either one to answer, but nothing happened. I went back inside and headed to my room to lie down.

About two hours later RonRon came into the room and woke me up.

"Tera wants you to come gets her from Aunt Laurie's house," he told me.

"Alright," I said, getting up and rubbing sleep from my eyes. "Let me throw some water on my face and I'll be right out."

When we pulled up to the house, cars were parked everywhere. I pulled in the middle of the street in front of the house and got out. I went inside to pay my respects once more. Cara grabbed my hand and introduced me to her family members from different states. I saw some relief in her eyes, but the pain was still there.

We walked into the room where her aunt sat on the bed crying. I just stood by the door. It was the room that Ronnie had slept in. They had neatly folded up the sheets and blanket that was on the bed and placed them in a suitcase.

As I was about to tell Cara I'd see her in the morning, RonRon burst in the house shocking everyone. "Anthony is outside," he yelled. "He's cut up and bleeding."

Everybody rushed outside. Two white guys and Hakeem helped Anthony inside the house.

"What happened, Ant? What happened to you?"

His mouth was bloody and the side of his eye-lid was split. He was hurt pretty bad. Cara called 911 and we waited for them to arrive. They tried to comfort Anthony until the medics got there.

The ambulance pulled up before the three fire trucks and two police cars. RonRon had to move the Hummer out of the street. The two police officers didn't show any concern as they questioned everyone. I didn't want to talk to them. RonRon and I eased back into the house.

Cara and her aunt rode in the ambulance with Anthony; back to the same hospital where Ronnie had just died.

"Damn, I thought leaving St. Petersburg was going to be for the better, but seems not," I said rolling up an El Producto.

"You got to feel these niggas. They want respect even though they are wrong as hell," RonRon said. "You cross the line then somebody has to pay."

"Yeah, I feel you," I agreed. "Anthony went out for justice and failed."

"Let's bounce," RonRon suggested.

"Yeah. Come on."

We rolled around a couple blocks just to smoke. We couldn't take part in a battle that had already formed before we arrived.

Cara called to tell us the same people that shot Ronnie were the ones who jumped Anthony. It happened because he was trying to find out who shot his brother and asking around Crenshaw. For no reason, a dude named Sweetman, walked up and punched him in the face. People with Sweetman started kicking Ant in the head while he was balled up on the sidewalk covering his face. They all ran once the two white guys pulled up.

"Anthony will be okay. He just has a bruise on his side, stitches over his eye and a swollen bottom lip where they kicked him in his face," Cara relayed.

"That's fucked up," I said.

She sighed tiredly. "I'm going to spend the night with Aunt Laurie. She needs me."

"I understand. I'll see you in the morning," I said. "I love you."

"I love you too, bae." We hung up.

The next morning, I sent RonRon to the meat market to grab some steaks and chicken. I planned to fire up the grill. I got things started before he left. Tera and I played cards until he returned. When he got back, I seasoned the meat then let it marinate in my homemade barbeque sauce. He and I played Madden while Tera put it down in the kitchen, hooking up some potato salad.

After we finished everything, I placed the card table on the patio, under the tent in the back yard. Cara pulled up shortly after things got underway. Tera placed the food on the table and blessed it then we all grubbed out.

"Damn, Tera, you did your thing with the potato salad," Cara complimented.

"Yeah yeah," RonRon and I agreed.

"Well, thank you guys, I try," she replied.

Everything was delicious. We ate and got full then we fired up a blunt. We played a couple of games of Spades. RonRon and I were partners. We beat the ladies at every game except the last one. We couldn't tell them shit as they gave each other high fives across the table.

We went into the house and tried to get another game going, but they didn't want to play anymore. I took out the trash and put the leftover food away. RonRon sat at the table and tried to reach Derrick and Jermaine. He still received no answer.

Cara and Tera sat on the floor in front of the entertainment system looking through our CD's. They looked higher than a motherfucker. We just laughed at them, walked past and into the bedroom.

"Yo 50ty, I'm going to stay up here for a couple of weeks with you, homey," RonRon said. He sat in my office chair in front of my computer, turning it on to browse the Internet.

"Alright." I pulled out my bag. "Help me count my money, RonRon," I said. "I lost count." I threw the bag of money across the floor. Luckily, I had rubber bands around every hundred grand stacks. I pulled out my calculator. We sat and counted all of my cash which totaled eight hundred and ninety-seven grand. I was spending like crazy.

"Damn bro, you going broke," RonRon joked.

"Yeah right," I replied.

He reached inside his pocket and pulled out a stack of hundreds.

"Here, let me make you another millionaire." He gave my two hundred grands along with the additional two dollars.

"Give it to me at a later time," I said, tossing it back at him.

That night while everyone slept, I played the PS2 and thought about my brother and Derrick. After the funeral, I planned to go to Bainbridge to see what was going on. After a few matches on Mortal Combat I went to shower then got into bed with Cara and fell asleep.

The next morning, two days before the funeral, we all went to Aunt Laurie's house to visit Anthony and pay respect to the family. The out-of-town visitors were still there. When Cara and Tara got out, RonRon and I parked the Hummers side by side in the front yard.

I noticed that Cara didn't have any younger family members. Anthony and Keem seemed to be the youngest in the house. That showed me that they really didn't have anybody to ride for them, plus the police wasn't doing their jobs.

Anthony was a good person. I knew he'd tried to handle Ronnie's situation even though it was a no-win situation. I didn't know what he was thinking of, going up against them when he didn't have any backup or weapons. He was lucky they hadn't killed him.

RonRon stayed on the porch while Tera and I went inside with Cara. When I stepped in the house, I heard people talking amongst each other, wondering who I was. I guessed it was because of my appearance. I wore a Versace three pieced suit with a pair of Perry Ellis shoes. Diamond earrings shone from my left ear. My arm showcased three Rolex diamond bracelets. Two diamond pinky rings and thumb rings adorned my hands. To top it off, I wore three platinum necklaces that I'd recently bought.

"Hey you, young man," a lady said. I turned around and there were two older ladies standing behind me.

"Ma'am?"

"How old are you?" she asked.

"I'm twenty-nine," I answered.

"You're not from around here, are you?"

"Mom," some guy said. "You're asking this man too many questions." He looked embarrassed.

"It's cool," I told him. "I don't mind. I'm from St. Petersburg, Florida, ma'am," I answered.

I entered the kitchen where Cara and the rest of them were. They were still talking about the guys who jumped Anthony, saying they were the same guys that killed Ronnie. I turned around to head back outside, but Cara stopped me.

"Hey Terrill. Come in and say hi to Anthony." She grabbed my hand and walked back into the kitchen.

"Hey Anthony, how are you feeling?" I asked giving him dap.

"Hey 50ty, I'm okay." he replied, trying to sound brave.

RonRon walked into the kitchen. "Yo Anthony, what's going on, pimping?" he asked.

"Hey RonRon." he greeted. He smirked and shrugged as if to say, "It's all good."

The doctors had fixed him up nicely. You could barely see the stiches in his face. Plus, the swelling had gone down.

I walked back outside to the porch and tried to call Jermaine and Derrick again. I even tried calling Los to see if he'd heard from them. No one answered.

Damn, nobody is answering their phones. Shit did Georgia get blown off the map and we haven't heard about it?

Cara came to the screen door. "Baby, me and Hakeem going to go to the store." she told me.

"I'm going too." Tera said. The three came outside.

'Okay. Bring me back a two liter of Mountain Dew. I'm hot as hell up here in California. It's no different than the Florida heat. I should be used to it," I said.

They hopped in RonRon's Hummer, because mine was stuck between his truck and one of Cara's family member's cars.

While I sat on the porch to wait for them to return, the two elders approached up.

"Hey there 50ty, that's what you call yourself right?" Frank asked. They both sat in the two wooden chairs on the porch.

"Yeah that's right." I answered. I tossed RonRon an amused smile.

"Damn there are two of you now huh?" Tom said. Looking at RonRon.

I introduced the two elders to RonRon and he greeted them with handshakes.

"Young man ever since you been here you been seeing some shit after another. I told you, L.A is a rough city." Frank said.

"Yeah it's rough everywhere you go. It's about the same in Florida. But this been going on before I got here." I replied

Anthony came outside and sat on the steps with us.

"Damn Anthony, you all fucked up in the face." Frank said tactlessly. "What the hell happened to you?"

Anthony just laughed then explained what went down.

"Somebody is going to fuck all those niggas up over there one of these days. Watch. Y'all will see." Tom said.

Cara's aunt was standing at the door and heard him. "Karma is a word that a lot of people don't understand." she said sadly.

Frank nodded. "They will meet their match."

I just remained quiet. Revenge only caused more pain. Only under certain circumstances would I pay a motherfucker back for what they'd done to me or my people. I understood how the elders and Aunt Laurie felt though.

We chilled on the porch for a while. Cara hadn't made it back. I tried to call Derrick and Jermaine again and still received no answer. I was tripping because there was so much on my mind. I got a bad feeling and turned to RonRon.

"RonRon, let's roll up to the store. Anthony, you can ride if you want," I told him, walking to my truck. They both jumped up and followed me.

"You guys be careful," Aunt Laurie advised and the elders nodded in agreement as we drove off.

We stopped at the corner store and I sent Anthony in to buy some Blunts. We cruised around smoking and getting our minds right. While I bent a couple of corners my cell rang.

"Terrill, these motherfuckers slapped Hakeem and fought me and Tera like we were men," Cara said. She was crying and talking loudly. I could hear Tera in the background yelling and swearing.

"What? Did they hurt you? How's Tera?" I asked.

"We're okay," she said. "We're at the Stop-n-Shop around the corner from my aunt's house."

"I'll be right there," I said stiffly and disconnected the call.

"What's wrong, 50ty?" Anthony asked. By the expression on my face they knew something was wrong. I calmed down.

"Nothing. Just chill out," I said.

I pulled up to Stop-n-Shop and we all got out. RonRon stood by my Hummer because L.A.P.D. was on the scene. I really didn't give a fuck.

One of the dudes walked up to Hakeem and slapped him right in front of the police.

"Hey you come here," the officer yelled rushing to Hakeem's side. The dude ran across the street laughing. The police didn't do anything, just asked Hakeem if he was okay.

"You soft scary motherfucker," Cara swore. "Why do they have to jump people?"

Hakeem had a red bruise on his cheek that Tera rubbed while he cried. I got mad but tried not to let it show. I let the officers do their jobs and just chilled as they talked to Hakeem, Cara and Tera. Anthony stood by the Hummer with RonRon. The police finished up their hopeless report then took off.

"Them boys crazy," Anthony said, looking out the window.

"Yeah, they stupid," Hakeem responded. Tears fell from his eyes while he held his cheeks.

Tera and Cara rode with RonRon while Keem, Anthony and I rode together. Tera had a bruise on her jaw and Cara had a red bruise on her chin. By them being light-skinned it showed.

When we pulled up to Aunt Laurie's house, Cara walked up to us.

"Don't tell Auntie or anybody anything, y'all," she told Keem and Anthony. "There is enough stuff going on right now."

"Okay. We'll keep quiet about it," Anthony said and Hakeem nodded in agreement.

"I love you two," she said, giving them both a hug. "See y'all later."

She got into the truck with me. "Somebody needs to do something about this because they are acting like they run this whole area," she said looking at herself in the mirror. "They aren't scared either. Once the police leave they will be right back out on the corner like it's nothing."

133

We stopped at the liquor store and bought a fifth of Hennessy then went to the crib. Cara and Tera talked about what happened while we just listened and smoked.

Within a couple of hours, we had drunk the whole bottle of Hennessy. Tera and Cara were in the room lying across the bed watching a movie.

Later that night after Tera and Cara had fell asleep I called RonRon into the kitchen

"Let's go see if we can go find them niggas," I said simply.

"Cool," he replied. "That's right up my alley." An excited glint entered his eyes.

We went into my room and I grabbed my two bulletproof vests and gave him one to put on. I got my 3030 and two 9mms. I called Anthony, but he didn't answer the phone so we decided to just ride over to his house.

Hakeem was sitting on the porch alone. I told him to get in and ride with us. Just as I was shifting into drive, Anthony came outside.

"Come on," I called to him and he hurried and got in.

No one spoke as I drove. Our first spot was where Ronnie got shot. There wasn't anything out of the ordinary happening there. We saw the blood that was still on the wall and sidewalk where Ronnie had stood. Anthony and Keem gazed at it, sadly. Ronnie's funeral was in two days. I didn't want to bring up memories of him so I pulled off.

Next, we went to the place where Anthony had gone to confront them. Anthony pointed at the dudes that stood on the corner.

"They all are together," he said.

I drove a couple blocks to Stop-n-Shop and we saw that the police were gone. Two of the dudes that were down with the others were at the store chilling like nothing had happened in that area.

"Damn. Where are the main hardcore motherfuckers at, like Sweetman?" RonRon asked.

After riding around for two and a half hours we decided to try finding him another time. As soon as we got ready to head out the neighborhood Hakeem spotted Sweetman on the other side of the street, posted in front of a hole-in-the-wall joint.

"There that nigga goes," he said pointing.

I pulled up to a neighborhood convenience store that wasn't far from their house.

"Hakeem and Anthony, I want y'all to get out and go on home," I told them. "Let us handle this."

"Are y'all going to kill him?" Hakeem asked, looking scared.

"We're just going to talk to him like men," RonRon answered calmly. "Now, go home like 50th told y'all," he said evenly. They got out and ran.

I turned around and drove up on Sweetman and his partner. RonRon pulled out the 3030 determined to just get it over with. As soon as he let the window down in order to aim at them, Sweetman and the dude walked into the club.

I parked right in front of the club and gave RonRon the MPA-10.

"Leave the 3030 in the truck," I said and he nodded.

We checked our clips for ammo. They were stacked with hollow tips. I pulled out both of my 9mms and placed them in the holster under my jacket.

"You ready RonRon?" I asked.

"Fo shows 50ty. Since you're living here now, pimping, I can do this by myself. You just keep the truck running," he told me.

"Fuck that. Since these niggas want to act bold and brave, we got to match their asses," I said.

We got out and walked into the strip joint. I examined the club and saw there were only a few people inside. That would make it good and easier. All of them inside wore blue bandanas. I spotted

Sweetman in the back by the pool table. I signaled for RonRon to follow me.

"Who got next"? I asked as they shot pool.

"I do," Sweetman answered. He sat on a stool beside of the pool table.

"Cool," I replied. Because RonRon and I were dressed stylish, they didn't pay much attention to us or give us further thought.

"Corner pocket, right," one of the players said getting ready to shoot.

"You're going to miss that, homey," I said and sat next to Sweetman.

"Who the fuck is you, homeboy, sitting close to me like that?" Sweetman asked.

I smiled at him. "That's all I need to hear." I snatched the pool stick from the player that called the shot and swung with all of my strength. The pool stick hit Sweetman straight in the forehead, knocking him backward off the stool. He hit the floor, hard.

RonRon jumped on top of the pool table. "Motherfuckers, get the fuck down!" he yelled. He started shooting up the bar with the MPA-10. Everybody ducked and tried to hide under something. I grabbed Sweetman and forced my 9mm into his mouth.

"Get the fuck up, nigga. You about to get your whole life dysfunctional if you try to be a hero." I snatched him up from the floor.

I walked out of the bar with my gun still jabbed into Sweetman's mouth. RonRon was behind me aiming at the people that remained in the bar.

"Hey, what the fuck is going on?" His words were muffled. We didn't answer, just threw him in the back of the Hummer.

"Payback is a mutherfucker," I said and smiled at him evilly.

RonRon sped off in a hurry. "You picked the wrong mutherfucker to fuck with," RonRon told him, laughing.

"What? I don't know who the hell you niggas are," he replied staring from me to RonRon.

"No, but you know my family, bitch," I said and dialed Cara's number.

"Who is your family?" he asked. "I have never seen you guys before."

"Just shut the fuck up, nigga," RonRon told him. He kept talking until I punched him in the mouth.

"Shut up. Why should we tell you that, so you can pay them a visit later?" I snapped.

"Hold up. Man, who are you guys?" He wouldn't stop talking even though his mouth was bleeding.

"You shouldn't have fucked with us, nigga," RonRon repeated in a low tone. He drove up Crenshaw Blvd.

"Hello?" Hakeem said answering the phone. I put my cell phone on speaker.

"Do you recognize the voice, fool"? I asked, aiming at his temple.

"No. No. Who is that?" Sweetman cried.

"Keem, put me on speaker phone," I instructed. Sweetman looked very nervous after I mentioned Hakeem's name. "I want everybody in the house to hear this."

"Motherfucker say what you did," I told him giving him an evil look.

""What are you talking about man? I didn't do anything."

"Hakeem, whose voice do you hear, dawg"? I asked.

"That's Sweetman's voice," I heard Anthony answer.

"I didn't do anything to y'all, cuz. You got the wrong nigga," Sweetman said, lying with a straight face.

"You the one who jumped me, my cousin, Tera, and Anthony," Hakeem said in the background.

"I don't know what you even talking about. That wasn't me," he denied.

"Fuck it, 50ty," RonRon said, making a complete stop in the street. "Drive, homey."

I hopped in the front and drove. RonRon had gotten into the backseat with Sweetman. I knew it was a terrible idea, but so what.

"Bitch, tell them what you did, motherfucker," RonRon yelled.

"What the fuck did I do? ARRGH!!!!!!" he screamed. RonRon poked him in the thigh with his knife. While Sweetman screamed in pain, RonRon stabbed him two more times to let him know we meant business. "Bitch, talk," he said tightly.

"Ok, ok, ok," he cried. "I did it," he finally said.

RonRon punched him several times. "Motherfucker, you did what?" he yelled.

"I killed Ronnie," he sobbed.

We heard people in the back-ground mumbling to one another as they continued to listen.

"Just to let you know, Ronnie's mom heard you, you punk ass bastard," RonRon said and stabbed him again. As bad as I wanted RonRon to stop I refused to make him because they went for bad and didn't care about Cara or her family.

I drove under a bridge on the outskirts of L.A. While they were on the other line listening, I had to bring the show to an end.

"Apologize to Ronnie's family, for coming here for a funeral and not a family reunion."

Sweetman began shaking and crying. "I'm sorry." RonRon glared at him and stabbed him again. "Now apologize to my wife, Cara, and lil Hakeem for fighting them like they were men." I reached over the seat and punched him a couple of times. "And to Anthony," I told him.

"I'm sorry," he apologized and I got out of the truck.

"That's good for his motherfucking ass," Frank said in the background. I heard others agreeing. I disconnected the call. They didn't need to know what happened next. No one did.

CHAPTER 12

The next day it was broadcasted all over Los Angeles and surrounding areas.

"A young man's body was discovered before dawn this morning under a highway in Los Angeles. Witnesses said the body was found hanging on a wire fence. There were multiple stab wounds to the torso. Police will not release the identity of the victim until they notify family. They currently have no leads. If anyone knows anything about this crime, they are asked to contact the Los Angeles Police Department."

Cara and Tera stayed at Aunt Laurie's house until it was time for the funeral. The police were the least of our worries. We just hoped that Sweetman's men didn't know anything about our retaliation.

The city was in silence and things were moving slowly, or so it seemed. However, we kept on our bulletproof vests and stayed strapped, just in case. We instructed Cara and everyone else not to call or look for us. They were to stay focused on the funeral that would take place the next day.

We wanted to stay low key. Without giving word to anyone, RonRon and I fled L.A. We figured it was best to get out of town until things died down. We headed to Bainbridge to see what was going on with Derrick and Jermaine.

Landing in Tallahassee, I tried calling Derrick and Jermaine again and still received no answer. We went inside and got a rental. I tried calling Los again, but got no answer from him either.

We left the airport and stopped at a restaurant and went inside to eat.

"Damn 50ty, maybe their phones are off or something," RonRon said.

"Nah, I find that hard to believe. Derrick, Jermaine and Los's phones off at the same time? Something is going on," I replied.

"Let's go check out Derrick's homeboys with the SUV first to see if they know anything," RonRon suggested.

"That's sounds like a plan." We stopped talking and finished eating in silence.

After leaving the restaurant, we went straight to Bainbridge. I pulled up in their driveway and parked directly behind the SUV. I got out of the rental in a way that nobody would recognize it was me. I knocked on the door twice before I spotted someone peering out the window. Eric opened the door.

"What's up, 50ty? It's been awhile. How are you?" he asked.

"I've been chilling doing my thing, homey." I cut straight to the point. "Where is Derrick and Jermaine?"

"Damn 50ty, I thought maybe he was in Cali with you, dawg. I've been trying to get at Derrick for about two weeks now and he never answers his phone," he replied. From the look in in his eye, I knew he was telling me the truth.

"I see," I responded looking up the road in thought.

"I went by his house a couple times," Eric continued. "I saw him and your brother's cars parked in the driveway, but nobody came to the door when I knocked. I asked Rodney if they went to L.A. and he told me he didn't know."

"Alright, dawg. Thanks," I told him and headed back to the car.

Hmmm. Maybe they went to St. Pete. They probably got too hot up here are something. But how, when both of their cars at the house? I thought.

"50ty, maybe if we called the police station we could find out if they are locked up," RonRon mentioned after I got in the car.

After leaving Eric and Rodney's house we went to Derrick's house. His Cadillac was parked in the driveway in front of Jermaine's car. I drove past the crib to the neighbor's house then parked. I checked out the surroundings. Everybody was in the house or minding their business.

We went to three different houses on the block and asked if they had seen or heard anything from either Jermaine or Derrick. Everybody had the same story: they haven't seen either for a couple of weeks.

I got one of Derrick's females on the block to call the police station. She relayed that they said they didn't have anyone by those names in their system. I even had her call Los again from her number, but she received no answer either.

RonRon and I went back to Derrick's house to find clues or any sign of breaking and entering. I checked both the front and back doors of the house and both were locked. I checked the windows and they were closed tight and locked, too.

"Hey 50ty, check this out." RonRon stood by Jermaine's car. "His car is unlocked and the keys are still in the ignition."

"Now, this is really strange," I said grabbing the keys and walking up to the front door. I used them to unlock it.

"Derrick's car is locked so they were getting ready to head out in Jermaine's car. They were probably getting ready to go to the airport," RonRon said.

Inside the house, nothing seemed to be moved or touched. I used the house phone to try to reach them but still got no answer.

"Damn, RonRon this is weird. I don't know what could have happened to them."

"Strange, pimp. I don't know either," he replied.

Derrick's money was in his room and all my guns were still in place as well. I grabbed everything from the drugs, guns and money. I placed it all in his bag and put it in the trunk of the rental. We drove back to Tallahassee in silence, wondering what the hell happened to Derrick and Jermaine.

While we were in the room, I spread Derrick's money out over the bed and RonRon and I counted it. There was one million one hundred and seventy-seven dollars.

"Damn it man. Derrick is putting down up here," RonRon said, smiling. We placed Derrick's money back into his bag.

"Yeah just like you are in St. Pete.," I told him.

With nothing else to do, I called Cara and RonRon called Tera. They were both happy to hear from us. We told them that we were in Bainbridge and that we still had no clue on where Derrick or Jermaine were. After talking to them, we just called it a night and went to sleep.

The next day we got up and went back to Eric's house to chill for a while. They were inside playing Spades and smoking. I didn't gamble but RonRon did, so I played as his partner. He took a chance with his money, not really caring whether he won or lost. I played smart as if it was my own cash.

"Hey, how are Cara and Tera?" Rodney asked.

"They're good. They are both in South Central at a funeral," I replied. I mentioned the situation concerning Ronnie but didn't tell them about Sweetman or his clique.

"Damn it man. I knew it was rough in California. Shit, they have riots damn near every summer in L.A," Eric said, rolling up a blunt and smoking another one at the same time.

143

"Life is how you make it though. As long as you stay away from the bullshit, everything will be cool," Rodney said not knowing that RonRon and I had already gotten involved in it.

We played a few games and won about a grand from them. RonRon split it with me.

"Since Reco vanished, the money spread all over Bainbridge. Rodney and I have a lot of clients coming," Eric said

"I see that," I nodded.

"Just keep it moving, though. Y'all don't want to get the spot hot," RonRon advised.

They were doing their thing in Bainbridge. They made a good seven to eight hundred grands while chilling in the backyard. It was really low since woods surrounded the area. They only had one sheriff that patrolled the area and he was clueless. I gave them their props on keeping it just how it was no matter how big their pockets became. Neither Rodney nor Eric had jewelry, rims, a big house, or fancy shit that would call attention to them. They just lived regular lives.

"I guess we'll head back to L.A. tomorrow to see if shit has died down," RonRon said.

"What? Y'all got problems up there?" Rodney asked. "If you need help with some shit we are always down, homey."

"Well that gang shit that's going on, I'm not trying to get involved in it. But they put their hands-on Tera, Cara and her family. Man, that set it off right there."

"Nigga, let's go finish this unsettled situation tonight," Rodney suggested.

"For real. They fucking with Cara and Tera. Nigga let's go do this," Eric replied.

I told them the whole situation and they got just as mad as RonRon and I had. The conversation varied. RonRon told them that he got married and how there was a lot of different opportunities up there. He thought we should just open one big trap up there and leave it like that. I felt it would never happen because that really would be a trap. We would either get robbed or killed. Eric and Rod listened more than they talked. The only thing on their minds was getting at Sweetman's people.

"My take on the situation is that we just lay low for a while and see if it dies down and end. If not, then we set it off up there," I said. RonRon and I got ready to head back to Tallahassee.

"No doubt, just holla at us before y'all head back to California," Rod said. He and Eric walked us to the front of the yard where we had parked.

"We'll be back over in the morning. If y'all hear anything about Derrick and Jermaine let me know," I said.

"Word."

"One."

"Peace," they said and went back inside.

On our way back to Tallahassee, I stopped at the pawn shop where I'd brought my guns and sold them back to the dealer. Placing thirteen hundred in my pocket wasn't a big deal. I just had to get rid of them before we headed back to California the next morning.

A block from the hotel we stopped at a convenience store. I stayed in the car while RonRon went in. I switched on the radio for entertainment. A few minutes later an undercover cruiser pulled up directly behind me. I just watched him through my rearview mirror. Before anyone got out the car I noticed two more police cars pull up beside the undercover car. They all got out of their cars and started making their way toward me.

I tried to figure out my next move, but I was too late. The officers passed by my window and looked inside the car as they continued walking into the store. I spotted RonRon at the door. He made a quick U-turn and went back inside. My heart start thumping and beating off track while the officers went inside the store. The other police stood by his cruiser.

I thought about ramming the undercover car out the way and speeding off or just jumping out and running. I noticed the other police cars that were silently surrounding the store in case of someone striking out. I just bowed my head and took a deep breath to try and get myself together.

Minutes later, one of the police officers came out the store and looked straight at me. The other one walked out with RonRon in handcuffs. RonRon stared at me as they placed him in the back seat of one of the police cars. I had to do something. I took another deep breath then got out the car and went over to the police that had RonRon. People started gathering around just to see what was going on.

"Officer, what's going on?" I asked. "Why are you arresting my brother?"

"We are not arresting him yet, son. He is suspected of a breaking and entering that occurred this morning," the office said.

"What? We are not from around here," I told him.

"So, what does that mean?" The other officer asked sarcastically. I didn't want to piss the police off so I stayed calm.

"It means, why would we want to break in somebody's property when we don't know them?"

"That's something you need to tell me, son." The first officer said.

As I talked to the police trying to convince them we didn't do anything, another police car pulled up and flashed a bright light on us. They took RonRon out of the back seat and sat him on the curb. RonRon wasn't saying anything, just doing what they instructed him to do.

I spotted the police take someone out of the car. The person looked over at us then they placed him back into their car and drove off.

"We're sorry to take up your time, guys. We have the wrong person. Let him go," the undercover said to the police that had RonRon.

"Damn motherfuckers need to get the suspect's identity right," I swore as they uncuffs RonRon. They didn't say anything as they got back in their cars and drove away.

"Well that was a wasted hour," RonRon half-joked.

"Them motherfuckers don't have anything better to do," I replied.

We were both exhausted by the time we got back to the hotel. I rolled up a blunt, got comfortable and just chilled. Sleep was written all over our faces and smoking the blunt didn't make it any better. RonRon was out cold in no time. I was getting ready to fall asleep myself until my phone rang.

"Terrill, they just shot up my aunt's house twice in a row," Cara said frantically. "They were in two Cadillac's." That woke me up completely.

"What? Is everybody alright?" I asked.

"Yeah. They just pulled up in the front yard and started shooting."

"Okay Cara. Don't tell anybody that you talked to me, okay? We're on our way back," I said.

"Okay, Terrill. Be careful," she warned. "I love you."

"I love you too." We disconnected the call and I turned to RonRon. "RonRon, get up."

"What?"

"Let's go to the airport, dawg. They just shot up Aunt Laurie's house," I told him.

"What the fuck? Did anybody get hurt?" he asked, leaping up and grabbing his belongings. I grabbed my stuff too and we rushed out of the room to check out of the hotel.

147

I took Derrick's cash with me just in case the neighbors noticed that nobody was there. They might try to snoop around knowing he had money. While sitting in the lobby I called Anthony.

"Yo Anthony, what's up homey? Are you alright?" I asked.

"I'm straight, 50ty. Those dudes that shot up our house are rolling in two Cadillac's. They are Sweetman's friends," he said.

"Anthony, save the information, playa. I'll give you a buzz soon when I'm near L.A.," I said interrupting him. The cell phone was the worst thing to chat on if the conversation was critical. We could be bugged. You just never knew.

RonRon and I got on the plane after waiting two and a half hours. I called Rodney and Eric and told them that we had an emergency and had to head back to Los Angeles. I promised to call them the next morning.

We arrived in L.A. around midnight Saturday morning. RonRon's Hummer was parked in the airport's parking lot. We got in it and he drove straight to the crib.

After walking inside and putting our stuff away along with Derrick's cash, I noticed that Cara had cleaned the place from top to bottom.

RonRon and I decided to lay low for a couple days. We really didn't have any reason to go anywhere because of the attention. We just plotted and planned our next move on how we were going to handle things.

"Man 50ty, we are at war, basically," RonRon said.

"Yeah, I know, but something has to be done, bro. I don't want things to become more serious than what they are now," I replied.

"Oh, it's going to get serious," he said. "Believe that."

CHAPTER 13

A whole week passed and Cara and Tera were still at Aunt Laurie's house. We hadn't given anyone notice that we were back. Only Anthony and Cara knew we'd returned. We hadn't even gone over there to see what had been shot up.

I just spent a lot of time thinking. RonRon and I seemed to be up against the entire city. I didn't want them to keep rushing Aunt Laurie's house because somebody was going to get killed and that would make me snap.

I got up early and called Anthony to tell him that I would be coming over to pick him up.

"Don't tell anyone and be ready to come outside when I call you again," I said. After hanging up, I went to wake RonRon.

After eating breakfast at McDonalds, we headed to Aunt Laurie's house to get Anthony.

"So 50ty what is we going to do?" RonRon asked. I gave him a blank look.

"I really don't know yet. But I don't want this shit to get any worse than what it is now," I said.

He shook his head, seemingly worried. "You don't think we can just go up to them and they will just drop all this and everybody walks away freely, do you?"

"Man RonRon, I just want you to feel me, homey. I don't want to go to war with these dudes and I don't want Cara or nobody else to get hurt either. Somebody got to stand up and squash this shit," I said distressfully.

I called Anthony on my cell. He did exactly as I had instructed him to do. He was already standing outside on the side of the house. It was a good thing that nobody was on the porch at the time. He saw us when we rode past and stopped at the corner. He ran up and got in the truck.

We drove up to the corner store where Sweetman's friends hung. I noticed the looks on both Anthony and RonRon's faces but ignored them because I wanted the shit to end.

I grabbed my 45 and placed a bullet in the chamber, just in case. RonRon grabbed the 3030 and did the same. By the look on Anthony's face, he was scared as hell. I opened the door and got out.

"Keep the truck running," I told RonRon. "Anthony, get out."

Once they saw Anthony come from around the truck everybody stopped what they were doing and began to walk toward us. I was ready to quickly pull out my gun, but I waited for a reason to.

"Anthony, you got nerves to come around here, nigga," some dude wearing an all-blue Dickie outfit said.

"We're not here to start shit, playa. We just trying to squash this," I said as they stood in front of us.

"Lance, my brother didn't do anything to y'all. Neither did me or Keem. Y'all started with us," Anthony said from behind me.

"Man, y'all got nerves coming around here and y'all killed Sweetman," another dude said. He was trying to scope the inside of my Hummer. RonRon was kneeling in the seat so nobody could see him.

"This is not going to be the last man standing here. It's just respected the minds of real niggas. We just came to make peace with y'all. Shit, there is money to be made out here. Why fuck that up?"

They walked up on us as if they were going to just jump on us and beat us down like they did Cara and Tera. I pushed Anthony back.

"Get in the truck," I said when I spotted a black Cadillac coasting up the street.

"That's one of the cars that shot up my aunt's house," Anthony said, standing by the passenger's door. They must have called them. I couldn't really see through the dark tint. I started walking backwards. As the car stopped, the windows slowly rolled down. I saw the barrel of a gun hanging out.

"Run," I yelled at Anthony. I pulled out my 45 Magnum and started shooting at the car. Lance and his crew weren't strapped so they ran off in the other direction. I ducked behind my truck, out of the Cadillac's range. RonRon bust out the back of the Hummer holding the 303O and started ripping shots at the Cadillac. He continued to shoot up the Caddy until they sped off.

I saw Lance making his way back toward us holding a gun in his hand.

"RonRon, shut the back door," I yelled, hopping into the driver's seat from the passenger's side. RonRon hung the 3030 out of the back window and shot some more toward the Cadillac. They burned rubber as they turned right at the corner. I turned left.

I had a clear view of the road and slowed down quickly. L.A.P.D came in a large group, soon taking over the area. I slowly drove right past them without being detained.

"Damn 50ty, that was close," RonRon said as I parked in my garage.

"I told y'all they weren't going to squash anything," Anthony said calmly getting out of the truck. I didn't respond. I just walked in the room and called Cara.

The phone only rang once before she answered. "Hey, Terrill," she said in a relieved tone. I could tell she was happy to hear from me.

"Hey baby. I think you should bring your aunt over here," I told her. I explained what happened earlier. She understood that I didn't want anybody to get hurt.

"We saw on the news that there was a shoot out across town," she said in a low voice.

151

"I know," I told her. "Everything's cool. I'll see you when you guys get here." I knew she wanted to know if everything was alright, but I didn't want to get into it over the phone.

Anthony paced back and forth in the living room while RonRon lay on the floor searching through my DVDs for a movie to watch. I just sat in my Lazy Boy in a deep thought, wondering what those dudes' next move would be.

Cara called me back. "Yeah baby," I answered.

"Terrill, my aunt told me to tell you that nobody is going to run her away from her house." Women, I said to myself.

"She said she will call the police department for supervision, but she is not leaving her house," Cara told me.

"Tell her to do that," I said, feeling wary about the decision. But, I couldn't make her leave her home. Even though I felt there was danger on the horizon, I could only pray that everyone would be safe.

I was lucky that they didn't know where I lived, but I knew it will only be a matter of time before they found out. I couldn't relax. I felt more scared than anything. RonRon was younger than me so I guess he really wasn't paying it any attention. I tried not to let them see how nervous I was so I got out of my chair and walked back into the bedroom.

"50ty, are you ok?" Anthony asked as he stood at the room door a few minutes later.

I straightened up quickly. "I'm cool, homey. Come in, what's up?" I replied.

"Nothing. I'm just thinking about my family," he said. Anthony carried a lot of weight on his shoulders and could not do anything about it. I felt his pain deeply.

RonRon came into the room after I turned the stereo on. I went in my drawer and pulled out an already rolled blunt.

"Hey 50ty, let's go get Hakeem, dawg. I haven't seen my buddy in a while," RonRon said.

"Cool, y'all stay here and I'll go get him, Cara, and Tera too." Even though RonRon's Hummer was over there, I still didn't want them leaving the house just yet.

"Aiight, whatever," RonRon replied grabbing my blunt. I laughed and grab my keys then walked out the door to the garage.

On my way to Aunt Laurie's house, I saw that polices were all around the area. I drove past one of them going opposite ways. He looked at my truck suspiciously then made a U-turn and got behind me. I continued driving normally. The cop stayed behind me for at least three to four blocks. My heart raced as I tried to stay calm. I decided to turn off the main road and the police turned behind me and flashed his lights.

Damn, I said to myself. I quickly placed my gun underneath my seat and fastened my seatbelt. I let my window down then placed both of my hands out the door to show signs of peace.

"I see you've been in this situation before," the officer remarked, walking up to my vehicle slowly.

"It's not that officer, but you pulled me over for no reason, so I'm thinking you are out to start something," I responded.

"Do you have any drugs or concealed weapons on you?" he asked.

I gave him a strange look. "If I did, Officer, I wouldn't have stopped that easily. No, I do not have any drugs or concealed weapons. But I do have my license, insurance, and registration."

"I don't need those. Just go ahead. You're free to leave," he said all of a sudden and walked back to his cruiser. I breathed a sigh of relief and sat for a couple of seconds longer. After I pulled myself together I drove off.

My phone rang. I thought it was Cara, but saw an unknown number. I pressed talk but didn't say anything. It was the operator stating that I had a collect call from Bainbridge Correctional Institution from somebody named Ramon. They instructed me to press 1 if I wanted to accept the call. I pressed 1 but, I still heard silence.

"Hello?" the unknown voice said over the line.

"Who is this?" I asked.

"You don't know me, cuz. But your brother is locked up down here in Bainbridge with no phone privileges, him and Derrick," he informed.

I cut the conversation short after hearing that. "Thanks Ramon," I said, quickly disconnecting the call.

Tons of shit started running through my mind. I began driving slowly wondering why they were in jail and Jermaine's car keys were left in the car. I made a complete stop and got out of my truck. I placed my cell phone under my tire then got back in the truck and rolled over it.

I pulled up in the back of Aunt Laurie's house while the police were posted on the corner. I walked in from the back door which was always left unlocked. Everybody was in the living room watching television.

"Hey baby," Cara said, excited to see me. She ran up to me and gave me a hug and kiss.

"Hey 50ty, where is my husband?" Tera asked with a smile.

"He's at the crib with Anthony watching the football game," I replied.

"We were wondering where Anthony was. He had us scared," Cara said, relieved.

"Son, can I talk to you personally in the kitchen?" Aunt Laura asked as she walked past us into the kitchen. I followed her.

"Baby, I know that you are not a bad person, and my niece loves you so much," she said grabbing a chair. "Have a seat, son." I sat down. She opened the refrigerator and grabbed two sodas. "The mad spree that you are on is not going to change the way things are up here in Los Angeles," she said, sitting in a chair next to me.

"Well, how can it end?" I asked.

"It doesn't never end, Terrill. It only dies down, until some jerk brings it right back up," she answered.

"I understand that, but they not even hearing me when I try to make peace for you and your family." I said

"Ronnie, rest in peace, was my oldest nephew. He maybe thought I didn't know or tried to keep it from me, but he was out for bad too," she said. I just listen as she spoke. "He probably done something to them boys and they thought he was a push over. He stood his ground against them and they weren't going for that." She took a deep breath and continued. "Sad nobody duke it out anymore. They are quick to grab a gun." I felt her one hundred percent.

Hakeem walked into the kitchen. He had a worried look on his face, which he tried to hide.

"What's wrong Keem?" his aunt asked.

"Nothing," he answered.

Nothing he didn't want her to know about. I could tell from the way he looked at me when he said it that something was on his mind.

"You don't have to worry about a thing Hakeem. I won't let anything happen to my nephew," Aunt Laurie said as she left the kitchen.

"What's up Keem? Are you alright?" I asked.

"Nothing. I'm just tired of being in the house. Where is Anthony?"

"Him and RonRon at the house watching the football game," I answer.

"I want to go over there when you leave."

"Alright, playa. No problem."

I chilled with them for a couple hours. The two elders hadn't been over since the shootout. The gunfire had both of them running and

155

diving inside the house. I guess they were waiting to see if anything else happened before they decided to return.

I sat on the porch with Hakeem and watched two policemen parked on the corner side by side. Cara came outside and told Hakeem to go inside so we could spend some time together and talk.

"So how is everything going here since I left Cara?" I asked.

"If you really want to know, I'm scared shitless, not of just for me, but for my aunt and cousins," she answered.

"Yeah, them niggas is not trying to hear shit since Sweetman vanished."

"Terrill, let's go home. Tera wants to see RonRon anyways and I just want to go home. My aunt will be alright with the police patrolling the area," she said.

"Okay bring Hakeem too so he can get out the house for a while."

Cara and Tera rode together in RonRon's Hummer. Hakeem and I rolled in mine. I pulled up in the garage and Tera parked in the drive way. RonRon came to the door with a smile on his face. He was happy to see Tera. She hurried and jumped out of the truck and ran to him. They started kissing and hugging.

Anthony was on the couch in the living room asleep. Everyone had relieved looks except me. They knew something bothered me. I guess the devil rode my back at night and fucked with my mind through the day.

Later that night we ordered two large pizzas and two 2-liter soft drinks. We chilled and watched some movies that RonRon had picked out. We smoked a couple of blunts in a row.

Hakeem wanted to hit the blunt so bad but didn't want Cara to know he smoked. I was tickled off that because I was high. The contact probably had him feeling good though.

"Well guys I'm glad that we are all back together," RonRon said sparking up another joint.

"Me too," I replied. I decided to let them know about Jermaine and Derrick. "I have some bad news. Derrick and Jermaine are locked up." All eyes turned toward me.

"What the fuck happened?" RonRon asked. I had everyone's full attention.

"I don't know, but they are in Bainbridge Correctional, without phone privileges."

RonRon pulled on the blunt while shaking his head.

"How did you find out, baby?" Cara asked.

"I received a collect call from there, from a dude named Ramon. He was discreet about it," I said.

"Damn, so now what?" Tera asked looking at me and RonRon. I looked at her and said.

"I'm going to start looking into getting a lawyer tomorrow."

RonRon stood up. "So that explains what happened to Los then," he said.

Everything was getting out of hand. I sat in my room alone thinking on what could have happened, but it didn't make any sense to me. Did Los snitch or did the law enforcement find out about what happened in Atlanta? Jermaine didn't have anything to do with any of that. Why did they have him and if it was because of St. Pete drama, Derrick didn't have anything to do with that. Because they didn't have phone privilege, I really didn't understand.

I'll hire a good lawyer. I was willing to spend everything I had to free them.

"Are you okay?" Cara asked walking into the room and closing the door.

"Yeah, I'm fine. I just can't stop thinking about Derrick and Jermaine." She sat behind me on the bed.

157

"I know." She placed both of her legs around me and started rubbing on my shoulders. I could feel the tension in my body. I just leaned back on her because it felt so damn good.

"I'm going to search around for a good lawyer, even if it has to be more than one. I'll get them out of jail," I said. Cara continued rubbing on my shoulders. "It's like me and Jermaine been going through so much more drama and chaos since my mom passed that we forgot reality. We really don't even see each other often even when we stayed together. He's a good person. He doesn't belong in jail. I'd rather serve a million and one years in order for him not to do any time."

"He's older then you, right? Cara asked.

"Yeah, but I've done some terrible shit in my life. He hasn't done anything out the way," I told her.

"Oh, okay."

"Cara," I said as I sat up to face her. "I'm sorry for everything that I got you and your family into."

"Shh!" She placed her index finger on my lips. "None of us blame you. Do you know that every time you are around us, we feel safe and secure? When you came in from the back door to the living room where we all were at, our faces lit up. You are my knight in shining armor, 50ty." I looked away from her and laughed. "It's true. You are so strong and brave. You and your sidekick, RonRon," she joked.

I wasn't being brave, I just had my back against the wall. I felt cornered and had to defend myself. That was not being brave, more like being scared half to death.

"You just need to clear your mind and place all your worries to the side tonight. Be under my control," she said.

"Baby why you never-"

She interrupted me by placing her tongue in my mouth. She paralyzed me with a kiss that I couldn't resist. Everything from my thoughts to my clothes dropped as she climbed on top of me. She started kissing me from my neck and shoulders to my stomach. The wetness from her pussy soaked through her moist panties onto the bottom of my stomach once she mounted me. She moved her panties to the left and slowly placed my dick inside her warm pussy. She gave a quiet moan that only she and I could hear. My dick stood up in her like a light pole, full of energy. She was turned on. She squeezed me trying not to scratch me because she was taking in a lot of dick. I loved every bit of it. It was the first time I really fucked her instead of made love. Every man needed to set it off from time to time with their lady. Sometimes they want it rough.

The next morning, I found myself waking up alone. Cara was already up. I went into the bathroom and washed up. RonRon and Tera were in the other room still asleep while Hakeem and Anthony were in the living room asleep.

Cara knocked on the bathroom door softly.

"Come in, baby," I said.

She placed her head in the door. "I found you a lawyer that Oriel deals with. He said he can see you anytime this morning or make an appointment to see you when you're ready," she said.

The thing about Cara was when it was time to be intimate she turned into a sexy fine loving machine, but when it was time to face reality she gets very serious and handled her business. It was good to have a powerful woman on my side. It made my job much easier.

I dressed professionally, putting on my Perry Ellis suit. I placed two pens in my top pocket and a mini note pad to take notes.

Crossing the San Francisco Bridge reminded me of the Skyway, but it was a little longer distance. The Skyway was higher though.

"California is so beautiful, Terrill, but I Love St. Petersburg better," Cara mentioned.

I looked at her and smiled. "Why?

"I don't know. I guess because staying on the beach and seeing the lights were amazing."

"Especially from the airplane flying over Tampa," I replied.

We rode through the finer parts of San Francisco. I let Cara drive because she loved the Hummer plus she had the directions on how to get there. San Francisco seemed to be a lot quieter and safer than L.A. I liked the environment.

We arrived at the lawyer's office in about two hours. Cara and I signed in at the front desk then sat in the lobby to wait.

"I hope he can get your brother and cousin out of jail." Cara said placing her hands over mine. I just gave her a half smiled. I hoped the same.

After we'd waited a couple of minutes a tall O.J. Simpson looking brother approached us.

"Hi. My name is Thomas J. Harrell," he greeted us with a handshake.

Tom, huh? I thought.

"My name is Terrill and this beautiful lady is my wife, Cara." Cara blushed and couldn't hide it.

"Follow me to my office," he replied walking off.

His office was no joke. It was laid out lovely. I thought it was nice that lawyers got broken off mad loot just for saying the right words to set people free.

"So, what's the problem?" he asked, getting straight to the point.

"I have family in Bainbridge, Georgia locked up. I don't know why, but they are in jail without phone privileges," I said and began pacing around his office.

"That's strange," he remarked.

I know what he was thinking: M.O.B., money over bullshit.

"How much will it cost just to find out what is going on?" I asked.

"Well we are talking about two clients, correct?" he asked, leaning back in his high chair and folding his arms.

"Right," I answered.

"It's not a big deal to find out exactly what's going on, but the traveling will get to be a problem," he said.

"Look Tom. May I call you Tom?" I asked, not wanting to assume. He nodded. "Okay Tom, can you offer me a settlement to fight for my family down there?"

"Terrill, honestly it depends on their charges," he said firmly.

"I feel you on that, but let me be directly up front with you." I stopped pacing and stared at him. "I'll give you fifty grands to fight for them and fifty more if you win."

He stopped leaning in the chair and got an excited glint in his eyes. "You have a deal. Just give me all the information that you have of them and I will do my part on helping you, Terrill."

"Say no more." I ripped off a couple pages from my notebook pad and wrote down all the information that I wanted him to have on them.

"I have your number. If I need any other information, I'll give you a call," he said, smiling from ear to ear as he shook our hands.

After we left Tom's office we went to Red Lobster to grab something to eat.

"I felt like crying today, baby, when you called me your wife," Cara told me.

"That's been on my mind now for a while. Cara, I'm ready to be your husband truly and honestly. Are you ready for a commitment?" I asked. She looked at me and I could see the tears forming in her eyes.

"Yes, yes, and hell yes!" she screamed running around the table to give me a hug and kiss me all over my face. Everybody stared at us.

"We're getting married y'all," I yelled. I picked Cara up and carried her outside to get some fresh air. We stayed outside until we'd both calmed down and then we went back inside.

I couldn't stop smiling because I could see how happy I'd made Cara.

"Baby, we are going to have a big wedding in a church up here," I said. She was all ears as I told her how I wanted our wedding to be.

"Congratulations guys," the waitress said as she placed our food on the table.

"Thank you," I replied. Cara gave her a joyful look and said thank you as well.

I remembered while growing up I always said that I wasn't going to ever get married. All that changed once I became rich. Plus, I had a beautiful woman that was smart and sexy. She had my mind in the clouds, but I would never lose focus on who I was and what I was about.

Cara was already affiliated with the lifestyle that I had her in. I didn't want to know about the men she'd been with or who she loved the most out of them. All I wanted was for her to stay focused and be true to me. I had no problem trusting her and giving myself to her completely.

A Time to remember

CHAPTER 14

May 21st 1999

Three weeks later

It was my mom's birthday and every year around this time Jermaine and I would get together. There would be the two of us, and we'd do something fun like fish, drink, or play music just to stay happy because that's all Mom wanted us to be. Today the tradition failed because we were not around each other to say happy birthday.

"Happy birthday, Momma. I miss you and sorry about the lifestyle that I'm in. I'm going to change for the better," I said aloud.

I got up and dressed without waking Cara. RonRon, Anthony, and Hakeem were in the living room playing the Playstation2, Madden. The aroma of sausage and bacon was heavy. Tera was putting down in the kitchen. I didn't bother to walk in there because it would have made me hungrier then what I was.

"What's up y'all?" I asked, sitting on the couch beside of Anthony. "Who's winning?"

"Anthony got me by a field goal," RonRon answered. Anthony had Oakland. RonRon had Tampa Bay.

"What is this, a battle of both cities?" I jokingly asked while they played their real-life home teams on Madden.

"Yeah, I spotted him a touchdown in the first quarter of the game. Now it's the second quarter and he have me by three points. It's 27-24.

"So, have you heard anything from the lawyer Tom?" RonRon asked, focusing on the game.

"Nah, not yet. I'm not going to get in his way. I'll just give him some time to work alone on the case. He has all the information he needs," I said.

"Damn, I can't wait until they get released," RonRon said.

"When I get them out of jail, I'm going to see if Jermaine wants to come up here and stay with me."

"That will be straight. Shit, nothing like being around your people through good and bad times."

Cara peeked into the living room to see if I was there.

"Hey baby," I greeted her with a kiss then walked back into the bedroom with her. "What's going on?"

"Nothing, baby. Do you want to ride over to my aunt's house with me? She just called."

"Cool. We'll leave after Tera finishes with breakfast. I'm hungry," I told her.

After breakfast Cara and I flexed over to her aunt's house. It was good to see the two elders back on the porch together.

"Hey there, son," one of them greeted me. I smiled at both of them.

"What's going on with you guys?" I asked.

"Son, I know you heard about the rampage those fools went on last month, right?"

"Them idiots had bullets flying everywhere on this damn porch. They had some big guns," they said. "Real big guns".

"Damn, are you guys okay"? I asked. I didn't want to burst out laughing.

"It's crazy how they did it, son. We were just talking away on a calm bright day and Laurie had just got up and went inside the house. Thank God for that," one of them said.

The other continued with the story. I was all ears because I knew they were going to tell me some funny shit. I just waited for that free laugh so I could get it out the way. It was hurting me to hold it in and they knew it.

"There were two Cadillac's. The first one was all black or blue one. Couldn't really tell because it happened so damn fast. Anyway, it stopped right in front of the house. We thought maybe it was you and Cara. Hell, we didn't know and really didn't pay it close attention until another Cadillac pulled up. Then we started to be concerned. We were like 'who in the hell is that pulling up and stopping in the road like that without getting out?' So, I stood up to get a better look inside the damn car and then the driver's window eased down slow and I saw a guy with a mask on. Then I yell out... DRIVE-BY!!!!

"Soon when I heard the words drive-by, shots were being fired and I jumped through the front door like I'm was in the movies, son, and his old ass jumped in right behind me tripping and falling, rushing into the house," the other one finished.

"I tell you today, I felt a bullet graze me in the ass, son," the first elder told me.

I couldn't hold it anymore and fell out laughing. They seemed more tickled than I was. We all laughed until it hurt. Cara and her aunt came and stood at the door and joined in on our conversation.

"I just had got up to go pee and soon as I sat on the toilet, I heard gunshots. It sounded like the war in Iraq. I never ducked to the floor that fast in my life. Didn't have to pee anymore because it scared the shit out of me," Aunt Laurie said.

I jumped up really quick and ran to the sidewalk because I was laughing so hard. Cara had never seen me so tickled and I had never seen her so tickled.

165

"Baby, me and Tera hit the floor and we crawled into the kitchen with Keem and Anthony after we seen them jump into the living room," she said. "I thought they were shot until I heard them cursing."

We ended up having a good time on the porch on my mom's birthday. All I needed was to get out and have a good time and that's what happened.

It was good to know that it would take more than a bullet to stop the two guys from coming over to Aunt Laurie's house and chilling on the porch.

My phone rang and I answered. "What's up RonRon?"

"Where are you guys?" he asked.

"We are at Aunt Laurie house for a bit."

"Okay. I'm going to take Tera, Keem and Anthony to the movie, homey. We're going out to eat too. Y'all want to meet us somewhere?" he asked.

"Nah go and have fun. Plus, I need some quality time with Cara anyway. Be safe, pimp," I replied.

Cara family was cool and the two guys were funny as hell. I was glad they didn't mention anything about Sweetman even though they knew what the deal was once the body had been found the next morning.

I went inside to talk to Aunt Laurie. I told them that it was my mom's birthday and that she would have been forty-seven. They wished her happy birthday and said RI.P. Aunt Laurie offered us something to eat but Cara was ready to go back to the house. We gave her a hug and I shook the elder's hands and told them that I would be back over soon.

Back at the house it was just Cara and I. We felt relieved even though having everyone over didn't bother us.

"Terrill, I have something that I want to discuss with you now that we're alone," Cara said quietly.

"What's wrong, baby?" I asked.

She gave me a happy but worried look. I could see the tears starting to form in her eyes. I walked over to her and gave her a hug. "What's wrong, ma?

"I'm— pregnant," she said then started crying.

"Hey, hey why are you crying, Cara? Calm down," I sat her down on the couch and sat beside her because she became really emotional. She looked in my eyes to see any signs of rejection, but there wasn't any. I was happy than kids on Christmas, especially hearing this news on my mother's birthday.

"Should I have it, 50ty?" she asked.

"Yeah baby, damn right you should have it," I answered giving her a serious look. I leaned over her and asked, "Are those tears of happiness or sadness?"

"Well if there is anybody that I would want to have a family with it would be you, Terrill. But, how will it change our relationship?" she asked.

"You don't have to question that, babe," I assured her. "You are mine, so whatever is a part of you is a part of me, too. I love you. That's why I want to marry you."

She smiled when I reassured her. "Don't tell anybody yet. I want them to just see me get bigger," she told me. She cleaned her face with a napkin that I gave her.

"Okay. So, this means no more smoking and no more smoking around you. We will just tell them that you quit for a while, like nine or ten months, but you will be back," I joked.

"No, Terrill, they'll know something is up if I tell them nine months," she replied laughing. "I'll just tell them I quit."

"That will work," I said then gave her a kiss and went into the room to lie down and think some more. I still wasn't going to let anything get in my way of happiness today. I felt as if I was one of America's Most Wanted from all the drama I'd been through. I knew there wouldn't be a happy ending from the chaos, but by Cara being pregnant, I had to stay focused and free.

I wondered if my mom was still around, would I have ever become rich and have the world in the palm of my hands or would I be out there on somebody's job miserable and upset because I worked a nine to five with minimum wage. I guess that would have been okay if I hadn't met Cara and fell in love.

Mama, I'm sorry. But please understand that this life isn't meant to be peaceful for me.

I was determined to never let another man run over me and think he was better than me. I would maintain. I stopped thinking and turned over to fall asleep.

The next morning Cara was on the phone talking to the lawyer. RonRon had dropped Keem and Anthony off at their aunt's house. I went into the living room where Cara was.

"The lawyer said that he called to verify that they were still in the county and not sent to prison or anything. They are still there waiting on a court date," she informed.

"Not to change the subject, but just give Tom some time to do what he has to do. All of this makes me want to go out there and flip a million for you and the baby," I said giving her a hug.

"What do you want us to have, honey?"

"It doesn't matter. Either way he or she will be set and ready for the world. I will put that on my entire life," I promised.

"I want a little girl so I can do her hair and show her how to do hair and dress her up in girl stuff," she said.

Shit having a girl sets a man on a mission and that's dangerous in my book. I wouldn't want to have to cut someone's life short over my little girl.

We sat hugged up together on the sofa and watched cartoons until RonRon and Tera got up. The smell of bacon and eggs banged through the house.

"Good morning, guys," Tera said smiling away as she walked past the hallway into the bathroom. RonRon went into the other bathroom.

Cara had cooked grits, eggs, bacon, and diced ham. We ate at the kitchen table like we were characters on the Soul Food series.

"So, when are you guys going back to Bainbridge?" Tera asked.

"It's up to the lawyer to make that decision," Cara said.

"Hey 50ty, I want to open up a Laundromat up here on Harmony, homey. I saw a lot of vacancies available on the block."

"Get the prices together and see what you can work with. That will be a good idea though because I haven't seen any Laundromats' up there," I told him.

Mind over matter was how I lived. I thought about investing myself. Having Jermaine and Derrick on my mind made it difficult. I'd wait until the outcome of the situation. I'd call the next day or the day after, giving the lawyer some time to work on the case.

Cara decided that she wanted to spend the day with her aunt I didn't care at all because Tera had things that she had to do herself. That gave RonRon and I some P.I.C. (Partner and Crime) time, so it was straight.

We chilled together for the whole day smoking and talking shit.

"Through the past year we established a couple million, homey. That's mad crazy," RonRon said excitedly rolling up a blunt to smoke.

"It's crazy but it damn sure came in handy," I replied.

We pulled out our cash and counted it for the hell of it.

"After I pay this lawyer off I'll have nine hundred and eighty-nine grand left. I know it's all going to be well worth it. Derrick is a hustler. Jermaine will get a job and straight chill. I will hold him down until he gets to where he wants to be."

I noticed a car pulling up in the driveway. "Who is that in the driveway, RonRon?" I was prepared for whatever.

With both of the Hummers gone and no other car in the driveway, how would they know if somebody was home? I grabbed both of my guns swiftly and RonRon grabbed the thirty-thirty.

We peered out of the window of the living room. RonRon spotted Hakeem getting out of the car first.

"That's Hakeem and Anthony," he said.

I was still looking out of the window and noticed a red Corsica parked on the corner. I didn't pay it much attention until it pulled off after Anthony and Hakeem walked into the crib. I didn't say anything about it, because maybe I was tripping.

"What's up, 50ty"? Hakeem greeted as he entered the kitchen where I was still peering out the window.

"Chilling, what's going on with y'all?" I asked.

"Nothing, just swinging by to see what you guys up to today," Anthony replied.

"I see," I said. I tossed him a cigar and a bag of weed.

"Where is Tera?" Anthony asked RonRon.

"I think she went shopping and shit," RonRon answered.

"What's Cara up to over at your aunt's crib, Anthony?" I asked.

"When I was there, she was helping my aunt clean up the house and wash the dishes," he said.

After we chilled for a couple hours just talking shit and smoking as usual Tera arrived. My crib smelled like L.A.'s best weed.

Tera walked into the smoked-out house and saw that we were higher than a motherfucker. Even Hakeem was exposed.

"Damn, y'all. It looks like a home invasion went on or something," she mentioned, carrying her bags into the room.

RonRon and Hakeem helped her grab the rest of the bags out of the car. She was gone a long time just to have a few bags. But with women there was no telling.

"I got some Hennessy and a twelve pack of coke for chaser."

"Well, I'm going to head out, 50ty. I'm going to see what they doing over there at my aunt's crib," Anthony said. He and Hakeem stood up to leave.

"Cool," I replied walking them to the door.

I watched as they pulled off and told them to call me once they got home. After Anthony drove out of view I went back inside.

RonRon and Tera were in the room looking through the clothes and stuff she'd brought for them.

I didn't want to bother them so I just went into my room and rolled me a solo blunt. My phone started buzzing on the coffee table in the living room.

It was Hakeem.

"We just got into an accident, 50ty. Up the street from your house. Damn. I knew I shouldn't have let Anthony leave just now because he was high as hell," I stated.

"Are you guys okay?"

"Yeah. Anthony is helping the people that we ran into out of the car."

"Okay Keem. I'm going to ride up there."

"Alright."

"RonRon, Anthony and Keem just got into a car accident up the road. I'm going to ride up there just to see if they are alright," I told RonRon.

"Oh my God. Are they okay?" Tera asked.

"Well Keem sounded okay. He said that Anthony is helping the people that he crashed into out the car so I don't know how bad it is."

"Okay 50ty, do you want me to ride up there with you, pimp?" RonRon asked.

"Nah, I'll be okay. Stay here with your wife. I'm going to just go and see if they high asses alright," I joked, laughing while passing Tera my joint and grabbing RonRon keys off his dresser.

I popped the lock from the key switch as I walked outside to the Hummer. Once I open the truck to get inside I heard a car pull in front of the yard. When I turned and looked back toward the street I saw it was the red Corsica. Two niggas jumped out in a hurry. Both had guns. I hurried and jumped into RonRon's Hummer and ducked down to the floor. They started shooting up the truck. They both aimed for the left side of the Hummer.

I knew if I stayed in the truck I would get shot so after I heard the first hit the truck, I jumped back out on the passenger's side. I fell to the ground with my forty-five cocked back. I rushed to the back of the Hummer and aimed at one of the dudes. I had a perfect shot but the other dude quickly crept behind me and shot three times. I felt something hit me in the back and I dropped to the ground. I quickly rolled under the truck. They ran back to the Corsica. I started shooting at them, hitting one in the leg.

RonRon swung the front door opened to start shooting but it was too late. The Corsica sped off. The police were on the block and they rushed after them.

"50ty! 50ty! Are you okay?" RonRon shouted as he ran over to me while I lay on the concrete. My back was bruised from the burns but my bullet proof vest saved my life.

"I'm cool, RonRon," I said.

"Who were those dudes?" he asked, helping me get to my feet and walking into the house.

"I believe they were Sweetman's homeys," I said. Tera stood in the hall, looking terrified. "I'm okay Tera," I reassured her. "Them motherfuckers shot me in the back, but my vest saved me," I said so she would calm down. I took off my shirt and saw that my back had three burn marks on it. It wasn't a serious burn, but I could tell where I got shot.

Two police pulled up in front of the house. I told RonRon and Tera to stay inside while I handled it.

"Sir, did you know the guys in that red Corsica?" A woman officer asked.

I had to make it quick so I could go see Keem and Anthony. "No ma'am, I don't know them nor do I know what happened. There was an accident up the street earlier. They're my brothers and I have to go and see if they're alright," I replied, getting into the Hummer.

"Wow," the male officer exclaimed. "They shot up this truck pretty bad. Do you want to make a report?" he asked, holding his notepad in his hand. I paused for a second then looked at him.

"I can't right now, sir. I need to go check on my brothers please. I will come to the police station after I see that everything is alright."

"You don't have to give a statement on what happened, sir, because I saw everything," the female officer said. "Do you know a Cara?" she asked.

I paused instantly and looked at her. "Yeah I know Cara. Why?"

"She had us patrolling this area and her Aunt Laurie's area."

Smart idea, I thought.

"Well, sir, we have all four of the suspects in custody," the male officer said.

The lady officer quickly examined the truck. "They were really after you. That's attempted murder," she said.

I didn't say anything else until they finally left. RonRon came outside to look at his truck.

"Damn! I'm glad you're okay. Shit, this will be fixed later," he said.

Tera quietly stood at the door.

"I'm going up there to see how Keem and Anthony are," I said.

RonRon refused to stay. He jumped in on the passenger's side.

When we arrived at the accident scene there were people everywhere. Keem and Anthony sat on the curb. Anthony's car was demolished. The rescue workers were tending to a lady and a man. They both wore neck braces. They drove a Lincoln Town Car that was smashed from the front. It was a pretty bad wreck from the looks of it.

RonRon walked over to Anthony and Hakeem. I walked over to the man that was in the Lincoln Town Car.

"Wow this was a terrible accident. What caused it?" I asked just to make sure they didn't think Anthony was at fault.

"Well all I know is when we were turning left at the green turning signal, I saw a car coming toward us at full speed and Bang!" he said.

The woman was placed in the ambulance. The man got in back with her.

The tow truck arrived.

"You guys should go to the hospital and get checked out," I told Anthony and Hakeem.

They said that they are okay, but they're young and the pain hadn't crept up on them yet. It would though. I'd been in the situation plenty of times so I knew.

"We have the people that caused this accident. They were in red Corsica, right?" The officer asked Anthony.

"Yeah that's them. They hit us on the side knocking us into the other lane where we hit the Lincolnton Car," Anthony responded.

I called Cara to tell her what happened. Immediately, I knew I should have waited because she started to panic I tried to assure her that everything was alright.

"Don't work a nerve. I don't want you upset because of the baby," I told her. I let her talk to Keem and Anthony so she would calm down. I never told her about me getting shot three times. She probably would have had a miscarriage. I'd wait to tell her about that later, in person.

We went to the Hummer car lot and switched Hummers until they repaired RonRon's truck. Then we went back to the crib.

"My neck is starting to hurt now," Anthony said.

"My neck hurts too, and my back," Hakeem complained.

"Cara is going to take you guys to the emergency room," I said as we pulled up on our block.

My Hummer was parked in the drive way. We pulled in behind it. Cara rushed out the door and ran to us.

"Anthony and Hakeem, are y'all alright?" she asked, giving them both a hug at the same time.

"No, they're actually not, baby. Their necks and backs hurt. They need to be taken to the emergency room," I told her.

"Okay, baby," she said. She grabbed my arm as I tried to walk past into the house. "Let me see your back," she said. I pulled her to the side and showed her my back. She placed both of her hands over her mouth. "Cara, I'm fine, ma. You wouldn't have ever known about this if Tera wouldn't have told you. I don't want you to be upset because of the baby, Ma. Take it easy please for me and the baby. Everything is cool," I told her, removing her hands from her mouth. "Go take them to the hospital to get check out and call me. I will be home waiting on answers, okay?"

"Okay," she replied. I could still tell she was worried, but she let it go. She walked back to the Hummer with Anthony and Keem. Tera went with them to the hospital in RonRon's rental.

Hour passed and RonRon was in the room asleep. I dozed off in the living room. I heard a car pull up in the drive-way and saw the lights turned off. I quickly grabbed my gun and looked at the clock on the wall. It was three o'clock in the morning. I peered out of the window and saw Cara and Tera. I hurried to open the door for them.

"How is Hakeem and Anthony?" I asked after they entered the house.

"The doctor said that they will be fine, just minor injuries. The doctor prescribed them some pain pills. I placed the prescription at the Walgreens by my aunt's house," Cara said. "Are you okay, baby?"

"Yeah I'm fine. I'm glad that I had on my bulletproof vest though."

She was silent. Tera went in the room with RonRon. I sat back down on the sofa to watch television. Cara turned the light on in the room and I heard her mumbling and sniffing. I just listened for a minute but couldn't really understand what she was saying to herself or what she is doing in the room with the lights on so late. I got up and went in the room.

"What's wrong, Cara?" I asked, noticing the tears on her face. She walked up to me.

"I don't want to stay in California any longer."

"Why? It's cool up here, plus I'm fine," I replied.

"No, you're not, Terrill. Understand, baby, you could have died." She placed her hands over her mouth trying to keep from crying.

"Cara," I said grabbing both of her hands. "I love you. Just know that, okay? I don't want you to ever think that it's your fault every time something happens to me or your family because it's not. Okay?" She nodded. "Besides, I'm glad to be here and help out with this bullshit they put your family through."

"Thank you," she said, placing her head on my chest.

We sat on the bed. I started rubbing on her stomach. "I want you to be happy, ma, because I'm happy that I have you on my side as my lady. If I can start over, I would love to have you again in my life," I told her. Every word was from the heart.

"I love you too, Terrill. I just don't want to lose you," she said quietly. She was in tears again.

I took a deep breath because that was something I couldn't promise. In this world nothing is promised. "It's late, baby. Let's lie down fully dressed like we did on our first stay together," I joked.

As I got ready to jump in the bed she stopped me by grabbing the back of my pocket.

"I don't think so," she said. She removed my shirt and unbuckled my belt. "We're both going to bed in our birthday suits." She gave me a passionate kiss. That's all it took to get me nice and hot.

CHAPTER 15

I got up early the next morning to call the lawyer Tom. When I entered the living room I saw that RonRon was up playing the PlayStation and smoking. I quickly closed the room door so the smoke wouldn't enter the room.

"What's up, pimp?" RonRon greeted, passing me the blunt.

"Nothing. I'm just going to call this lawyer to see what he's going to do about this case."

"Alright dawg," RonRon said and went back to the game. I got on the phone with Tom.

After talking to Tom, I told RonRon about Tom's trip to Bainbridge on the upcoming Friday.

"Are going to go down there with him?" he asked.

"No, it won't be worth it because I wouldn't be able to see them."

I grabbed the other joystick and we played Mortal Combat. I always beat him with Lu Kane. His main man was Raiden.

"Switch up, 50ty. Why do you always get Lu Kane," he asked jokingly.

Growing up playing video games was all we did in St. Pete. But RonRon never realized that I was the man in Mortal Combat.

After we played three matches, Cara was up. She came into the living room to see what was going on.

Hi, baby. I'm sorry RonRon woke you up," I said. RonRon threw me a comical look and smiled. "Because right now he is collecting an ass whipping." They laughed.

Friday came along, and we stayed at the crib for the day. Cara and Tera cooked a nice meal of fried chicken, homemade mashed potatoes, and sweet peas to eat later in the evening.

Tom will call once he arrived in Bainbridge. I will wait on the outcome of his visit with Jermaine and Derrick.

"I'm thinking about going to Florida to see what's going on with my lil homeys. I want to see who needs work there," RonRon told me.

We sat at the kitchen table while Tera and Cara were in the room talking.

"I'm going to keep Derrick hustling for me when he jumps," I said.

Money, money, money was on my mind. Derrick had well over a million dollars so he should maintain his position in Bainbridge. My main goal was to make money and stay on top of the game.

My phone rang, seeing that it was Tom I answered it quickly.

"Terrill, I have wonderful news," he said.

"And what's that?"

"Your brother and Derrick are in holding cells waiting to be released," he told me.

"Hell yeah!" I yelled with excitement. RonRon looked at me. Tera and Cara walked into the living room to see what was happening "Thanks Tom. I will be on a plane heading to Georgia to see them ASAP," I replied, hanging up with him. I turned toward everyone. "Derrick and Jermaine are free. They are waiting to be released now. I'm going to Georgia tonight to get them," I went to pack for the trip.

"Word," RonRon said, as he sat on the floor, between Tera's legs.

"That's wonderful news," Tera replied.

"Good, baby. I'm going with you. I want to go see my friends in Bainbridge," Cara said, coming into the bedroom.

"That's cool," I said, glad she'd be traveling with me. She smiled and got a suitcase from the closet.

On the way to the airport we rode in RonRon's rental. "50ty, while you guys are in Georgia, me and Tera will be heading to St. Petersburg in the morning," RonRon said.

"Cool. I'll call you tomorrow morning or later tonight whenever I see them," I told him.

"Tell them I said hello."

"Cara, tell them hoes that I haven't forgotten about them. I just didn't have time to call none of them yet," Tera said.

"Okay," Cara responded laughing.

RonRon went to spark up a blunt but I had to stop him before he fired it up. "RonRon let's chill out for now, homey. I have a headache," I lied. I just didn't want him smoking around Cara while she was pregnant.

"Cool," he replied, pulling up in front of the airport.

We hugged and gave each other dap. We'll see you guys soon. RonRon, how long are you planning on being in St. Pete?" I asked.

"We'll probably stay a week or less. I have to see my grandmother too," he said.

"Tell her I said hello and that I'm keeping you out of trouble, alright?" He laughed and helped me grab our bags out of the back of the truck.

Our plane arrived thirty minutes after we entered the lobby. I was so excited and couldn't wait to see them. I kept a smile on my face which made Cara smile. I even had a glass of wine. I felt good the whole trip to Tallahassee.

As we departed the plane Eric called.

"What's happening, Eric?" I asked.

"Yo 50ty, me and Rodney at the jail picking up Derrick and Jermaine," he said.

"Alright cool. We're in Tallahassee right now getting a rental," I told him as we walked into the rental center.

When we got to Bainbridge we went straight to Cara's friend's house so she could see them. We pulled up to a white house with a gate around, and flowers on both sides of the sidewalk. It led to the front door. I'd never met her friends before. A light skinned girl came to the door. I couldn't really get a good look until she saw that it was Cara and she ran out the door screaming. Damn she was fine as hell, and thick, too. I slowly got out of the car as two more ladies came outside. Wow! All of them were model material.

Cara introduced me to all three of the beautiful ladies.

"Baby, meet Tiffany, Tasha, and La' Keisha." Neither looked better than my baby, but they were running neck to neck though. Instead of shaking hands, they gave me a hug. They smelled really good, too.

We stayed at their house for over an hour before Eric called me again.

"50ty, we have Derrick and Jermaine and we're headed to my house. I'm not going to tell them that you are here so just come up to the crib in about an hour and surprise them," he said then laughed.

"Okay. That's cool," I replied.

I sat in the living room a little longer and listened to the women talk. It was good to see Cara happy around her friends. She never told them that she was pregnant because it would get back to Tera for sure.

"Cara, I'll be back. Stay here with your friends and I'll return in a couple of hours." I gave her a kiss then left them in the living room gossiping about everything under the sun.

The first place I went was Derrick's house just to check out the area. The block was still silent. Just for the hell of it I tried calling Los. As I figured, there was no answer.

Two hours passed and it was time to make my move to Eric's house. I couldn't wait to see my brother and cousin.

With a full moon, silent streets, and no traffic it was crazy. It felt like Georgia really did get hit by something.

I pulled up to their house, and saw that everybody was in the backyard. I parked out of their view then got out the car. I walked to the other side of the house to look and see who was in the backyard. I spotted Jermaine sitting on the bench next to Rodney. Derrick was in the house with Eric. I eased back to the front of the house. I knocked on the door hard as hell then quickly ran to the side of the house to hide.

Eric came to the door and opened it just a little bit.

"Whose car is that in our driveway?" he yelled. I snuck to the back and saw Jermaine and Rodney go around the other way walking toward the front of the house. I quickly entered the house from the back door. As I crept to the living room, I saw Eric and Derrick standing at the door talking to Jermaine and Rodney outside. I walked up on Eric while he was standing in the doorway. As soon as Derrick walked outside, I grabbed Eric by his shoulders and pulled him inside the house slamming the door and locking it. He started to panic until he saw that it is me. Derrick tried to open door, but couldn't. He started pounding on it.

From the living room window, I saw Jermaine and Rodney rush to the backyard. As they rushed inside from the back door, Eric and I ran upstairs to hide in his room. I got in the closet and Eric hid on the side of the bed towards the wall.

"Yo, Eric, where are you?" they yelled, searching for him downstairs.

I heard someone coming up the stairs and then heard the sound of a gun clicking. The door silently opened and Derrick looked inside the room. He held a three-eighty in his hand. I would have jumped out and scared him but he was strapped. That could lead to an accidental death. So, I waited for him to turn and walk out the room.

The house phone rang. He stopped at the top of the stairs and put his gun in his pocket. Now it was time for me to act. When he took his first step to go down the stairs I grabbed him and turned him around fast with a shocking shake by his arm. As he screams he went for his gun before he noticed it was me, I grabbed his wrist.

"Cuz, good to see you, pimp," I said laughing because his eyes were wide with fright.

"Damn 50ty, you almost got shot for that" he said, laughing in relief.

"Derrick, are you okay?" Rodney asked from the living room.

"Shh." I pulled Derrick into the room.

Both Jermaine and Rodney came up the stairs. Jermaine came into the room first and I jump out from behind the door at him. He and Rodney both jumped back in fear.

"50ty, you scared the hell out of all us," Eric said, laughing.

"Sorry about that, but I had to do something exciting. Plus, I'm glad to see y'all niggas again."

"Shit, bro, I'm glad to be out of jail," Jermaine said, smiling.

"Hell yeah," Derrick replied. "They locked Los up in Atlanta to. That's weird."

"So that's why he's not answering his phone," I said.

"The word in the county is that the police found out about Reco's death, and that he is calling out names, cuz. He mentioned me and you," Derrick said.

Motherfucker, I thought.

They didn't have anything on my brother. I guess they locked him up to keep from letting me know what was going down.

"They tried to keep us in jail on lock down until they found you but they never could find out where you were located. They were in St. Pete on a manhunt for you," Jermaine said.

"We told them that we didn't know anybody by the name of 50ty, but they weren't trying to hear that at all," Derrick mention.

"Thanks for having Tom get us out of there though. He did his thing in court and they released us."

We sat in the backyard all night talking until Eric and Rodney went to bed. I called Cara and let Derrick talk to her. I told her that we would be heading out in the morning. RonRon was in St. Pete at his grandmother's house with Tera. They said they would be back in a week.

"Derrick, how did you get that dude to call me from the county?" I asked.

"The dude Ramon there is a trustee and he always came to my cell to give me cigarettes. I didn't trust him from the start, but after a while of getting to talk to him at lease 5-10 times a day, I got to know that he was cool. I gave him your number just to test the waters and had him tell you that we were locked up. I hoped it would work and it did," he replies.

"I see, because once I got the message I hired a lawyer."

"True. Where is Cara?" Jermaine asked.

"She is at her friend's house chilling."

"I know whose house she's at, Tiffany and her sister, Keisha," he said.

"Yeah that's where she is and they fine as hell, too," I mentioned.

"I have your cash in the trunk, Derrick. We didn't want nobody taking your goods, homey."

"I was thinking about my money every single day, 50ty. Boy good looking out, I haven't been by my house yet. I'll head out there in a minute," Derrick said.

"Yo Jermaine, will you come to California with me, bro, I have room for you?" I asked just to see what he would say.

"Yeah, I will come up there for a while, but I'll have to let them peoples know if I'm leaving Bainbridge," he replied.

At three in the morning we decided to call it a night. I gave Derrick his money and dropped him off at his crib. Jermaine and I went to Tallahassee and got a room. I called Cara to see if she was doing alright. She was half asleep so I told her I'd see her in the morning. Jermaine fell asleep quickly. I took a shower then went to bed.

The next morning Cara called and woke me up at 11.am.

"Hey, baby, I'm glad you called and woke me up. Shit, Jermaine is knocked out," I said getting up to head for the bathroom.

"I knew you probably were still asleep. Tiffany said that she can bring me to Tallahassee, if you want," she states.

"No, have her drop you off at Derrick's because we're headed over there to tell him bye."

"Oh, okay then. I'll get dressed then. I love you and I will see you when you get there."

"I love you too, ma. Bye."

Jermaine got up after I came out of the restroom. He went in to shower then got dressed. Once he'd finished, we were ready to go.

After leaving the hotel we went up Monroe to a fast food restaurant to eat lunch.

"Damn 50ty, I haven't eaten like this in a while. This is what people be needing in jail, for real," Jermaine said, pigging out.

"Yeah, I feel you. Cara is at Derrick's house waiting on us to get there. She'll be okay so there's no need to rush. Derrick will entertain her," I said, sipping on my soda.

We sat at the restaurant talking for about ten minutes after we'd finished eating. We left a tip and headed out, driving straight to Derrick's house.

Cara was already outside when we pulled up to the house. Derrick sat on the steps. Jermaine got out, going straight to his car to examine it.

"I locked the door because you left the key inside, Here." I tossed him his car keys.

He tossed them to Derrick. "Hold them down, homey, until I return" he said.

"Hey Jermaine. How are you?" Cara asked, giving him a hug.

"Free at last, free at last," he replied making us all laugh.

"Well, cuz, when you get yourself together, you should swing up to California as well," I said to Derrick.

"You already know I'm coming up there soon," he replied giving me and Jermaine a one- armed hug and hugging Cara. "I'm going to handle my business first then I'll come up there."

"Cool," Jermaine said

"Alright, cuz, take care of yourself. Holla at me if you need me and tell Eric and Rodney that they got the number, use it sometime."

I took the rental and dropped it back off at the airport in Tallahassee. Derrick had a lot of trips to make in order to drop off packages.

I was stress free now that Jermaine was going home with me. Cara and I held hands the entire trip home. I called RonRon to tell him we were on our way back to Los Angeles. I took a nap after I talked to him. Cara was already asleep.

After arriving in L.A we waited in the lobby for Anthony to pick us up.

"Wow, I can't believe I finally made it here, Y'all, I'm sorry that we missed RonRon's wedding," Jermaine said.

"He understood. He wanted you out of jail just as bad as I did," I told him.

Not too much time passed before Anthony called Cara and told us to come outside to the pickup area. He and Hakeem were waiting on us.

Jermaine looked out the window as we rode around for a few showing him the spotlight of Los Angeles. We stopped at a corner store to grab a blunt and some bottle water.

"I can't believe Los went out like that Jermaine," I said. "I thought he was a real ass nigga."

"Yeah, a real lying ass nigga is what he is," he replied as we pulled up in the front of my house.

"Whose Hummers are those?" he asked. I gave him a baller look.

"The red and black one is mine and the other one is RonRon's"

"Oh damn! Where is mine?" he asked jokingly.

"I'll go get you one right now," I said laughing.

"I'm just kidding, bro," he replied as we walked into the house.

Jermaine stood in the living room and examined the stereo set and the fountain in the middle of the floor. "Damn Bro you and Cara got it looking nice, he complimented. "When is the last time you been home?"

"Been awhile. I only been back and forth to Bainbridge looking for y'all. That's it. Why? What's up?

"My dumb ass baby momma got her phone off or disconnected. I want to check on my kids."

"Here," I gave him three grands. "Go and check on them. Tell them I'll be down there in a minute to get them and take them shopping."

I loved my nephews. Both were bad as hell. Lil G was the oldest at ten, and Jamal was only six.

"I'm glad I didn't get cased up at RonRon's birthday party," he said bringing that back up.

I had totally forgotten all about that shit. I noticed the expression Jermaine gave me because he'd brought that up.

"Yeah, it's all good, bro. I'm glad that you're good to go down there in peace. So, what are you going to do?" I asked.

"Since I can't get in touch with them, I'll call RonRon to see if he can go over there and have her call me," he responded. He gave the three-grand back to me.

"I feel ya. I pulled an already rolled blunt out of my top pocket. "Are you going to bring them up here if you go down there?" I asked, following him into the kitchen.

"Depends on how they're living down there. If my baby mom is doing her job taking care of them the right way, then it's all good," he replied.

"Let's go sit outside on the back on the patio," I said. I didn't want to smoke around Cara.

It was four o'clock in the evening. Cara was tired after the trip from Bainbridge. We weren't but we let her rest.

"Bro, Cara is pregnant," I said because I didn't keep anything from him. "She is three month. That's why I don't want to smoke around her."

He laughed. "Damn, bro, now you are finally going to see what it's like raising a kid. Congratulations," he said.

I smiled. "See the difference with my child is they are going to be set. And so are my nephews once everything falls into place. You'll see." I gave him my cell phone. "Call RonRon and tell him to go by your baby momma's house now, bro. Shit, I want to talk to Lil G and Jamal since you got them on my mind."

Jermaine called RonRon and asked him to swing by his baby mama's house and to call him as soon as he got in front of her house. We sat out back for a couple of hours until Cara came to the back door. She didn't have to say anything because I already knew what was on her mind. My baby was hungry.

"Hey, ma. I know you're hungry. Let's go to KFC. "

She smiled at me and Jermaine. "Okay. Let's go," she said.

"I know you're pregnant, Cara," Jermaine told her. "You're carrying my nephew or niece. It doesn't matter which, Uncle J will be there," he said, walking past her and into the house. She playfully hit him on the back and laughed.

We decided to eat at KFC. Cara talked to her aunt while Jermaine and I stood in line for our food. Once we got our order, we joined Cara at the table she'd picked.

While we were eating the chicken RonRon called. I gave the phone to Jermaine.

"Knock on her door, homey then give her your phone," Jermaine said to RonRon.

That's a smart way to do it I thought.

Jermaine got up and walked off from the table as he talked to his baby mama.

"Are they good to each other, baby?" Cara asked, watching as Jermaine carried on his conversation.

"Jealous. She is so controlling and insecure. Hoes be all up on him and she thinks he's cheating on her. He never denied it. He just let her say and think however she wants. You know how that goes," I replied.

After having a long conversation with his baby mama, Jermaine finally came back to the table and gave me the phone.

"Lil G wants to talk to you," he said. I smiled as I took the phone.

"Hey, lil nigga. What's going on with you?" I asked.

"Hey uncle, 50ty," he responded.

"What I told you about calling me Uncle 50ty? Boy, it's Uncle Terrill. You know better than that," I scolded. "Are you being good in school?"

"Yeah. I made the honor roll three times already and Jamal is doing good too," he said cheerfully.

"Oh yeah? Alright. I'll be down there with your daddy soon. I'm going to take you shopping, nephew. You can get whatever you want, okay? And tell Jamal to be good. Uncle will see y'all soon."

"Bye Uncle 50- I mean, Uncle Terrill," he said.

"Bye Knucklehead." I handed Jermaine the phone so he could end the conversation with his family.

CHAPTER 16

A week passed. Basically, we stayed home watching movies and chilling. Cara spent most of her time at her aunt's house. RonRon and Tera finally made it back to L.A. and went to check out their new crib. Cara had called her landlord and inquired about a property for them. Lucky for them she had one for sale not too far from where we lived.

I was in the bedroom reading a book when my house phone rang.

I got it, bro," I yelled through the house, picking up the receiver.

"Yo, 50ty, the crib is nice, playa. You should come and check it out," RonRon said, excitedly.

"Cool. Jermaine and I will head over there right now, pimp." After I hung up, I told Jermaine and we headed out.

We drove up the same street that Aunt Laurie lived on to RonRon's house. I noticed that his yard was bigger than mine. Cara stood at the door talking to Tera as she planted flowers in the grass.

"What's up, pimping?" RonRon greeted Jermaine, giving him a one-armed hug. "I missed you, boy."

"Yeah I'm back now. RonRon, this is a nice crib you have," Jermaine said.

"You like it?" he asked.

191

"Yeah, this is straight, homey. All you need now is a Pitt Bull for protection," Jermaine said.

"That will be straight. I think I'll get a female and a male so I can breed and sell them for like four to five hundred a puppy," RonRon said.

Another part of a hustler's field was breeding Pitt Bulls, gambling and drag racing. We used to stop at the red-light side by side while people stood on the curb watching. When the light turned green, we'd shoot up the one way at full speed, driving down a one-mile stretch. Whoever won got up to $200 a bet.

Back then, I had a Park Avenue Buick that kicked up dust. I raced from First Avenue across the Howard Franklin Bridge and won. I stayed in first place.

While we stood outside reminiscing about the races and gambling bets, the women finished in the yard and went inside. Not too long after, we headed inside too.

Cara and Tera were decorating the living room and bedrooms. Since we didn't want to get in the way, we decided to go to San Francisco to visit Tom. I wanted to thank him in person and see what he knows about the situation.

"What's the deal with this lawyer?" RonRon ask when we pulled into the parking lot of the lawyer's office.

"I'm going to find out what's the deal now," I told him. Sometime it was better to face-off with people dealing with certain situation than talking over the phone.

We had to sit in the lobby for a couple of minutes before Tom came out to get us.

"Hello Terrill and Jermaine," he greeted, shaking our hands. I introduced him to RonRon and they shook hands then we went in to his office.

"I'm glad to be out of jail and out of Georgia," Jermaine said, sitting down in the office.

"So, what's the plan now?" I asked just to get on the real reason why we were in San Francisco. "I don't want Jermaine or Derrick going back to jail."

"Terrill, basically everything is on a "he said, she said right now concerning Carlos's situation." We all looked at each other, puzzled.

"How do you know about Los?" I asked.

Tom smirked. "In order to free Jermaine and Derrick I had to go into full detail on the matter and reasons of them being detained," he said.

Since Carlos's name popped up in the situation my trust in Tom became limited. "Okay, Tom, now what's the deal?" RonRon stood up, getting straight to the point.

"I'm sure you guys know enough about him to know that he's an Atlanta police officer," he stated. We didn't say anything and he continued. "Carlos has mad pull in Atlanta, from the streets to the police department. Now he is in jail for murder." He gave me a weird look.

"What's that look for Tom?" I had to asked.

"Terrill, I'm going to be straight up with you, okay? He doesn't know where you are or anything. But the police there are looking for you and it will only be a matter of time before they show up in California to find you," he answered.

"How will they find me?" I asked, just to see if he would show any signs of turning me in.

"Well as I said, Carlos has pull at the police department. Somebody there is keeping him well informed, it seems," he said.

"Well they don't have anything on 50ty. He has pull, so what? He got cased up on some bullshit and now he's trying to bring other people down with him," Jermaine replied angrily.

Tom stood up and went to his closet which was near the door of his office. "That's the problem," he said stopping in front of me. "He has something in the closet.

"What does that supposed to mean?" I asked.

"He has some kind of evidence or proof on you," he answered.

"How will they find me in California?" I repeated.

"You have to understand, Terrill, they wait. Eventually people will turn themselves in." We gave him a crazy look and he laughed. "It's true. They turn themselves in by getting caught up at the wrong place, at the wrong time," he finished.

I felt Tom to the fullest but I also knew where he was going with the conversation. "So, what are you doing, Tom, profiting off of me now?" I asked.

He laughed again. We just stared at him with a serious look on our faces. "I wouldn't put it like that, son, but you will need somebody on your side to defend you. You already know that."

"I just gave you fifty grands for helping me to get them out of jail. I'm going to give you fifty more once they are done with this matter. I thought you were on my side," I said.

"That was the deal for representing Jermaine and Derrick," he replied.

"Carlos don't have shit on me so fuck his reason." I said getting up to leave.

Jermaine and RonRon stood up too.

"It is what it is Terrill." Tom said.

"Fuck that," RonRon replied.

Tom stared at me as if I was going to give in and pay him extra cash.

"I'll call you sometime this week for the court date, Tom. Be easy," I said then walked out of his office.

Back in L.A. we went to the movies then to the club to get our minds right. "Do you believe that motherfucker?" RonRon yelled as we sat at the bar waiting on our drinks.

"I don't trust him, bro," Jermaine said.

"I don't trust him either," I replied.

The beautiful waitress returned with our drink orders. We waited until she placed them on the table and left before we continued our conversation.

"We will probably have to get another lawyer. Shit, Tom did his job," I said, sipping on my Hennessy.

All I could see was Tom facial expression. That dude didn't give a damn about his clients, all he wanted was money. I'm glad he didn't have my address. I'd only given him the address in St. Pete.

I made a mental note to have Cara call Oriel and have her tell Tom that she didn't know us. We'd paid for our house and RonRon's crib in cash. She should be cool on keeping silent.

We got wasted at the club. Jermaine dropped RonRon off then we went home.

Cara wasn't there. She was probably still at her aunt's house. I was too drunk to call her so I just fell asleep.

About an hour later Cara snuck in quietly, but I know she's there. After the conversation with Tom, I was on top of everything even when I was fucked up or high.

"Damn baby, you smell just like liquor," she whispered, removing my shoes and socks for me. I pretended to be fucked up. She lit a candle to try to kill the alcohol smell. "Baby," she said nudging me and trying to wake me. She smacked her teeth in disgust. I tried to keep from laughing but she spotted the smirk on my face. "Terrill, I know you're not asleep. I see you smiling." I started laughing and I sat up. She gave me a kiss and sat beside me.

"I went to talk to Tom today," I told her. "He is acting really strange."

"How?" she asked.

"Well first, he knew about Los and what he was in jail for. I believe he did some research on other situations concerning us just to get more money from me."

"So, you think he's a bad person and will set you up?"

"I don't know, but I don't trust him anymore. I want you to call Oriel in the morning and tell her if Tom calls her asking for any info on us, don't give him any," I said.

"Alright," she told me. "Now, what are you going to do about your breath, baby?"

I just laughed. "It's that bad, huh?" I got up, grabbed a wash cloth and towel, and went to take a shower. I didn't want my baby to be miserable because I smelled like alcohol.

When I woke up the next morning I quietly got out of the bed and went into the living room. I turned on the PlayStation and let it play on its own. I fell into deep thought. What choices did I have concerning me, Jermaine, and Derrick? What plans did Los have on setting me up to go down with him? Just because he couldn't clean up his mess good enough not to get caught, why bring people down with him?

I called Derrick and told him everything that happened with Tom. He felt the same way about Tom. He said he didn't trust him either. That's all I needed to hear.

I was going to stop fucking with Tom and let him ride on the 50 grand I gave him for getting them out of jail. I'd get another lawyer to fight for their freedom.

I played the game solo until Jermaine came into the living room and grabbed a joystick. "I just got off of the phone with Derrick and he said that he knew something was strange about Tom. He said he don't trust him either," I told Jermaine. Tom was a black man with greed and that could get him in a whole lot of trouble.

We heard the sound of brakes in front of the house. I got up and peered out the kitchen window. It was Anthony and Hakeem.

"What's going on, y'all?" I asked, meeting them at the door to let them in.

"Nothing just left my aunt's house to see what y'all up to today," Anthony said.

"I'm just in here walking the dog on Jermaine," I bragged. "I'm killing him on this video game. You hear me?"

CHAPTER 17

We decided to just leave Tom alone. He called a few times but I never answered Cara explain everything to Oriel and asked her not to give Tom any info on us. She understood and agreed.

Cara was five months pregnant and was starting to show. She tried buying bigger clothes which worked for a while. But it was only a matter of time before someone noticed. That person was Aunt Laurie. We went over to her house one day and found out that she'd known all along.

"Hey Terrill and Cara. How are you?" she asked, letting us in. We sat on the couch and watched whatever movie she'd been watching.

"So, what's the plan for the baby?" she asked. Cara choked off her own air and so did I.

"Huh?" Cara asked.

"When was you going to tell me, Cara? I waited for months for you to say something about you being pregnant and you or Terrill didn't tell me. I didn't want to just bring it up in front of everybody. Now I have both of you here so this is a good time to bring it up," she replied. "I'm listening," she added.

"Oh Auntie, I'm five months pregnant," Cara admitted. "We don't know what we are having right now, but I go to the doctor every month. I have a private doctor that Oriel introduced me to." I looked at Cara because I didn't know that.

"Well, that's good to hear and from the looks of it, Terrill is not going anywhere so you will be alright," she said with a smile.

"This is my first and only child. This means the world to me," I told her while rubbing on Cara's thigh.

"I'm glad to hear that son. Glad," she said happily.

A week passed. Cara and Jermaine were at RonRon's house. At home alone, I talked to Derrick for a minute. He was waiting on the court papers to arrive. We still hadn't found a good lawyer but the trial date was far enough off it gave us time to search for one.

While I was talking to Derrick Anthony called on the other line. I switched over and answered. "Anthony, what's going on, homey?"

"50ty, I'm at the club P. J's and Sweetman's homeboys in here. I'm alone and they spotted me when I came in. They're following me around the club and I think they're waiting to see who I'm with or waiting for me to go outside."

I was already running out the door to get in my truck before he could finish telling me what was up. "I'm on my way, Anthony. Stay inside until I get there alright? If they try to pop off in the club run to the police there, but don't make a scene if it's nothing. Stay by the phone. I'll call you when I want you to come outside."

I swung by and picked up RonRon and Jermaine then headed straight to the club. Once in the parking lot, RonRon and I put on our bulletproof vests and got out. Jermaine jumped out with my 45 in the waistband of his pants.

"Jermaine, police are up here, bro. Don't cause a scene if we don't have to," I cautioned. I waited until I got to the door then I called Anthony to have him come outside.

Anthony came out the club in a hurry with four dudes following him. As soon as Anthony got close to RonRon, Jermaine rushed the four dudes.

"What's up niggas?" Jermaine asked, showing the handle of his forty-five.

"What to do, pussy?" RonRon yelled.

They dudes began talking trash to RonRon. They weren't scared that we were strapped. People gathered around to watch the altercation.

"This Kat want a straight up fade. Back up and let me fight this dude," RonRon challenged, taking off his jewelry and handing it to Anthony.

The dude punched RonRon in the face as soon as he turned back around. RonRon swung back, missing him. Then the dude grabbed him and tried to scoop him up, but RonRon kept his weight down over the dude while upper cutting him in the forehead and ears. He kept hitting until the dude let him go in order to block some of the punches RonRon threw. RonRon slung the dude to the ground. We kept our eyes on the other Kats. Another dude stepped over the boy RonRon beat up and told RonRon it was his time.

"What's up, nigga?" the dude said as he got ready to rush RonRon. He walked past me, swung, and missed. That had to be the oldest trick in the book so I was ready for that move. As I moved away Jermaine stuck the dude with a powerful right hook, knocking him to the ground.

I swung on the dude next to me with all my strength, trying to knock his head off. His legs gave out, bringing him down to one knee. RonRon did a Bruce Lee sidekick, kicking the dude in the face. It took him down. He was hurt, rocking back and forth on the ground.

The police came out of nowhere, rushing us. I eased into the crowd then took off running. While I ran across the street, I spotted police running behind me, shining a flashlight. I rushed on across the other lane of the street almost getting hit by a car. I ran between two buildings in back of a neighborhood. I kept running between houses. I spotted police on every block and knew they were looking for me.

Damn. Is it that serious? I thought.

Lights flashed everywhere. I kneeled between a house and a fence. It was a good thing no dogs were around. I just stayed there for a while watching the helicopter circle around in the sky. I turned my cell phone off so it wouldn't catch anyone's attention. I saw the police coming up the alley and scurried under the house.

After being under the house for a while, I came out slowly and noticed the alley was clear. I walked up the alley and spotted three dudes walking past. One looked over at me. I tried to hide, but he saw me.

"That's that niggas right there," he yelled.

I faded off in the darkness between two more houses. I wasn't worried about them, but I had the police on my mind. I did think about being unarmed when all three of them were probably strapped.

I climbed a big oak tree in a yard next to a house with a barking dog. The barking dog brought the three dudes in my direction.

"We just want to talk to you, man," one said. I guess he figured I'd just say, okay and give myself up. Dumb ass.

I took a quarter out of my pocket and threw it behind the guys. When it hit the ground, they turned around swinging their guns. I knew they were strapped.

I tried to see where I was so I could tell RonRon to come get me, but I couldn't tell from the top of the tree. The leaves and darkness covered everything.

"Oh, shit there goes the police!" one of them yelled and they took off.

The police cruised up the alley slowly. I know they saw the dudes take off, but didn't go after them. The helicopter came back flashing their lights over the area where I'm hiding. When I saw three police cars come up the alley, I knew it was going to be a problem. I spotted the K-9 dogs. I called RonRon and told him to meet me on the block where the club was located.

I climbed down the tree slowly before the K-9 got near enough to smell me. I ran off toward the front of the house. Looking over the hedges I spotted police on both ends of the corner. The K-9 moved in on me from the backyard.

I knocked on the window of the house which was a dumb idea. The person cut the front door light on and opened the door.

"Who is that knocking on my window?"

I heard talking on a Walkie Talkie coming from the backyard. I hid in the hedges while the police officer went to the guy at the door Lucky for me he was by himself. I eased up on the officer from behind. I ran up and tackled him to the ground like a football player, grabbing his gun and Walkie Talkie.

"Go back inside, man, before I shoot your ass," I told the startled older gentleman. He shut the door quickly.

I handcuffed the officer and told him that I would shoot him within one minute if he said one word. I ran across the street at full speed. I heard the K-9 barking and the police. I quickly removed my shirt and placed it over my face. I heard the dogs rushing toward me.

After I jumped a fence the K-9 were in clear view. They were a half of a block away rushing toward me. I knew I was caught until I spotted a big Pit Bull tied to a tree. I quickly rushed toward the Pit as the K-9 jumped on me and started biting on my shirt.

I turned the dog, swinging him toward the Pit. The Pit grabbed the K-9, snatching him off me. The police rushed the alley and saw the K-9 under attack by the Pit. I ran to the front of the yard and jumped the fence. While I continued to run, I heard a gunshot which brought the police on the corner and the helicopter to the alley.

I didn't stop running until I got lost in the crowd at the club. I put my shirt back on and spotted RonRon in his Hummer at the corner.

I heard the police on the Walkie Talkie stating that the suspect went back to the club. I quickly jumped into the back seat of some female's car.

"What the fuck are you doing, nigga?" one of them asked.

"Please, baby," I begged, breathing hard. "Just drive normal." I pulled out $200.00 and gave it to the driver. "The police are after me, ma. Just let me lay low and I'll gives you another hundred once you get me out of here."

"Shit, I need that money," the driver said and they all laughed.

"Damn, you dirty as hell," the girl sitting in the back seat with me said.

"I know. I was hiding under a house," I responded. But they could tell that I was about money because I wore an expensive G-Unit outfit. Plus, I had on a lot of jewelry.

I climbed into the trunk from the back seat, just in case. I turned the Walkie Talkie's volume down just so I could hear what the police were talking about.

"The suspect is still around the club or inside the club. We have the entire area surrounded. Don't let anybody leave until he is in custody."

The female just drove off normally. As we left, a light flashed in our direction. It was the police I started to panic. I turned the Walkie Talkie off and listened to what they told the officer.

"Hello, ladies." the police said, flashing his light inside the car. I held my breath in silence.

"Damn Mr. Officer, why you flashing that bright ass light on us?" the driver asked.

"As you can see all the cars that are leaving the club are getting pulled over," he replied.

"I see that, sweetie. But why are you pulling us over? I'm the designated driver," she responded. "See, my girl in the back seat is tore up from the floor up. I got to get her home before she throws up everywhere in my shit," the driver told the police officer.

"Yes, I understand that pretty lady. But, we have a murderer from Georgia that is on the loose," the officer said.

Damn, why in the hell does he think I'm a murderer? I thought.

"A murderer? Who got killed, Officer?" the passenger asked.

"I really don't know, but we have word that the suspect is here in Los Angeles. They said they made an arrest in Atlanta. A police officer there was accused of killing a man. He said that his partner is here," he replied.

"Well all I can say is welcome to the murder capital. Shit, people get killed every day here," the driver said laughing as if she were innocent.

"Well ladies, I'm sorry to have taken up your time. Be careful out there and drive safe," the officer said then left.

Damn! That motherfucker Los got Tom on his side.

After we pulled off the girl in the back seat let the seat down for me.

Damn, boy, who you killed in Atlanta?" the girl in the back seat asked.

"I didn't kill anybody. The police officer they have in jail in Atlanta is the one who killed that man, not me. I didn't see him shoot him. I don't want to get involved in the shit," I replied.

"So, he got cased up and now he trying to bring you down with him?" the driver asked.

"Pretty much, but I really don't know what's the deal," I said.

They dropped the girl in the back seat off at her house. I gave her a hundred-dollar bill and thanked her for the help.

"Do you guys want to stop at a restaurant and grab something to eat?" I asked the other two ladies.

"Sure, let's go to Denny's," one of them suggested.

I called RonRon and told him to meet me at the restaurant alone. Lucky, I had on a black T- shirt under my G-Unit shirt because it was dirty as hell and my T- shirt didn't have anything on it. I took the G-Unit shirt and trash it as we walk pass the trash can inside of the restaurant

After we placed our orders, we chilled and talked for a bit.

"So, do you have a wife Mr.?"

"Just call me 50ty. That's what everybody calls me," I told the beautiful lady. "Yes, I'm married. But, it's kind of like I'm not. I just don't want to hurt her by getting taken away forever, so I distance myself from her at times," I tried to explain. I felt like I was talking too much, so I changed the subject. "How about you two, where are the men in your lives?" I asked.

"We're lovers," they said. It brought flashbacks of G-Rod's mother, Sasha, and her lady friend. The two ladies were both young and beautiful. I wondered if the girl we'd just dropped off joined their love voyage on the love boat.

"So how does your wife look, 50ty? I bet she's beautiful," one of them asked.

"Yes, she is an angel sent from heaven. Her name is Cara, and by the way, what are your names?" I asked.

"My name is Ashley," the driver of the car said.

"My name is Jasmine," the other replied.

Jasmine was Puerto Rican with a sexy body and the pretty face of a model.

The two ladies knew they had me wrapped around their time of chilling.

The waitress returned with our food and drinks at the same time RonRon came into the restaurant. I signaled for him to spot me at the table with the two fine ladies. He gave me a 'what the fuck are you doing' type of look. His face expression changed quickly as the ladies looked over at him.

"Hey, ladies how are you tonight?" he asked as he sat in a chair next to me.

"We're fine. How about yourself?" Ashley responded, flirting a bit.

"Order you something, RonRon," I suggested while getting ready to grub out on my food.

"I already ate before I left the crib," RonRon replied.

"50ty, that's a very unique name for such a tall guy," Jasmine said, sipping on her glass of wine. I just smiled stupidly and RonRon shook his head.

"50ty, they pulled every car out there tonight even our car. We just knew that they caught up with you," RonRon said.

"Yeah, it was pretty close, homey. I thought I was a goner for a second there."

"How did you manage to get away?" he asked.

"We hid him in the trunk of our car," Jasmine answered.

"These beautiful ladies and their friend saved me. I'm dedicated to the both of them. "How do y'all want it?" I asked, smiling.

"Let's take it to the house and see how we can get it," Ashley replied.

Jasmine gave RonRon a sexy look. "Sorry Ron, but the ring on your finger shows you mean business and this is pleasure," she said.

I laughed as we followed them out of the restaurant.

"What do you want me to do, 50ty?" RonRon asked.

"I'll call you a little later," I responded, getting into the back seat of Ashley's car.

"Do you smoke, 50ty?" Ashley asked.

"Yes, I smoke. Bring it on because I need to relieve some of this stress." They had some pretty good green that I could smell as soon as Jasmine fired it up.

Ashley pulled up to an all white house surrounded by roses and other flowers. It resembled what the Garden of Eden would look like.

"Those are a lot of flowers," I said.

"Thank you. They're my babies," Jasmine replied.

"Be careful. We have a vicious dog, Melisa. She is a mean ass whore," Jasmine said, unlocking the door. She and Ashley laughed.

Man damn! I hope they don't have a Rot, or a bull dog.

I didn't feel like running anymore that night, but after Jasmine unlocked the door I stepped back getting ready to make a move toward the fence.

Once the door opened the loud vicious, mean bark ready-to-rumble, dog came to protect the house. It was a well-groomed all white poodle.

"Hey baby," Ashley said, kissing the dog.

"Don't worry. She won't bite you this time," Jasmine said, giggling.

"I was prepared to see a big dangerous dog and you guys have… a damn poodle," I said.

"Come on inside," Ashley said laughing. She put the poodle in another room.

The two entered the restroom together. "Make yourself at home, 50ty," Ashley yelled through the wall.

I sat on the fluffy couch and turned on the television. I switched to the news and they were running the story about the fight at the club. They showed a sketch of me, that didn't really look like me.

"Officials are looking for this person for several reasons. He's wanted in another state, in connection to a murder. He has allegedly been connected to a few murders in the Los Angeles area," the news reported stated. "If you have any information regarding this suspect, please contact the L.A. Police Department. The suspect may be armed and dangerous. He attacked an officer tonight, stealing his gun and Walkie Talkie. Here's what the officer has to say regarding this suspect." The camera turned to the officer that I'd attacked, zooming in close.

"I feared for my life tonight when this guy snatched my gun. If it wasn't for the team being in the area, he probably would have killed me," he said.

"Damn, I should have done his ass a favor since he just lied on me," I said angrily. I quickly turned the T.V. off.

The ladies came out of the restroom. "It's your turn," Jasmine said, handing me a towel and wash cloth. With so much running through my head, I didn't really think about what I was getting ready to do. I just flowed with it and went to take a shower.

After taking a shower, I put on an all-black robe with a pair of brand-new boxers. I walked out of the bathroom and into the dark hallway.

"We're in the bedroom. Come here," Ashley called.

I walked into the room and saw that they were in the bed under the covers. "Have a seat in the chair in front of the bed," Jasmine instructed. "Have you ever seen two women make beautiful love?" she asked.

"Well not really. I only saw them kiss and stuff like that," I answered. Thinking about Sasha scene back in St. Pete.

"Well sit back honey and enjoy yourself," Ashley said.

Jasmine grabbed the remote and turned the radio on low. Smooth grooves and weed smell filled the bedroom. I sat back and watched them as they did their thing.

Jasmine placed the front part of Ashley's panties in her mouth then pulled them off of her slowly. Then she started kissing Ashley from her feet on up to her thighs. Ashley moaned from the sensational feelings. Jasmine then started kissing her around her belly button, to her stomach Ashley moaned louder.

Ashley leaned over and placed her tongue in Jasmine's mouth. I was rock hard watching them kiss and rubbed on each other.

Jasmine started kissing on Ashley chest, sucking her nipples softly. Jasmine's right hand rubbed her clit, while the other one caressed Ashley's right breast.

Jasmine switched positions with her fingers. The finger she had on her pussy, she placed in Ashley's mouth. Ashley slurped it as if it was one of her favorite lollipops.

"You like this 50ty?" Jasmine asked while Ashley was still sucking the pussy juice off her finger.

"Hell yeah," I replied.

Jasmine placed her head between Ashley's legs and started kissing her around the pussy before she ate her out. Ashley moaned and moved up to the head of the bed. Jasmine followed with her mouth still on her pussy, working her tongue. When Ashley got to the top of the bed and couldn't move anymore, Jasmine took full control.

Jasmine had Ashley moving all over the bed as if she were having multiple orgasms. Jasmine looked back at me with a sexy smile. Ashley's moistness was around her mouth. They knew that they had me where they wanted me.

They switched positions. Jasmine sat up on the bed while Ashley got on her knees in front of her and went straight to work. The entire time Ashley ate Jasmine out, Jasmine had her eyes on me. One finger was in her mouth while she softly moaned.

Seeing that I had my hands in my pants Jasmine said, "Pull it out." I couldn't help it because my dick was on rock hard. I pulled it out, holding it in my hand. "Hmmm," Jasmine moaned, while watching me jack off.

Ashley looked over at me. The two stopped what they were doing, got out of bed and approached me. Just as I was about to put it back in my pants, Jasmine pushed me back into the chair. Ashley took my dick and slowly placed it in her warm mouth. My body felt weak, leaving them in control. Jasmine started working on my upper body while Ashley gave me some bomb ass head. I felt the passion flow through my body from both angles.

After Jasmine realized that I wasn't trying to resist them anymore, she went down on her knees to help Ashley. Ashley had one side of my dick while Jasmine was on the other side. They stroked me up and down in opposite ways, taking turns.

It was hard trying to stop myself from screaming with passion. Just as they almost made me burst, my phone rang. It was Cara. I looked at them. They understood what time it was and sat on the bed in silence as I answered.

"Hey, baby," I said.

"Hey Terrill. I'm still at my aunt's house waiting on you to take me home."

"Oh okay. I'll come get you, ma," I replied, looking at Ashley and Jasmine tongue kiss each other.

After I hung up with Cara they continued sucking my dick. I positioned myself in the chair for both of them to enjoy. It would be the first and last time they would see me. After about five minutes, I felt the pressure rush from my body to my dick. I was about to cum. Jasmine stood back. I yelled with pleasure. I tried to push Ashley back, but she continued sucking until I came in her mouth. She sucked it all up. "Dammit man!

I sat for a second feeling a head rush. Ashley wiped the side of her mouth then smiled at my puzzled expression. I took a deep breath and stood up.

"Y'all are wild. I loved every minute of this West Coast style loving y'all got. But I got to go and take my girl home from her aunt's house." They gave me their number and told me whenever I was around to call them.

I called RonRon and told him to come back to Denny's to pick me up. Ashley and Jasmine stayed with me the whole time. We talked until RonRon pulled up. They waved at RonRon then blew me a kiss and drove off.

"What is that about, 50ty?" RonRon asked when I got into the truck.

"Peer pressure, homey. Peer pressure," I answered. He laughed as he drove out of the parking lot.

"So, are you going to tell me about it or not?" he asked, staring at me while heading back on the road.

"Tell you what, pimp?" I asked innocently.

"Nigga you were with two fine ass hoes and they took you home for some erotic pleasure. So, what happened?"

"Well, I didn't have sex with them if that's what you're trying to ask me," I said.

"You telling me that 50ty was in the house with two bad bitches and didn't fuck? That's hard to believe, cuz."

I looked at him and smiled. "Well I didn't fuck.... but I got my dick sucked damn near off the bone," I told him and we both laughed.

"Nigga, Tera or Cara better not find out nothing about this shit. Boy, all hell would break loose," he mentions.

"Don't nobody know shit but us, pimp. Just be cool," I replied.

I called Cara and told her to have Anthony take her home and I'd meet her at the house.

Jermaine put some steaks and ribs on the grill. Anthony pulled up a minute after we did.

"Hey baby," I said giving her a kiss. She gave me a weird look and she gave RonRon the same look. We both looked at each other. "Why you gave us a look like that?" I asked. She continued walking toward the house. I looked at RonRon and he shrugged.

"I don't know what's wrong with her," he said. "Where's Jermaine?" he asked, following Cara. I just stood outside in front of the house and waited on Cara to come back out to tell me why she looked at us like that.

She came back to the door and just stood there giving me the same look.

"What's wrong with you, ma?" I asked. "Why are you looking at me like that?"

"Terrill, we always meet up at my aunt's house. You're never late and you never told somebody else to bring me home," she replied.

"I know, ma. I just ran into a little problem today and had to lay low for a second until everything died down." I walked up to her and gave her a kiss. "I'm sorry." I knew that females get very sensitive when they're pregnant. They let their emotions get in the way. I know I fucked up, but I would stay by her side until her spirits came back up. " I'm sorry, baby, I won't fall off track no more. Please forgive me," I said, smiling to show her that I loved her. She smiled back and gave me a kiss.

"I'm sorry for snapping, baby. I'll tell RonRon that I'm sorry for blaming him as well," she said.

We went in the house. Jermaine and RonRon both had a plate and were eating.

"I made enough for everybody, bro. You an Cara can eat whenever, "Jermaine said, holding a rib in his hand.

"RonRon, I'm sorry for giving you that evil look," Cara told RonRon. "Baby, I'll fix you a plate," she told me and smiled.

I shook my head at RonRon, letting him know she don't know anything about Jasmine and Ashley. I followed Cara into the kitchen where she was fixing us a plate. Even though I wasn't hungry because I ate earlier at Denny's, I just made it seem as if I was waiting on her to eat with me tonight.

We sat at the kitchen table and ate together. I was starting to believe that a woman's instinct really was a reality check. All the time we'd been together, I'd never saw Cara really mad or acting strange. It was weird that it happened on a night of cheating.

"Baby, so how was your day at your aunt's house?" I asked just to spark up a conversation.

"I'm still upset about the way things are happening to the family. We don't deserve this much drama in our lives," she said.

I understood that clearly. From what I could see, they were not thugs or gang bangers. Anthony was just a young man living his life day-by-day and hanging out with his little cousin, Hakeem. What harm was that? They were not bad guys at all, just innocent people caught up in bad situations.

"It's like we can't turn our backs or let our guard down because we will get cased up in some mess," Cara said.

Cara calmed down when we started sharing funny stories about growing up. We went to bed on a happy note. At least Cara did. I was pretending to be happy because I had so much on my mind that it was crazy.

I woke up the next morning feeling angry and vengeful. I leaned over and gave Cara a kiss and told her that I had some business that I needed to take care of with Tom and a couple more things that I needed to do.

I got up and took a shower. I thought of my next move once I got to San Francisco. While I dried myself off, Cara walked in. Without saying a word, she walked up to me and pushed me down on the toilet. She pulled the towel from around me, exposing my nakedness. She placed my dick in the palm of her hand and started slowly stroking it until I got on hard. She placed it in her warm mouth.

Damnmit man, what is this? Give 50ty head week, I thought.

I leaned back and let her do what she wanted to do to me. I wasn't in the mood, but I wouldn't let her know that. A hard dick can set it off alone. So, I just managed to keep my dick up.

After the main event of me getting my nut and Cara getting her orgasm, we both came out the restroom looking crazy.

"Baby, I'm going to head out now. I'll call you later in the day. If you need me just give me a call," I said, grabbing my jacket and bulletproof vest.

"Okay, Terrill. Be careful," she said, walking to the door behind me and watching me drive off.

Life was like gambling, everybody had to play to win. I made sure that my guns were in my truck and that they were loaded with hallow tips and had extra clips in the glove compartment.

I called Derrick to see what was going on with him.

"What's up, cousin?" he asked.

"I just got Tom on my mind, man. I had damn near every police on my ass last night at this club where a minor fight broke out that I was involved in. I need to find out what the cause for the whole force to be after me, so I need answers."

"You better be careful on whatever is going down," he warned.

"Yeah I will tighten up once I see what is going on with Tom," I said. We talked for a while longer then hung up.

Once I arrived in San Francisco, throughout the whole day, I followed Tom around. I trailed him from his office to his girlfriend's house where he dropped her off some Chinese food. I followed him back to his office. I knew he was going to be there for a while.

I got a hotel room in San Francisco for just a couple of hours.

Cara called. "What's up baby?" I answered.

"Nothing. I'm just letting you know that Jermaine and RonRon are going to St. Pete. Tera said that she will go if I do."

"Well okay, ma. Do you want to go with them? If so, it's cool with me."

"I thought maybe you would want to come down there too, to see your nephews."

"I do, but I have a few things that I need to take care of first. Like I promised Anthony and Keem that I'd take them to a San Diego football game."

"Well, will it be alright if me and Tera went down there with them?"

"Yeah baby go. You need to get out of California for a while anyways because you been stressing lately," I said.

"Okay, Terrill. Be careful because you're alone. I love you."

"I love you too, baby. I'm not alone. I got Anthony and Keem here with me," I reminded her. She laughed then we hung up.

I lay back on the bed, deep in thought. Why would Tom want to bring me down when he didn't really know me? I gave him a lot of information because I trusted him and he turned that against me.

I jumped up in anger, ready to go face him but then I thought about it. It wouldn't be a good time. I sat back down on the bed and decided to call his office. I acted as if I was one of his clients when his sectary answered. I wanted to find out what time he got off.

I had seven hours to wait. I left to grab some food from an island restaurant then went back to the room. After eating the food, I lay down after setting my watch an hour before it was time for Tom to get off.

CHAPTER 18

Opening the door blindly, Tom flicked the light switch in the darkness and the light didn't come on. "Shit, when did the light bulb blow?" he whispered in the dark as he made his way to another switch. He flicked it. Still nothing. "What in the hell is going on? I know I paid the light bill. Why are my lights off?"

He felt the wall as he made his way down the hallway to the kitchen. When he reached the kitchen, he flicked the kitchen light and the lights came on.

"How did two light bulbs blow at the same time?" he wondered aloud.

Turning on the kitchen light brought a little brightness to the living room. When Tom walked into the living room, he looked in the darkness part in the corner and spotted my feet. I guess my body casted a shadow. "What... the... who is this in my house?" I heard the fear in his voice. I stepped out the darkness and into the light, with my hands behind my back. "Terrill, is that you?" he asked, trying to make his way to the front door. I brought both of my hands from around my back exposing my 45 Magnum.

"Sit down Tom. I just want to talk to you for a minute. That's all."

"How did you get into my house and why haven't you called or came by my office?" he asked.

"Okay, I'm here now. Do you have something to tell me?" I asked, sitting down in his love seat.

"Well I thought you and your brother were going to come see me. "

"I decided to come alone instead," I said, interrupting him.

Somebody knocked on the front door. "Can I answer that?" he asked.

"Who is it, your girlfriend Karen?" I asked.

"How do you know her?" he asked.

"All these questions with no answers are a problem," I said. "If you want her involved, by all means let her in," I said, giving him a smirk as I stood by the door.

"No. I don't want her involved," he replied quickly.

She knocked a few more times than she walked around to the back of the house. "She sees my Porsche parked outside. She is not going anywhere because she knows that I'm in here," he said.

"Well let me open the door and let her in. I have things that I have to do and I'm in a hurry."

He gave a strange look which was similar to the look he'd given me the other day at his office.

"You can make peace with her after I find out what I need to know. When we're finished, you can call the cops and I will be long gone."

"No. I'm not going to do that, Terrill. You are a good man and I don't want to see you go down," he said nervously. What he didn't know was that I saw the lie written all over his face. His girlfriend knocked on the door again and called his name. "

"Cool. Let me open the door and let her inside," I replied.

I opened the door and saw a pretty blonde white lady standing there. Black lawyer white girlfriend. It happened every time.

"Are you looking for Tom?" I asked.

"Ah. yes...I'm one of his clients, as well," she lied.

I stepped to the side and told her to come inside.

"Hi Tom. I didn't know that you had company. I just stopped by to see you for a sec about my meetings," she said. I laughed.

"It's okay. You can come by later and we'll talk," he replied, business-like.

The look on Tom face wasn't a happy camper look. "Are you okay, Mr. Tom?" I asked to throw that look off.

The facial expression that I gave Tom made him straighten up. "I'm fine, just had a busy day. that's all. I'm a little tired. The guest lady took the words right out of my mouth.

"Tom, are you going to introduce me to your client?" she asked.

I looked at Tom, smirking. "Yeah, Tom, introduce me to your girlfriend," I said.

"She's my client," he insisted.

"What kind of client Tom, Physical Body Therapy?" I joked.

"I'm going to go. I'll see you later, Tom," she said. She gave him a seductive smile as she showed herself out. I listened as she started her car and drove off.

"Good, our little visitor is gone," I said.

"What do you want from me, Terrill?" he asked, standing up angrily like I screwed up his date.

"What is it, Tom? Isn't my money good enough for you?" I asked.

"I don't understand what you're talking about."

"Tom, I don't want to be all rude and start cursing and slinging shit around. So, I'm going to try to stay calm with this. You set me up after taking half of the hundred grand that I'm paying you and you turned against me."

"How did I set you up, Terrill?" he asked with a confused look.

"That's a question that is already answered in your head. You need to tell me why you set me up. I have a slight clue on why you did it. It will really piss me off if I have to answer any questions that I'm supposed to be asking," I snapped.

"I don't know-"

I clicked my gun back bringing a bullet into the chamber. "Should I answer your question Tom?" I asked in anger.

"Why are you doing this and why are you threatening me?" he asked.

"Honestly, I didn't come over here to kill you. I just wanted answers but I see it's not happening with you the way I thought it would." I stood up and walked toward him. "I only have just enough patience's to ask you one more time. Why did you try to set me up after I paid you to help me?"

I…. didn't set you up. I'm just looking into the case just to see what I'm up against in order to fight for you."

"I probably would have believed you if you told me that earlier and not had the police come looking for me out in L.A. You lead me to believe you were a good lawyer. Come to find out you just are as crooked as me."

"I'm sorry that I didn't let you know earl-."

"I don't give a fuck," I interrupted. "I'm sorry for putting my life in a black man's hands.

"I got your brother and Cousin out of jail, Terrill," he said in a tone as if I'd offended him. I looked him in the eye. "I would have done the same thing if I knew I was going to profit from it. Fuck how we feel about the situation. Let me guess. In the end, everybody goes to jail while you live the lavish life of a millionaire off their cash. Is that it?"

I pulled my black pouch from the inside pocket of my jacket.

"What's that, Terrill? What are you going to do to me?" he asked, panicking.

"Good question. I'm not going to kill you, but I'm going to tie you up."

After I tied him up he kept trying to explain himself. I remained silent.

"I'm going to place this duct tape over your mouth so you won't scream when I leave," I said, placing the tape over his mouth.

I walked into the kitchen and turn the kitchen lights off. All was silent. I could hear Tom trying to get a loose. A minute later he heard liquid splashing on the floor. Tom stopped trying to get loose and looked toward the hallway to see what I was doing. The smell of gas enters the Livingroom.

I splashed gasoline all over the kitchen and hallway, up to the living room. "What's wrong?" I asked as he shook his head for me to stop. "Do you want me to stop splashing gas all over the place?" I turned the whole can over his head. The gas ran down his face and body. "Okay, I'll stop".

I examined his house, taking all of his jewelry. I returned to the living room where he was still tied up at. "Well, I did say that I wasn't going to kill you, but I didn't say that I was going to watch you die." I pulled out a blunt and my lighter. Tom screamed through the duct tape, begging me to stop. I walked to the hallway then stopped and look back at Tom in the darkness. I fired up my blunt. "Tom, if you live, then I die," I said in sorrow. He started yelling even louder through the tape. "And I'm not ready to die." I flicked the joint up in the air. It landed in his lap and the entire living room lit up. I ran out the back door, vanishing in the darkness. I stood and watched has his house burned.

People soon gathered around the front yard while Tom's house was on fire. I felt there would be some Captain-Save-A-Motherfucker so I ran to the front of the house where everyone waited for help to come.

Tom's front door swung open and he ran outside on fire. People rushed him.

Shit, I said to myself. I pulled out my 45 and ran up to him. "Tom, it must not have been your time to die in there. But, the decision has been overruled." I aimed my gun at him. Everybody started screaming and running away. I shot him twice in the head and he dropped on his lawn. I turned around aiming the gun at the screaming crowd then I ran into Tom's burning house. I jumped the flaming area and headed toward the back door. I made it back outside and ran down the alley. I jumped into my Hummer which was parked near a gas station on the outskirts of the neighborhood.

I heard the sirens of fire trucks and ambulances racing through the streets. I quickly changed clothes in my truck and threw the other clothes in the nearest trash can. I eased off.

I saw what they meant when they said get rich or die trying. As a rich man I had gotten myself into a bloody war.

I went back to L.A., grabbed all of my stuff and got on Interstate 415. I didn't look back.

So much was placed on my brain, from my past childhood until now. I decided that nobody but the devil came home with Bosco. Bosco was already dead. I'd done dirt to a person who lost his life to make mine. G-Rod was on top of his game. How did he get caught up like that and why did his girlfriend have to be with him that night?

Tears dropped from my face as I thought about Sasha and G-Rod's daughter. Why did it have to happen like that? I asked myself, hitting my steering wheel as I drove. I pulled over at a rest area in Nevada. I never got out of the truck. I just sat there thinking while trying not to lose focus on reality.

I killed a man for the first time then got addicted and killed many more. I was dangerous and a threat to society. I didn't want anybody around me to get hurt or killed. I felt like I'd let Bosco die. I didn't want that to happen again. I thought about slaying my enemies and killing the Asian man who shot Bosco.

The gas light on my truck flashed, making noise. That brought me back to reality. Looking at the sign I saw a Texaco gas station coming up.

"Damn, how did I drive this far without noticing that I'm running out of gas?"

I pulled into the Texaco gas station to fuel up the Hummer. I spotted a hotel across the street and I headed over to get a room. I decided to stay a couple weeks in Dallas, Texas.

I took a long shower in the hotel room, letting the water run down body. I kept picturing Tom running out of his house on fire. I'd never seen anything like that before. The scream from the neighbor after I shot him was scary. I was lost in thought, itching to pay the Chinese people a visit.

After I finished showering, I counted my cash. I had eight- hundred and ninety grand of blood money. Money was power, and power brought respect. Jealousy, death and misery surrounded me. My mind, body and soul were overtaken.

I couldn't bring anybody down with me.

I'm sorry RonRon and Cara, but this is it the only way.

In order to get peace, is to make peace because you dam show can't earn it.

I started to dialing RonRon's number, but I hang up every time.

Leaving the pack

CHAPTER 19

Two weeks passed in Dallas, Texas. I only left the room to get something to eat. Everybody had been trying to get in touch with me, but I ignored all the phone calls. I felt bad not answering Cara's call, but I felt homicidal. And in a way, I also felt dead. I was really tempted to answer when my brother called just to let him know that I was alright.

I was in one of the biggest states in the United States and I didn't know a soul. One day I went to sit at a nearby park to watch as they played basketball. I needed to get my mind off of everything that was bothering me. I watched an entire game noticing that females standing around the court like they were real cheerleaders.

I was in a daze when I heard the sound of footsteps creeping up on me. Quickly, I turn and aimed my 45 at a kid and an older man.

"Whoa! Man, what's the deal with that?" the older guy asked, holding his hands out in peace.

Everybody on the court stopped playing and watched us. " I. I'm sorry," I said, getting up quickly and running back to the room.

I'm going back to St. Pete now.

Once in the room, I hurriedly packed all my shit, went to the office to turn in the key, then headed for Florida.

I drove from Texas to Louisiana without stopping once. I got really hungry when I arrived in Baton Rouge so I stopped at a M.C.

Donald's. I ordered my food to go then gassed up, got back on I-10. I continued driving until I made it to Tallahassee. I stopped at a convenience store to use the restroom and to get something to drink. Then, I was back on the road heading to Derrick's house in Bainbridge. I wanted to let somebody know that I was alright so they could tell Cara.

When I pulled up to Derrick's house there were two Cadillac's parked in the front yard along with his car and my brother's car. I also spotted the undercover car parked at the end of the street. I kept driving past, glad to be in my Hummer because the undercover couldn't get a good look inside.

I went back to Tallahassee and got a room at the Days Inn. Thinking smart, I called Eric and Rodney telling them to pass a message to Derrick in person. It was for him to come to Tallahassee and meet me at the Days Inn. They told me how the police pulled Derrick over damn near every day question him about me.

If they were bothering Derrick all the way over here and fucking with me in California then I wasn't safe anywhere I went. It was best to stay low-key for a while. However, I had unfinished business that had to be taken care of right away.

After I got out of the shower I turned on the television. I heard the room doorknob shake a little. I grabbed my gun, eased the bullet in the chamber. I peered out the window and saw the back of the person. I couldn't tell how many was out there. They turned the knob again then knocked on the door softly. I unlocked the door then ran into the restroom and turned off the light. They went to turn the doorknob again then knocked and the door opened. In clear view I had a good aim at the door.

Two hands came in the door first then I heard Derrick's voice. "50ty, it's me. What's happening?"

I breathed a sigh of relief. "Cuz, you could have got yourself shot creeping like that," I said coming out the restroom.

"50ty, I'm glad you are alright. Everybody is worried sick about you, especially Cara and Jermaine."

"Derrick I have unfinished business to settle in St. Pete.," I said, rolling up a blunt full of weed.

"I feel you, bro. Eric and Rodney outside," he said.

"Tell them to come in and what have you been up to?" I asked.

"Surviving to the fullest, cousin." He went to the door and told them to come inside. Rodney and Eric walked into the room.

"What's good, 50ty? Cara told us what happened with them in L.A. that's fucked up." Rodney said.

"Popos is on a mad hunt for you, 50ty. They even offered a reward on you. I told them that I hadn't seen or heard from you since you went to Arizona, just to throw them off," Derrick said as he hit the blunt hard. I just laughed.

"How did you know which room I was in, Derrick?" I asked.

"RonRon told me that you have a red and black Hummer. Rodney told me that you were here. I knew you would park your Hummer right in front of your room," he replied.

"Damn, cuz. You really do know me," I said laughing. "Is RonRon them still in St. Pete or back in California?" I asked.

"The last time I talked to Cara, she was at her aunt's house in L.A.," Derrick answered.

I grabbed another blunt and rolled up a fat one.

"So, what's the deal with Tom?" Derrick asked. The look I gave him showed what happened.

"Oh shit, 50ty. You knocked him off?" Rodney asked.

Eric and Rodney had been on missions dealing with Reco. I knew that they were cool.

"I'm at war now. I have unfinished business in St. Pete., then I'm going to finish up where we left off in California. If only I could put my hands-on Los, he would become history," I said flatly.

"If we could knock off the police that are out looking for you, that would be cool," Eric said causing us all to laugh.

"Once all this shit is settled and everything ends right, I will get back on the grind and push the heavy shit again," I said.

"Let's go to St. Pete., 50ty. Rodney and I will trail you and Derrick down there," Eric said.

"Alright. After we finish smoking out, we can do that," I said, passing him the blunt.

We left the hotel and headed for St. Pete on the same night. We arrived in Tampa in three and a half hours. We went to the Hilton on St. Pete Beach, spending four grands on four rooms. We were living the lives of ballers.

After getting settled in the room, we went to the pool. There were a couple of black women there swimming and playing around in the water.

"Hey fellows," one of the women said, smiling at us.

"The water is just fine," another said.

Derrick, Eric, and Rodney accompanied the women, while I sat on the stairs deep in thought.

The next morning, we were all set and ready to move on.

"Cuz, so what is the plan?" Derrick inquired.

"Whatever is necessary to get the job done," I answered, grabbing my keys off the dresser.

We drove to our destination with little conversation between us. My mind was set on what I had to do. Arriving in St. Pete, I pulled up to the back of the Asian store and parked almost in the same place I'd parked the day of Bosco's death. I glanced at the parking space in anger then got out of the Hummer.

Eric and Rodney went to the front of the store while Derrick and I went to the back to make our entrance. Rodney went in the opposite direction as Eric once they entered the store. Eric went to the counter and told the clerk that there were two guys in the back of the building tampering with shit near the trash.

It was 7:15am on my watch. I saw one of the Asian men come around the store while the other one came out the back door, just as I wanted them to. Derrick had his back turned on the one outside. I stood on the other side of the building with my eyes on both of the guys.

"Hey you, you got to leave from behind store now," the Asian guy that killed Bosco instructed.

Without even thinking I approached him from his blind side. He gave me a strange look.

"Do you remember me?" I asked while standing in front of him.

"Yeah, I remember you from that day I shot the kid for robbing my store," he answered calmly.

"He was a man not a kid," I said angrily. "And we're here to finish where he left off."

He went to run back into the store, but Rodney was standing behind him when he turned around. Rodney pushed the man outside, toward me. Derrick pulled his gun on the other guy that was already outside. We forced both of them back inside the store.

"Alright, bitch, get from behind the counter and come here," I yelled to the female clerk. Eric locked the doors.

Rodney tied both men and the lady up, placing them in the middle of the store. I walked up to the man who killed Bosco. "Who is he?" I asked him pointing my gun at the other man.

"He is my nephew," he replied.

"Well, Bosco was like a nephew to me. I felt the same kind of love," I said. He didn't respond. I glared at him. "I know that don't matter to you, because you didn't give a fuck about Bosco." I walked up to his nephew. "I'm going to leave you with the same headache and pain you left me with," I told the man who shot Bosco.

I stared the nephew straight in the eye. I looked back at Bosco's murder. "This is revenge," I said lowly.

I shot the guy twice in the head. When the first bullet hit him, his eyes flipped back. When the second bullet hit him, the Asian man and lady started screaming until Derrick placed a bag over their heads.

"Shut up or I'll shoot the lady," he warned. They both grew quiet.

"Now we're even," I mumbled.

Rodney grabbed all the cash out the register and safe. They must have been ready to make a deposit at a bank because the safe was unlocked. We ran out of the back door and vanished.

Back at the Hilton on St. Pete beach we quickly grabbed our stuff and got ready to leave St. Pete. Derrick and I drove back in the Hummer while Rodney and Eric followed in the S.U.V.

"Cousin, cousin, cousin, what would you do without me, homey?" Derrick inquired. I looked at him.

"What?"

"We would probably all be cased up right now if I hadn't grabbed the tape out of the camera," he said. I forgot all about the damn surveillance cameras in the store.

"Damn, good looking out, Derrick," I replied.

"I'm on top of shit, 50ty. We can't unfold and reveal our plans or plots of getting away from massive destruction, due to the time limit of incoming enforcement that can lead to a journey through hell or longer. We have family and loved ones so we will have to stay open minded," he said with pride.

I gave him a weird look. "Could you say that again?" I asked.

"Ah… that would be a difficult thing to do," he replied and we both burst out laughing.

"Man, you on some other level," I said, still chuckling.

Back in Bainbridge we met up at a park and chilled for a while.

"50ty, we should have eliminated them all, left no witnesses," Eric said.

"I'm sorry Eric. But I felt Bosco's pain so that dude will have to feel mine," I responded.

"Blood for blood is how I see it," Derrick said.

"I'm done on the East Coast. Now, I'm going back to L.A. to finish where I left off there," I told them.

"We're going with you this time, cuz. We going to get at them fools," Derrick said.

"For sure. We're going with you, homey. They shouldn't have put their hands-on Cara like that or Tera," Rodney said.

I just sat in silence not responding. We chilled at the park for a few hours then went to get a room.

When we got to L.A. we checked into separate rooms. I went straight to my room and called RonRon.

"Hello?' Who is this?" he asked suspiciously.

"This me, homey. Don't say any names. Meet me at L.A. Furniture." I said then hung up.

As I opened the door to go out, Derrick was about to knock on it.

"Damn, cuz. Good timing," he joked.

"For real." I said. "I'm heading to L.A. Furniture to meet up with RonRon."

"Rodney and Eric are in the room sleep. I'm bored so I'm going to ride with you," he replied.

"Cool. Let's bounce."

When I pulled up to L.A. Furniture I spotted RonRon in his original Hummer. The dealership had repaired all the bullet holes. He got out of the truck once he saw me.

"50ty, where in the hell have you been? You just up and vanished without a word," he said, giving me and Derrick a one-armed hug.

"I know playa. I called myself trying to stay away from y'all because of all the drama and shit. I don't know what I'd do if something happened to y'all," I said.

"50ty, it's ride or die with me and you homey. You know that. Man, Cara cried all day and night," he said. I didn't say anything, just continued to listen. "We didn't know if you got killed and ditched somewhere or if the police had you."

"I know homey. I just don't want y'all to get involved with the police and charged for hiding my where about," I told him as we walked back into L.A. Furniture.

We just walked around the store and I told him about Tom and the Asian man.

"When they had Tom on the news, we knew it was you because soon after you vanished," RonRon said.

"Man, I'm lost in my mind. I got nothing to lose now, homey."

"50ty, you just need to lay low for a while until the heat dies down," he suggested.

California was known for murders and drug dealers. I could say I would do what the rest of them did, just blend in. Thanks to Los I would have to get another lawyer to help me out.

"So, are you going to see Cara while you're up here?" RonRon asked.

"No doubt, RonRon. I have to face her eventually. I didn't mean to hurt her like that so that's an issue that I will have to handle."

We left L.A. Furniture and went back to the hotel to get Erick and Rodney. We all rode around Los Angeles.

Cara called RonRon's phone and I answered.

"Hey baby. How have you been?" I asked.

"50ty?" Cara asked. I just remained silent. "Terrill, what happened to your part ownership in our relationship?" she inquired. I was still silent listening to her talk. "Baby, I'm not mad just worried about you," she said.

"I'm the one who is mad and confused," I relied.

"Well, are you okay?" she asked.

"Yes, ma, I'm fine. I'm going to send RonRon to get you and bring you to me tonight."

"Okay," she said, excited.

"Well, I have to get off this phone. You never want to talk too long. I'll see you tonight."

"See you. I love you, baby."

"I love you, too." We hung up and I gave RonRon his phone.

"Alright, we need a strategy," I said. "Where these Kats be?" I asked RonRon.

"Anthony showed me where their spot is," RonRon said, "We're on their block now." He glanced to the left. "There go them niggas at the corner store." RonRon gave a wicked laugh.

"So, what do you want to do, 50ty?" Rodney asked.

"Let's go get them niggas now," RonRon said.

I stopped them. "Y'all motherfuckers are just as sick as I am. We are in the heart of these fools. If we get out right here and start blasting at them, we won't have a chance of surviving," I rationalized.

"So, what do you think we should do then, homey? Scout the area and see where we can start bombing on these niggas or just put it up for another day?" RonRon asked.

"Nah, RonRon I have a better idea. We're going to kidnapped them one by one," I explained. "Anthony and I will get to know them a little bit better," I said as we pulled out of the parking lot and headed back to the hotel.

"I like the sound of that," RonRon said and the rest of them nodded in agreement.

I returned to the hotel and took a long shower to refresh my mind, body and soul. I heard a knock at the door while I was in the shower. I hurried to get dressed. I opened the door for Cara. I just stared at her feeling guilty.

"Cara, I'm sorry-" I began. She placed her finger over my mouth.

"Terrill, I love you and I missed you. Just don't do that ever again," she said. I gave her a tight hug, showing her how much I missed her too.

"I'm afraid of getting you and others involved in my mess," I told her. She started to do what she does best…. cry. I gave her another hug.

"Baby, they don't have anything on you. Yes, there's a picture of a guy that looks a little like you but not much. There are so many people in California that looks like you. If they had a police lineup, it would be hard to pick you out the crowd," she rationalized.

I sat on the bed while she stood behind me and gave me her thoughts on the situation.

"So, what are your plans now since the heat is on you?" she asked.

"Sit down, baby," I said, pushing my Coach bag to the floor. "You are here with your family who love you. I don't want anything to happen to you or your family. I love you the same as they do."

"Do you?" she asked. Tears formed in her eyes again.

"Yes, I do baby. I called myself running away from all of this bullshit, thinking it would go away. Now, I know that it will only get worse."

"We wouldn't know what to do without you being around, 50ty. Every day we got together and talked about you, wondering if you were alright. Why do you take on so much by yourself? Jermaine said that you've been like that all your life."

"I just thought I was keeping everybody safe."

"The police are looking for you here baby. That's why I asked you, what your plans are?" she said.

"I know that. I'm going to stay low key for a while. I'm thinking about leaving and moving to New York— Manhattan. We can start over."

"That's a good idea," Cara said. "Let's leave today," she said excitedly.

"We can't. I have some unsettled business here that I need to take care of first."

Cara didn't ask questions, or prompt me to give answers that I didn't want her to know. She just let the subject drop. I loved that about her.

CHAPTER 20

The next morning, Cara and I went to her aunt's house. The two elders were there, sitting on the porch. I got out of the truck wearing a smile on my face. I knew they would start in on me. Cara went inside after speaking to them and I sat on the steps.

"Damn son, you came and turned L.A. out," one of the elder's said.

"I don't know what you talking about," I joked.

"Shit boy you are all over the news," the other elder said. "We told you to be careful of L.A. Shit, L.A. need to be careful of your ass." We all laughed.

Hakeem pulled up on his bike. "Hey 50ty, where have you been hiding, homey? Cara is going crazy," he said getting off of his bike and sitting on the steps beside me. I laughed at him because he thought everything was alright no matter what happened.

"Hakeem, let's ride around," I said. I got up, went into the house and spoke to Mrs. Laura, and told Cara that I would be back. She walked up to me and I put my hand over her mouth to stop her from say anything. "I promise you that I will be back. Keem and I am just going to ride around for a few minutes. That's all," I said, giving her a kiss.

I knew that I was taking a chance by riding around when the law was looking for me, but there was a 50/50 chance of getting caught when they had million motherfuckers out there just as worse as me.

"Where is Anthony?" I asked as we cruised the block.

"I haven't seen him today or yesterday," he answered.

"What the fuck, is he okay or what?"

"He's okay. He just ups and leaves like that sometimes when his girlfriend is in town."

"I see," I responded, turning on Sweetman homey's block. Niggas were up at the corner store deep, just hanging around and selling drugs.

"Is that their corner store and are all of them up there every night?" I asked Hakeem.

"Yeah, every night," he said as we rolled past. That's all I needed to know. I took Keem back to his aunt's house.

Back at the room I talked to Rodney and Eric.

"It's going to go down tonight," I said. I told them how we were going to surprise them and hit them all up at the same time.

"What about the kidnapping plan?" Rodney asked.

"Nah, this is better. It'll be quicker and this shit will be over."

"Alright. We're ready, 50ty," Eric said. "More than ready. Them niggas done fucked with the wrong ones."

Later we were at RonRon's house when I told him the plan. "We're going to get the mother fuckers tonight RonRon. Are you in?" I asked, speaking low so that Cara and Tera couldn't hear me.

"What you think, pimp? I'm going all out, homey," he said passionately.

RonRon was beating my ass in Madden until I gave up in the third quarter.

"So, what's up?" I asked before he went all crazy because he won.

"With tonight?" he asked, turning the game off.

"Yeah, tonight."

"50ty, I brought two more Teflon vests off the street for cheap," he replied.

"That's cool because it's time for these niggas to understand the power of war," I said.

"Nigga you finally woke up and smelled the blood on these cowards. Let's go get those fools now," RonRon said.

I chuckled at his enthusiasm. RonRon was always ready to do battle. "We'll get them tonight at midnight. Tell Tera whatever you need to tell her and be ready," I said.

When Cara dropped me off at the hotel I told her to get all her stuff together and to search the Internet for apartments in Manhattan. She said she would and gave me a kiss.

Back in the room I took a nap but was awakened by Derrick and Eric.

"What's going on?" Derrick asked, entering the room.

"Shit just woke up. Where's Rodney?" I asked.

"He's in the room sleep," Derrick responded.

"We just checking on the status for tonight," Eric said.

About thirty minutes before it was time to put our plan into action, RonRon arrived. He had a big green Army bag.

"What's in the bag, homey?" I asked.

He opened it and dumped out guns and bullet proof vests. I laughed. "You act like we going to Iraq or somewhere," I joked.

I called Derrick and told them to come to the room to go over everything one last time. We agreed that Eric would be the driver because he races cars in Bainbridge. Rodney, RonRon, Derrick and I put on the Teflon vests.

"Y'all ready?" I asked, looking at each of them. They all nodded. "Let's do this."

RonRon got hold of a Delta 88 Oldsmobile to drive. It would work perfectly. They wouldn't recognize the car. Two blocks from the corner store we got out and walked up the sidewalk. They were chilling at the store unaware of the tragedy that was about to happen.

I spotted Eric across the street in front of the store as if his car had broken down.

We walked in pairs up to the store. Derrick and RonRon were behind me and Rodney. As we walked on their block I looked back at RonRon and Derrick.

"Make every shot count."

Their guards were still down. When we walked up on them I quickly examined everything. Everybody was in perfect view. One of them was on the side of the store selling to a crack head. RonRon walked toward him.

After taking a deep breath I pulled out my 30/30 and yelled. "Alright, motherfuckers, you know what time it is!"

RonRon pulled out his Mac 11 and aimed it at the dude in the cut. While we were trying to get them all in the open to burn their asses, one of them boldly came out the store and started shooting.

With one single shot Rodney took the dude out. One of the dudes tried running across the street. Derrick was shooting at him but missing. The dude ran past Eric. Eric jumped out and shot him five times in the back. After a couple seconds of silence, we started shooting up the entire place, bringing them all down.

Rodney quickly ran inside the store and shot the clerk twice, leaving him for dead. We heard the sirens sounding in the distance. Eric jumped into the Delta 88 and mashed over the curb, stopping in front of us. We all jumped in and hauled ass.

"Make a right, right here." RonRon said as we rolled into another area. We pulled up to a small park. "Let me handle this shit really quick." RonRon jumped out the car. He ran up on two niggas that were smoking and chilling on a bench. I guess they thought RonRon was going to rob them, because they threw their hands up, giving him a perfect aim. He shot one in the throat then he quickly pulled out his knife and stabbed the other in the balls. That brought him down to his knees. RonRon then sliced his throat, dropping him instantly. He shot both of them again just to finish them off and jumped back into the car. We peeled off.

RonRon had us pull around another corner and told us to get out because he had his Hummer parked in the cut. We switched rides quickly then headed to the hotel room. As soon as we got to the room I turned on the news. We all watched in silence as the announcer spoke.

"Breaking news. About an hour ago eight young men were gunned down along with a store clerk at a neighborhood convenience store. In another area of the city, two more black males were found dead at a small park. The police don't know if the murders are connected, but they are investigating the matter. If you have any information on the tragedies that occurred tonight, please contact the Los Angeles Police Department."

"So, was that all of them or what?" Derrick asked.

I grabbed a blunt off the dresser and a sack of weed from RonRon. "We'll know sooner or later," I answered. "True," RonRon said, with a cocky smirk on his face. Everybody else wore a similar look. None of us had any fear in our hearts. We were ready to square off with anybody, even the police.

The day I was to leave for New York, I called RonRon and told him to swing by to get Jermaine and Tera and come to the hotel. I had everybody meeting me, even Anthony and Hakeem.

"Damn 50ty you got everybody here today. What is this about cousin?" Derrick asked.

I gave everybody a blunt to fire up except Cara.

"I have a couple of things I want to discuss with y'all," I said, getting their attention. "We all have been through some rough moments since we hooked up. I just want to say thank you guys for everything--for being there for me and Cara through all the bullshit. Even though we got rid of those niggas, we can't drop our guard. We are still at war. There are still things out there that will bring us down because we have money and are on top of the game. I'm not going to be around to ride and die for y'all because of the situation that I'm in. You guys already know the deal on that," I said. "It's time now to stay focused and realize this is real life. Those streets aren't a joke. "

"50ty, what are you saying man?" Derrick asked, hitting his blunt hard.

"We're getting back on the right track. We need to get our minds out of the gutter and put them back on luxury," I explained in the fogged room. "Cara and I are moving to New York," I said.

"Whoa, so you're relocating again?" Jermaine asked.

"Yeah, just to stay low key until we can change up plans," I responded. "But that's the outside information. Now, I'm going to reveal the inside information that I kept to myself. Cara and I are getting married tomorrow and you guys are invited. Well, y'all already know that." Cara placed her hands over her mouth, just as surprised as everyone else.

"For real?" Tera screamed, giving Cara a hug.

"Where will the wedding take place, in court or in a church?" Jermaine asked.

"I'm good friends with a preacher that I met up here. He prayed for me and you guys. He said whenever I wanted to get married he would do it for me."

"How did he know about me?" Cara asked.

"You are my lady. I told him how I truly felt about you," I replied. She gave me a kiss.

"What time are you getting married tomorrow?" Rodney asked.

"One o'clock. From there, we will make our journey to New York," I answered.

We sat around the hotel room talking and playing video games. Later, Tara ordered pizza and we all ate as we watched Def. Comedy Jam. Once everyone left my room I tried to go to sleep, but I was too excited.

I turned on the T.V. and kept tossing and turning. The wedding was the only thing on my mind. I knew my mom was happy that I'd taken the steps to marry Cara. But, I couldn't forgive myself for the man I had become.

I'm sorry, Mama. Please forgive me.

If I hadn't done the things I did, I wondered if I'd have money and live an average life. How would it have been? Would motherfuckers still respect me or would they try to run over me? Would Cara have paid any attention to me because she was used to drug dealers?

I didn't have the answers to the numerous questions running around in my head. I'd never have the answers so I decided to live for the day. Soon, I'd be a married man, and that was all that was important to me at the moment.

CHAPTER 21

The hotel's phone rang, scaring the hell out of me.

Damn, when did I fall asleep?

"Hello?" I answered.

"50ty, I'm on my way over there with the tuxedos, pimp. Jermaine is with me," RonRon said.

"Cool. I'm getting up now," I responded.

I got up and hopped into the shower needing to refresh my mind, body, and soul. It was 7:30 am. I felt nervous for the first time in a long time. Getting out of the shower I put on boxers and a tee-shirt until they arrived with my suit,

After getting myself together I paced around the room, waiting for RonRon and Jermaine arrived. I turned on the T.V. and the news caught my attention.

"Multiple murders are happening in the Los Angeles area. Two more young black men were gunned down early this morning. The murders began earlier this week when eight people were shot and killed at a convenience store along with the clerk. Two others were shot at a park nearby. The police caught two of the gunmen and have the two suspects at LA.'s precinct. "

"Damn. I wonder who the two guys are that they have in jail," I said aloud. I turned the television off.

My cell phone rang soon after I'd turned off the T.V.

"Hey, baby." I answered seeing that it was Cara.

"Baby, I'm glad to hear your voice. That's all I wanted. I love you," she said.

"I love you too, ma." I told her.

RonRon and Jermaine arrived with the tuxedos. We smoked and reminisced for a while before we got dressed.

"Today is your day big bro. You ready to do this?" Jermaine asked.

"If you going to change ya mind, you better do it right now," RonRon said. 'Go 'head and run. I'll hold the door open for you," he joked and they laughed.

"Man, y'all clowning'. No way in hell I'm going to change my mind." I shook my head. I wasn't all dressed up for nothing. Hell, I was going to marry the woman I loved, who was pregnant with my child. "Now, let's go grab something to grub on. That's where I'm running; toward some damn food."

At the restaurant, we got a lot of attention wearing our all white tuxedoes. Everyone kept staring at us like we were famous. The waitress that took our order even assumed we were rappers. She nervously took our orders.

"No. We're all dressed up and excited because my brother is getting married today," Jermaine said.

"Well congratulations," she said, shaking my hand.

Finally, it was time. We rushed to the church and they escorted us to a back room to meet with our female partners. We would be walking side by side into the church chapel. I was starting to feel a nervous fluttering in the pit of my stomach.

I could already hear the music playing as we approached the double doors of the church. I saw Derrick and a lady walk in together behind the flower girl. The church was packed with people.

I took a deep breath to relieve my nerves. Jermaine and another lady walked in behind me. I kept picturing my mother staring down from heaven at me, smiling. I spotted Aunt Laura on the front row. She was already crying. The two elders were in the second row. They were dressed to kill, which was amazing to see.

Everybody started taking pictures from both sides of the church. They were standing up when Hakeem entered. Then Anthony followed with his female partner. Facing the preacher while the music played, Cara and RonRon finally made it to the walkway up to the pulpit. I turned in looked into Cara's eyes.

"I got you now, motherfucker," she said. She laughed along with everybody else in the church. I started to panic then shook my head. It was only an instant thought that appeared in my head. I laughed to myself.

Man, I shouldn't have had those two Hennessy shots back at the restaurant, I thought.

We pledged our vows and became husband and wife. It was one of the happiest days of my life. I think I even shed a tear.

When we walked out of the church another Hummer was parked by mine. It had a ribbon on it.

"What is this for?" I asked looking back at everyone.

"That's for you and Cara. Derrick and I went half on it," RonRon said.

The Hummer was one of the newer models; a little smaller but better looking than the one I own. It had cocaine white rims.

We didn't need two Hummers in New York because my wife and I could share one. I looked at my brother, smiled, and tossed him the keys to the first Hummer.

"You can keep my truck, bro. Me and my wife will only need one ride and I'm loving the one y'all got me," I said. My brother grinned from ear to ear. I walked up to RonRon. "So, you just had to buy something, huh?" I asked.

"Yeah, pimp. Shit, you are on your way to the Big Apple. You have to go in style. So, get in where you fit in and go all out in fashion, playa," he responded.

"I'm going to miss L.A. for real, but know that I will be back to visit," I told everybody.

My plans were to go back to Georgia first and break bread with Rodney and Eric, then head to New York from there. Cara already had a couple of prospective houses lined up with Oriel's help.

Jermaine and I rode around in my new Hummer.

"Thank you for the truck and crib," he said. "I'm going to maintain up here because my job is great. We have a court date soon. When that's all over with I will be straight."

"That's right. I won't be making it to the court date because of my situation, but let me know how that shit turns out though," I said.

After dropping Jermaine off at his truck which was still at the church I went to spend the rest of my time with RonRon and Tera.

"50ty, you know if you need me holla. I will be on the next flight," RonRon said as we sat on the steps.

"I already know that, homey. I'm going to stay low key up there and chill and see if I can find a good lawyer," I replied.

"When you guys get settled in, Tera and I will visit. I'd never been to California and now I'm here. I haven't been to New York and can't wait to visit there," he said.

"For real y'all better hurry and visit because you know Cara and Tera can't be separated for long," I said.

We got on the 405 heading toward Arizona. Cara had fallen asleep. We made our way through California in no time. I was wide awake in deep thought as we drove through the states. We stopped in Dallas, Texas twelve hours later to get a room.

"Baby, I know that you're tired so go to sleep, but I'm going to the pool," Cara said.

"Okay ma. Be careful," I told her. She wasn't tired because she'd slept the entire time we'd been driving.

We got on the road early the next morning, determined to make it to Bainbridge at a decent time. When drove straight through, only stopping to gas up and take bathroom breaks. Of course, Cara slept the entire way. When we finally got there, we pulled up on Derrick's block. The police had the street roped off.

It wasn't long before Derrick called Cara and asked to speak to me.

"50ty, the red Range rover that's on fire, is one of Carlos's homeboy's ride. I remember the rims on it," he said.

"Why is it on your block?" I asked.

"His baby mama lives right across the street from me. I've seen him over there a few times," he responded. I notice a lady crying as she talked to one of the police officers. I guessed that was his baby mama.

Derrick got out of the rental and walked over to us. I gave him a one-armed hug through the window and Cara got out and gave him a hug.

After leaving Derrick's place, we went to Tiffany's house so Cara could spend some time with her before she left for New York. I got out of the Hummer.

"I'm going to go handle a few things with Rodney and Eric," I told Cara. "I'll call you later and let you know what hotel I will be at."

We took a small trip to Quincy on the other side of Tallahassee. We met up with some dudes that Rodney and Eric knew who wanted to

245

conduct business with us. We went to an all-white trailer home. Two dudes sat out front glaring at us as we pulled up into the drive way.

"Y'all niggas stop staring hard at us like we are some jack boys or the police," Eric joked as he got out.

"Oh E. You better identify yourself. This is real life, playa," one of them said as he flashed the handle of his gun.

"Them niggas there are as soft as cotton," Rodney told me as we sat in the car watching the exchange.

I laughed and just sat back and chilled until Eric signaled for us to come inside.

Inside the trap, I was immediately ready to leave. All types of people were inside doing some of every drug. There were big time hustlers, hand-to-hand hustlers, and even crack heads inside the trap. I felt really uncomfortable.

"I got whatever ya boys need, E." A dude, sitting at the kitchen table, said. It would only be a matter of time before the nigga got his shit kicked in because he had his spot wide open.

"Let us get two keys," I said. I wanted to make it a quick transaction, be in and out.

People in the house stopped what they were doing and started looking at us like we had money. I was strapped with my .45, but making it out alive probably wouldn't happen. I was ready for whatever, though.

I wore a white G-Unit jean set because it was cold, along with G-Unit shoes. I also wore the Teflon vest that saved my life in L.A. I hoped Rodney was right and the dudes didn't want to start anything because I was really not in the mood for bullshit.

"Two keys are going to cost you twenty-five grand, buddy," another person said.

Eric and Rodney looked at me waiting for a response.

"Shit, that's pricey as hell, man. But I don't know anybody else around that I could get it from," I said.

"Shit, we know other places, 50ty. Don't get it, homey, because that's too much," Eric said.

"How much you guys getting for Rodney?" The dude asked.

"Ten a key," I responded

"That's five grands off, Poppy. We'll move on. I just tried to put some cash in your pocket that's all. But that's too steep for us," Eric said.

Even though the twenty grands weren't too much of a problem because we were going to get that back and more, it was the principle. Eric was right. Why lose in a successful business that we were going to gain in? Fuck that.

As we were about to leave the dude stopped us.

"I'll give it to you for twenty-two grand. Take it or leave it."

"I just want the two keys," I replied.

"Just give me twenty grand this time, but I can't do it like that every time. Shit. I want to know who y'all be getting 1 key for 10 grands from. I'll make them rich." the dude said.

That's all I wanted to hear. We exchanged numbers, but I still felt uncomfortable. It would be my first and last time dealing with him.

"Cool," I responded. I waited for somebody to show me something.

"Where's the money?" Poppi asked.

"We're straight with the money, Poppi. You already know that," Eric said.

"I don't know you guys and you guys don't know me. Why would I want to pull out twenty thousand dollars in front of y'all niggas?" I asked with a straight face.

"Hell, yeah Poppi, this man doesn't know nobody in here. At least go into another room or we all can just leave you two to discuss business," the other guy said. I heard them mumbling. I just stared at them and waited for the first move to be negative.

Poppi kept his eyes on me. I was dead serious about mine. I kept my eyes locked on him just to see if he was too.

"Shall we cancel or continue?" I asked.

"Continue, no doubt. I need that cash," Poppi responded.

He made all of his people leave the kitchen. I told Rodney and Eric to go to the car and wait for me. Once everyone was gone, Poppi pulled the carpet back from the kitchen floor. He had a secret compartment in the floor. After he got his safe and opened it, he gave me a look. A homicide would go down if needed. He was ready because I spotted the A.K. on the other side of the safe.

I just acted as if I hadn't seen the gun and waited until he pulled out the cocaine. I tested it to see if it was real.

"Oh, this is the real deal nigga. You can see that. Why would I have a shit load of fake shit?" he joked.

"Cool. Could you just weigh it so we can go because I have other shit I have to attend to?" I asked.

"Aiight," he said, pulling out his triple bean from the kitchen cabinet. He weighed everything to the head. I pulled out my pouch which was under my G-Unit shirt.

I counted twenty grands in front of him to show him that I was straight. I gave him an extra grand to let him know I wasn't trying to knock his hustle if he pushed others for thirty grands.

"Sorry about the misunderstanding, homey. But you know how the game goes," he said. I agreed with him and gave him a dap, then walked outside the trailer to the car.

I felt as relieved as a person that just got out of jail. After we pulled out of the neighborhood I knew everything was alright.

"Damn that dude Poppi was a paranoid motherfucker. He kept his eye on me the whole time. I thought he was going to flip out and charge at me," I joked.

"Them niggas is soft 50ty. Ask Derrick. He'll tell you about them fools," Eric said.

We made it back to their house in no time and they were glad to be home.

RonRon called as I was getting ready to go inside.

"What's going on, RonRon?" I asked. I remained outside to talk to him.

"Man 50ty, Anthony told me that a blue car was following him around today. He said that he didn't know who it was so he didn't go home. Jermaine went to where he is," he told me.

"Y'all better be careful up there RonRon. Try to stay away from the drama. Let it die," I said.

"That's real. But I'm not going to let anything happen to them niggas, feel me?" he responded.

"Yeah, just keep your eyes open and stay focused. Watch out for them and keep them out of trouble. I'll call you when I get to New York."

I walked into the kitchen where Eric and Rodney sat at the table waiting on me to get off the phone with RonRon.

"Y'all ready to bake these pies to serve around the area?" I asked.

We cooked up the two keys within two hours. I split it between Rodney and Eric, twenty-eight grand a peace. They would be straight with that for a while.

"I'm going to head up to the Big Apple tomorrow morning and get myself together," I said, getting into the car with Rodney. I gave Eric a one-armed hug.

"Man, be careful and watch out for Rodney."

After Rodney dropped me off at the room I called Cara and told her which hotel I was located at. With Five hundred and fifty-seven grand I felt middle class, but I had a plan. When I got to New York I would invest in a studio since that was a known place for hip-hop and R&B. Maybe I would run into RonRon's uncle, Blitty. I know RonRon told him that I was on my way there. I hadn't seen Blitty in a long time. It had been at least five years since he'd visited his mom, RonRon's grandmother, in St. Pete.

He is wheelchair bound because he'd been shot seven times in Philadelphia. The person that shot Blitty got knocked off the very next day, and no one would talk. There were several more killed and some were missing and never found. They tried to pen it on Blitty, but he'd been hospitalized when it happened.

Blitty raised RonRon after RonRon's mom passed away. When he got shot, RonRon had to leave Philly and live with his grandmother in St. Petersburg. I definitely planned to look Blitty up when I arrived in New York.

CHAPTER 22

The next day I told Cara my plans. I wanted to stay in Bainbridge for a week to see if Rodney and Eric sales increased. Cara wasn't ready to go either because she still hadn't found enough houses in New York. Plus, she wanted to spend more time with her friends.

Derrick helped by putting them onto some of his connections. Rodney made his first sale in Chattochee, Florida. He sold two cookies which was eighteen hundred dollars up front.

A couple days passed. It was a day before we were going to leave. Eric and Rodney gave me thirty grands. Derrick gave me two hundred grands to add to the stack.

I just stayed at the room, sleeping, the whole day while Cara was at her friend's house. Derrick, Rodney and Eric showed up at the room around nine o'clock pm to say goodbye. We blazed up the hotel room while Cara went to pick up dinner.

They chilled for a while until Cara returned with the food. After they left, Cara and I ate, showered, and went to sleep.

We left Georgia at one o'clock in the morning and headed toward South Carolina. For six hours I drove. I couldn't really enjoy the sight because it was dark and I had to focus on the road.

Cara slept the whole time, from the minute she left the hotel and got in the Hummer. The temperature started to drop as we made our way through South Carolina. Cara woke up around 10 am.

"Damn, it's cold up here," she said.

I pulled into the next gas station and fueled up while Cara went to use the bathroom. I grabbed my jacket out of the back of the truck and gave it to her when she returned. We got some snacks then got back on the highway.

It started to snow as we made our way out of North Carolina. That was my first-time seeing snow. I pulled over at a rest area at 5pm.

I got out of the truck and looked up in the sky as the snowflakes dropped on my face. It wasn't heavy enough to grab so I just enjoyed watching it fall.

When we arrived in New York City it was snowing heavily. We got a room for a week in order to give us time to look at available houses. Cara had set up appointments to see some of the houses the following morning.

Before we settled down in the room, we decided to ride through Brooklyn and Harlem just to see the amazing traffic. Cara called her aunt and I called Jermaine and RonRon.

The streets were mad sick. I'd have to adapt to the lifestyle. Cara would never drive in New York; it was too rough for her.

We went to a place in China Town to eat. I really didn't do Chinese food but Cara loves it. I just watched as she ate everything on her plate. After we finished, we went back to the room.

I wasn't tired, so while Cara slept, I explored the city some more. Just looking at the view from the hotel was amazing. We were across the street from Central Park. I walked to Central Park and sat on a bench and enjoyed the Manhattan night. I could see what they meant when they said it was the city that never slept. Mad people were everywhere. They screamed and yelled the whole night.

It started to snow again. The first drop landed right on top of my head. I thought someone threw something at me from behind. I hurried inside the hotel once it started snowing heavily.

Cara was awake when I entered the room.

"Hey baby, I thought you were still sleep," I said, walking into the restroom to take a hot shower.

"Wow. It's still snowing outside," she said, looking out the window.

"Hell, yeah ma. It's colder than a motherfucker. When I walked outside the frost rushed my balls instantly," I responded. We both laughed.

Three days passed, but we couldn't look at any houses because we were trapped inside because of the snow. I'd never seen anything like it before, only on T.V. Other people were stranded as well. Cara and I seemed to be the only paranoid ones. Everybody else seemed calm and relaxed. The snow outside was four to five inches high off the ground. The snowmobiles were the only thing on the street moving. There wasn't a soul on the streets.

On the fourth day, the storm passed over New York. Even though it was still freezing outside we had appointments about some houses in Queens. We decided to catch a cab because of the snow. While we waited for the cab to arrive, we had a playful snow fight. Some others from the hotel even joined in.

Laughing and out of breath, we hopped into the cab when it got there. Riding through neighborhoods of Queens was disappointing.

"Baby, this neighborhood looks scary. We can't stay here," Cara said.

The cab pulled up to the address that we'd written down.

"Hell motherfucking no. We don't want it," I said aloud. The place was ghetto as hell. Trash bags were everywhere. It was most definitely out of the question.

"Hi are you Cara?" A man asked as he walked up behind us. We turned around to face him then looked at each other.

"I'm sorry. No, I'm not Cara," she lied. We hurried to get back into the cab and left the area.

"That guy looked as ghetto as his house," I said laughing.

We went to Harlem to check out another house. It was similar to the place in Queens. An all grey Jaguar pulled up as we were pulling out. The person flashed their lights as a signal for us to stop. I rolled down my window. A young white dude, looked like he was in his late twenties to early thirties, got out of the car.

"Hi Cara. I talked to you yesterday. I'm glad that you made it. Let me show you the inside," he said.

"I'm sorry to have wasted your time," Cara said. "But we are not interested in getting this house because it's too ghetto for us."

"I understand. You do realize that you're in New York, the city of fast living tall buildings and so on? This is pretty much what we have to offer. What are you trying to get?" he asked.

"We want a single house that is not connected to another one. We don't want to feel closed in and we will need our privacy," I explained.

"Well, I have houses all over New York, from the ghetto to the suburbs. What's your budget for a house?" he inquired.

"We can afford something nice. We want it away from shady motherfuckers. We don't want to have to watch our backs all the time," I replied.

He gave me a list of all the address that should be suitable for us. I thanked him and we got back into the cab. We headed for Long Island to check out the finer houses that New York had to offer us.

The cab driver pulled up to an all-white two-story house with a circular driveway.

"Wow, this house is beautiful. I like it," Cara said.

We checked out some of the others on the list, but Cara wanted the one in Long Island. She called the guy to meet us there. By the time we made it back to Long Island the guy was already waiting.

The man wanted eight hundred grands for the crib. I would have given it to him up front if I'd still had Derrick and RonRon hustling for me. Since I didn't, I decided to make payments until my funds increased. Instead of a month to month payment plan, I gave him a hundred grand to stay out of our hair for a while.

I drove to Brooklyn by myself. I had both of my guns and wore my bulletproof vest. I had my music blasting as I rode through the city. While cruising up an avenue, I spotted a vacant building with a for rent sign on it. I called the owner as I parked in front of the building. We agreed the he would meet me there in a few minutes.

An all red Caddy pulled up behind me and parked. A couple got out of the car.

"Hi. My name is Danny and this is my wife Clara," the man said.

"That's almost the same name as my wife. Her name is Cara," I replied, shaking their hands.

"So, you are interested in renting this building?" Danny asked.

I smiled. "I'll buy it if you're willing to sell it," I said.

All of a sudden, we heard three gunshots. I jumped to the side while Danny and his wife ducked down.

"Welcome to Brooklyn, son," he said, helping his wife up from the sidewalk.

"Well, you still haven't missed a sale. I want the building and the lot. A couple gun shots won't stop me from doing what I got to do. I need to get this building for major business," I told him.

We went inside to conduct business. I gave him fifty grand and told him I would give him fifty more in a month. That would square off the deal between us. I placed flyers over the windows leaving Cara's number on them and I placed a car magnet on my Hummer in case any rappers needed studio time.

I went to a music store and spent over another thirty grands on equipment. I purchased everything from a microphone, to tweeters, a computer, keyboard and other stuff to master the Cds. The building was already made for a studio with the foam and extra space to put the equipment.

Before I placed the stuff in the building, I got cage security. Without a key to the cage it would be impossible to break into the studio. I also placed video cameras inside and out.

After I finally got everything running perfect and ready to go, it was late. I had only talked to Cara twice because I was so busy. I picked her up from the crib and I brought her back to the studio.

Within a week people started coming to the studio looking for prices on beats. I'd been in the process of making beats since I got the equipment. I gave a free month trail to everyone that was interested in making music at my studio.

One Friday it was late. Cara was asleep on the couch and I had a group in the booth making their last song for the night. They were good as hell. I gave them their props.

As we were locking up the studio for the night two people pulled up on bikes. Cara freaked out. I looked at both of them with no fear and flashed the handle of my forty-five, showing them a sign.

"We're not trying to handle you kid. We're trying to see what's popping with the studio time B," one of them said.

"Not tonight. It's late and I'm trying to get my wife home. Come by tomorrow. I'll be here from ten in the morning to twelve at night," I said, walking to my Hummer.

"That's cool. Can you check out our CD and tell us what you think about it tomorrow?" the other one asked handing me the CD.

"Cool." I replied as they rode off.

I put the CD in the visor of my Hummer and drove home.

Eleven o'clock the next morning I got dressed and headed out to the studio. The two dudes that were there last night were in the parking lot when I pulled up. It reminded me that I had their CD but hadn't listened to it yet. They met me at the door of the studio.

"Did you hear the CD?" one asked

"I'm not going to lie to y'all. No, I didn't hear it yet, but I will let you guys freestyle over some beats that I made," I said. I let them inside after I turned everything on.

They freestyle over six instrumentals. I recorded them and kept their songs on file.

"You boys are nice. What do you call yourselves?" I asked.

"D.H.C. Meaning Da Hustling Crew."

"I'm feeling that," I said.

We sat talking in the studio for a couple of hours. I asked them why that they didn't have a producer or manager because they were very good at what they do. They were both twenty-five years old. Since they were basically on their own I believed that they were going to be my first artists. I told them to make a hot album then we would move it from there.

I closed up for they day because I promised my wife that I would be home early. We just spent four hours in the building.

Cara and I spent the rest of the evening in Long Island at a restaurant. Then we sat at a park until the sun went down. I told her about D.H.C. and how they were without a manager. I wanted to work with them as my main artists.

I couldn't say I was not trying to get my life together because of the situation that I was in. But I could say I actually had a job. I was putting in well over twelve hours a day in the studio.

The police were all over looking for me. I hoped they didn't catch up with me in New York. Even though I had been ignoring the situation, it was still active. I just stayed low and lived my life.

257

I spent over a month working with D.H.C. in the booth until they did a twenty-one-track album. I paid out of my own pocket to get their album copy righted under my production company which I name Misery-n-Pain Records.

We had upcoming shows that I paid for to start their journey of success. D.H.C. had shown from Brooklyn to Queens. They'd never been on stage before so that would be a big step for them to perform in front of a live audience.

I took them to Central Park in the Hummer so they could practice on their performance. I explained to them that they didn't need to pay the crowd any attention because they were up-and-coming rappers that were doing their thing and the crowd was their fans.

The first show was in the Bronx. RonRon and Tera flew in to accompany us to the club. They were to open up for a famous rap artist called Physical Madness. The little club was packed. Me, RonRon and Tera sat in V.I.P. We looked down at D.H.C. doing their thing live. They had the crowd's attention. Some already knew them as rappers. After they were done with their show Physical Madness came on stage.

Me and RonRon went backstage where D.H.C. were at.

"Yo y'all niggas killed that shit," I said, giving both of them a one-armed hug.

"Thanks, 50ty. It was fun," they replied.

I introduced them to RonRon and we went back to V.I.P. so they could see Physical Madness do his thing and take notes.

After Physical Madness was done, he came to V.I.P. with a few hoes with him. People from every angle were trying to get his attention. He was ignoring them. I was glad that Cara stayed home because the bodyguards started pushing people to the side. It became a problem when they pushed Tera. I jumped up without a thought and went to the bodyguard that pushed Tera. RonRon had gone to the rest room

"Yo nigga, what the fuck you think about pushing my people like a man?" I asked.

RonRon came back up the stairs and saw that I was going through it with the bodyguard. He stood beside me.

"Y'all niggas better step the fuck back and act right," the bodyguard said, mean mugging RonRon.

D.H.C. wanted to speak to Physical Madness but he was acting shady.

"I see y'all dudes think y'all the shit but I think D.H.C. is better than you. They just love you because you are known playa. I believe you already know what time it is. Try to ignore them, but they're still coming," I told Physical Madness while he stood behind his bodyguards.

"Whatever nigga. I'm there already. They won't never get there because they whack," Physical insulted. His bodyguard laughed while sipping on a drink.

"I bet y'all pussies too," RonRon said. Then we started laughing.

I turned around to go back to our table. RonRon reached over and knocked the bodyguard's drink out of his hand. The dude went to swing on RonRon, but Mike from D.H.C hit him in the head with his glass, knocking the dude to the ground. RonRon swung on another dude that was with them. I grabbed the dude when he went to react and slung him toward the stairs, almost throwing him over the rail.

Everybody started fighting in V.I.P. Tera stood in a corner out of the way.

The dude that Mike hit with the glass was getting up. I ran up and kicked him in the head with my Lugs knocking him back out. I grabbed RonRon and D.H.C. We snuck down the stairs and vanished out of the back door before the police arrived.

Back at the studio, I saw that I had blood on my shoes and RonRon's right hand was swollen. Tera wrapped it with a bandage that I had in the medicine cabinet. D.H.C. talked about what

259

happened and how soft Physical Madness was because when everybody started fighting he stayed out of the way.

RonRon and I just listened. Little did they know we'd been through some worse type of shit. But I wasn't trying to bring that to New York. This was the start of my new life. I had to keep the drama on the low.

I turned on the music and played a beat that I had just made. D.H.C. and RonRon went into the booth. RonRon always used to free style in St. Pete. I knew he was straight, but didn't know he wanted to make this a project. I put a rider beat on that was gangsta. RonRon took the first verse.

Oh no, Physical Madness Caught One in the Throat.

Lucky It was My Fist and Not My Knife That Made You Choke.

Blood for Blood Nigga You Brought War In Da Hood.

It's Murder We Wrote If We Catch You in The Hood.

I turned the music down. "Y'all niggas trying to start shit now," I said.

"Damn right 50ty turn that shit back up," RonRon said.

I laughed. "Fuck It." And let RonRon rip the track.

They killed the track and I spent over two days mastering it. I made it a single diss song with no plans on putting it on D.H.C.'s album. RonRon wanted D.H.C. featured on it, but he wanted to make his own album with the song on it.

RonRon spent an entire week in New York determined to make a whole album, which he did. Tera and Cara spent time together while RonRon and I stayed in the studio. D.H.C was out pushing their album on the streets.

RonRon made a thousand copies of his CD then went back to Los Angeles. Cara went back with them just to visit her aunt for a while. Being home alone in Long Island was cool.

I knew as a hustler RonRon was going to make moves on his album. I opened up shows in L.A. for him to attend. I didn't make it to the shows there but Jermaine, Anthony and Hakeem went. I just maintained in the studio and made beats.

I had a few more people from New York that paid for studio time and they were alright, but I only had D.H.C. and RonRon on my mind. Probably once we blew up in the game it would be much faster for me to hire more people. Basically, I was getting paid two to three hundred dollars a day once the news got out about D.H.C. and Misery-n-Pain Records.

Rodney and Eric had twenty grand a piece for me in Georgia. I was using all of it for the upcoming shows in Queens and Brooklyn which would cost three grand a night.

D.H.C. caught a flight to California to join RonRon for his shows there where he featured them. They could get known on the west side as well on the east. The five grand we'd made from the show in the Bronx made me want to push more shows, but I knew that would wear them out after all the shows they were doing in California. I'd let them rest for a while unless they wanted to push more shows.

CHAPTER 23

New Year's Day in the New millennium 2000, the day the world supposed to end.

I caught a round trip to Bainbridge. I thought about the law, but I had to go there by plane to get my money. I felt comfortable because nobody was paying me any attention. The flight was smooth and fast.

Derrick and Eric waited in the lobby in Tallahassee. I had two hours before my flight back to New York. I just stayed in the airport area. We went to eat in the food court.

"How will you be low-key in New York now that you've opened a studio?" Derrick asked sipping on a strawberry milkshake.

"I can't really. Being low-key will cause attention. If I'm looking over my shoulder with worry every time I'm on their street, people will start wondering what's the deal. That will get me cased up for real. I got to be calm and out in the open. But I have no identification on me. And I use my alias, 50ty," I replied.

I told them about RonRon and my artists, D.H.C. When I mention D.H.C. Eric gave me a strange look. "What?" I asked.

"Damn, 50ty, I heard about them Kats on the B.E.T.'s news brief. They are the ones that jumped on Physical Madness and his bodyguards'." he responded.

I laughed. "Man, that dude was scary. He left his bodyguards there and they were defending him. We walked the dog on them motherfuckers in the club that night," I bragged.

They were surprised that we were part of the commotion that was on national T.V. I told them about RonRon's up and coming show in New York.

My plane arrived and I gave them a one-armed hug, got my money, and went to get on the plane.

Back in New York, I went to the studio to make a couple more beats then worked on RonRon's single. I wanted more on the single and figured I needed to find a singer. I called a few club managers from a list I got off the internet.

I was put in touch with a group called Success. The group consisted of four male members. I heard how good they were so I called and asked them to meet me at Central Park.

I was all about networking. Once I got a couple more riders on the team, I would stop hiring and work with what I had.

I sat on a park bench on the side of the road as Success pulled up in an all-white Cadillac truck with rims. All four of them were together. I was dress as a business man wearing a black suit, with my jewelry to accessorize.

"What's going on guys?" I asked, shaking their hands. I introduced myself to the group as 50ty from Misery-n-Pain Records. We went to sit at a table in the park.

"The manager from the club uptown told me about you guys," I said. "I'm looking for some top singers to jump on a song one of my artist's is working on. Either, I can pay you guys for it or maybe we can work out a deal because Misery-n-Pain is blowing up. This will be your chance to success."

"Plenty people have told us that they were going to make sure that we reached the stars and we haven't done it yet," one of them replied.

"Yeah, that's why we're not signed now because of the way shit is running. Who can we trust?" another one asked.

"I know I can't tell you can trust me because you don't know me. But, I can say that in this life, you have to give people a chance to see what's up with them, especially when it's benefiting you," I said.

"True, we will do it but we will also need a copy of our song on file," they said.

"That will be no problem at all," I replied.

"We have a good industry lawyer as well and he told us to wait around before we just jump into anything. We will get in touch with him then get back in touch with you," the main speaker said.

"That's cool." I gave them all one of my business cards. Before I walked off, they gave me a CD to listen to.

Back at the crib in Long Island, I put their CD in my player. I just sat and listened to the whole album. I planned to make their next album ten times better. They were damn good singers and should be out there touring and representing themselves.

Three days later I was at the studio waiting for RonRon and D.H.C. to arrive from California. When they came into the studio they went straight to the booth. I showed them how to work the equipment. I let them mess around on the other beats I'd made.

Everybody that heard the CD that D.H.C. and RonRon made liked it. The response made them tighten up their game. When RonRon walked into any crowded area, niggas gave him dap and hoes gave him hugs. They showed him much respect because he put Brooklyn in his song.

Later that day D.H.C. left early because they had to perform at a house party. They got paid three grands in advance to do it.

RonRon and I were left in the studio. I was talking to him about the solo album and expressed how I thought about putting an R&B singer on it. Success called and asked if they could come to the studio to hear the beats to their song. They wanted to bring their lawyer along. I had no problem with that.

When they arrived, I introduce them to RonRon and they introduce us to their lawyer.

"We're here to hear the song and work with you to see where we'll go from there," the lawyer said.

"Cool," I replied. I put RonRon's beat on from his single and let it play.

"RonRon, go in the booth and show them what you got," I told him.

While everybody relaxed and listened to RonRon rap, Success started writing. Their lawyer wanted to talk to me in private. We walked outside and left them alone in the building.

"They told me to come by and check you out, 50ty, to see what we can work with," he said.

"I heard about your clients through Mickey at club Up Town," I replied.

"Yeah Mickey is a good man and by the way, my name is Tommy but you can call me Tom," he said.

"I want them to just sing on this single for RonRon because it's a slow song. He will need more than just hip hop on the track. That's why I was searching for some singers," I said

"Well you picked the right ones to do that for you. How much are you talking about for them doing this?" he asked.

"Well I could offer them an amount but the well can run dry feel me so I thought about doing their next album for them I can give them like a year contract or something and they will be set." I said.

They lawyer Tom started scratching his head. "Well we can see what happen." he said.

Back in the studio Success is ready to go back there with RonRon and show us what they had.

We set an listen to them do their thing in the booth. They are blowing that shit up nicely RonRon had his fist over his mouth with excitement I'm excited has hell to but I remain calm until I stopped the music.

"Oh my God!" I yelled. That's what I'm talking about y'all that will be the number one on the bill board right there. They are just laughing off RonRon because he is going crazy over that.

The lawyer told them what we had talked about and they are please with doing a contract with me for a year on their next album just to see how it work out but main thing now is to do the single for RonRon and we will start on their tracks. They sign the contract and we made our agreements and they left.

Me and RonRon went to the airport an picked-up Cara. We went an ate at a fancy restaurant.

"How is your trip ma?" I asked Cara.

"It is good baby my aunt is glad to see me and to know that everything is ok with us." She answers.

"Wait to you see our house RonRon we have a lot of room in it pimp." I said. We were dressed like stars.

Cara had enough for two peoples she is starting to get bigger we just laugh at her.

"What y'all laughing for I have to eat." She joked.

After we left the restaurant we went home. RonRon eyes are like whoa, because of the sides of the crib. I put on RonRon album an Cara went upstairs and we blazed some of Brooklyn finest green, that D.H.C. gives us from their neighborhood.

Cara love RonRon album as well she over cleaned up listening to the songs, I guess it is just something to do.

Jermaine is spreading D.H.C. cd around in Cali, selling them ten dollars a pop with the help of Anthony and Keem.

They will call me every day to told me how much they made of the cd's.

By them doing the three city tours in Cali that I set up for them they made around twenty grand a peace they broke me of from the split of sixty grand they give my twenty grand I just placed the money in the stash.

The ground is feeling light now that we starting to get reparation. I'm getting emails one after another for shows that they wanted D.H.C. and RonRon to perform I took down most of the numbers an called them to see which prices were better. I had a list of them. Washington had the best offer for ten grands just for a couple hours which would be only three songs.

Two weeks later, Cara and I got packed up and set out for Los. Angeles to meet up with RonRon, Tera and Jermaine to fly out with us to Washington.

We hit the club up in Washington, the connect spread all over California before it got around New York.

While D.H.C. is kicking up dust on stage I'm in V.I.P. with Rodney and Derrick drinking Hennessy. I notice three white guys dressed in suits go up to the bar and they said something to the bar tender an she pointed at us. I stood up catching Rodney attention an looking at the three guys that approach me. I looked down into the crowd to see if they had anybody else with them in suits. But it is fogged up from the smoke and it is dark as hell the only lights is on D.H.C.

"Yo what's up guys." Rodney said stepping in front of me facing them.

"Hi we are looking for the managers or the producers of them guys that's on stage," One said.

"What is this about?" I inquired as I grabbed my drink off the round table.

"Well them guys are hot to death and I think they are hot to death in their performance on stage." One said.

"What is this about?" I asked again.

"We just wanted to know if they had any record deals or anything that will help their career out." The same guy said.

"Their under Misery-n-Pain records." I replied with pride.

"Ok, ok." They guy said with understanding.

I guess since he is the only one talking the other guys isn't shit just witnesses.

"Well let me ask you something, how would you guys like to join a bigger company?" He asked.

I always learn to think things through before making fast decisions. They were in suits in tie but that don't mean a thing in these days of time, disguise is a flaw standard.

"I can't answer anything at this time, do you have a number and maybe we can get back in touch with each other." I replied.

"Well we are not here to rush into anything just looking for talent artist, an them guys out there caught my attention with their first two songs now listening to their third they have what it takes." He said.

As we chilled in the V.I.P. I give the three guys a drink. They left after D.H.C. last song played. They walked pass D.H.C. an went down stairs and got lost into the crowd.

I never told them anything I just kept it to myself for the time being.

RonRon got on stage and did his solo he is dissing Physical Madness hardcore. Rodney went on stage with him just to be there on the side of him as his homies should do. I'm shock when the crowd starting saying fuck Physical Madness along with RonRon. Shit, Physical Madness is all the way in Miami way out of the district.

Back in L.A. D.H.C threw a party at the Marriot Hotel, I just made a short visit an took a couple picture with them then I flex an went back to the crib to see Jermaine.

When I pulled up to the house him and Anthony were about to pull out.

"Yo where are you guys about to go to?" I asked while jumping out of the rental walking up to the truck.

"We are on our way to the Marriot bro." Jermaine answers.

I got into the Hummer with them an went back to the hotel. "Those boys are blowing up, up here 50ty." Anthony said with a smile. I just laugh.

When we pulled to the hotel they place got crowed with more people's since I left. We went straight to the room where D.H.C. and RonRon is at. The two staff that we paid a grand a peace for stood at the door keeping people's out the way of them. I notice the music and the video van out in the parking lot, they were inside talking to them I let them talk and stayed behind the camera. Tera kept calling RonRon phone which I had it on me while he is doing his interview I answers it on the last call just to let her know what is going on an her and Cara is alright they just checking in on us.

We met up at RonRon house after the show. We made about four more grand at the hotel because they charged ten dollars a head to come there and it is over packed. I gave everybody a hug, then me and Cara an D.H.C went an caught flight back to New York.

Pulling up on the block of the studio in Brooklyn there were a lot of people's in front of studio waiting on our arrival. Everybody is screaming an waiting to see RonRon and D.H.C. The staff members called the police to move the crowd back from the studio which I know is a bad idea but they're the only one that could do it. We stayed in the car the entire time until the police moved them far back.

I put my hood over my head an got out of the car, everybody started screaming for D.H.C. and RonRon. But RonRon isn't here he stayed home with his wife. But they are going crazy when D.H.C. got out an started waving at them showing their love. I bet people's in St. Pete is going crazy now that we are on the map. B.E.T. is waiting to meet and talk to both D.H.C. and RonRon but we are not ready for the spot of T.V. attention yet.

CHAPTER 24

The next day in the studio I'm mastering RonRon tracks. Success came over to do their part on the song which I already had RonRon rap on his part when he is here. Tom is with them in the studio and is happy to have join us. They dropped the song in no time.

"Only men make decisions, is a wrap." I said when they walked back into the room from the booth.

I told them that, that's it an now we can start working on their album which they aren't ready to start it until the weekend which is good timing because I will spend my time mastering the single song for RonRon.

I had a lot of mail I just packed them all up an gives Cara her first job and helping me out by reading them and make good choices on letting me know what there about if it is really not an eye catcher she can pass it to the trash. I had a lot of voice messages as well. I let the answer machine play on speaker while I continue mastering the single.

People's is all over D.H.C jock. Now I have everybody want to come to the booth an rap. Even though I heard the whole voice messages I couldn't place my focus on a small plate at the time, when we are eating off bigger plates.

As nice as everything is looking, I still see a clear view of reality. I'm in trouble an everybody knows it but we maintain. RonRon called me on my office phone in the studio.

"I'm going to kill the next track. 50ty watch me." He said.

"It's on for bigger and better things bro." I responded while searching through the letters Cara gave me that she kept from the stacks.

"Well I'm coming up there this weekend and chill with D.H.C. an go to a club up there." He said. Then we hung up.

I kept a letter stating that they want us to come down to Miami an do a video shoot. I called D.H.C, an told them that I wanted them to meet me at the studio Saturday when RonRon comes up here because I have something to tell them in person.

We had a free week to do whatever we wanted to do. I spent the whole week with my wife. She is happy to finally have time with me. She cooked Monday and we ate than watch DVD's and chilled at home the whole day. Tuesday, we went to the movies and Success wanted to see me which they called my cell I told them that I'm on vacation for the week and to call me Sunday. Cara loved the attention I'm giving her. Wednesday, we went to a play they had in Manhattan which was crowded, an Cara enjoyed the whole play. Thursday, we set at central park and had a picnic which it started to snow again screwing up our evening at Central Park we hurried an got in the Hummer an went to Long Island. Friday, I had a cold from getting caught in the snow yesterday an Cara fed me soup and crackers with some cold medicine. The week is fun an relaxing I enjoyed the entire week with my wife as she enjoyed it with her husband.

Saturday morning RonRon called and told me that he is in New York with D.H.C. and he will meet me at the studio. I got dressed an gives Cara a kiss and told her I'll see her later.

Back in the studio, I had all their attention. "They want you guys to come down to Miami an do a photo shoot and a video shoot next weekend." I told them straight up.

Everybody is silence until RonRon laughed.

"That's where Physical Madness from right?" Mike asked from D.H.C.

"Yeah, an? RonRon replied. That's right up RonRon alley.

"So, when are we going?" Wil asked from D.H.C.

"First of all, what do you mean that's where he from that's not his city, and second of all California, New York, Georgia, Alabama, to wherever, nobody going to stop us from doing what we have to do." I replied.

"Well 50ty we will all half to go down there homey just to be prepared as we always do." RonRon said.

I rolled up a blunt, RonRon rolled up a blunt and one of the staffs rolled up a blunt. We sparked it up at the same time. The studio got fogged fast as if the building is on fire and we just chilling inside the smoke. Mike placed a towel in the crack of the door so no smoke would get out.

We are all choking an laughing as if we were dying with happiness from the chronic. It was cool, until Wil just burst out of the door for fresh air, I laugh. Lucky the streets are cleared out an nobody is around but us.

We had the tickle me high laugh and is cracking up on everybody an everything. I had it bad because I'm laughing so hard that I'm crying my whole face is wet. After chilling damn near the whole day D.H.C and RonRon went to the party that they had to attend. I left an went home.

I will go back to the music store an get a studio for my empty room.

A couple days passed I worked with Success on the first two tracks which they already had their beats. RonRon went back to Cali. On Monday. I hooked my room up with the studio so I don't have to spend my entire time in the building to master tracks. I had the staff watch over the studio an take messages for me. I wrote a hook call Blood in Blood out which is gangster an threw it up for grabs which they all wanted to jump on it so I made it for D.H.C and featuring RonRon and me on it.

I ordered me and Cara a pizza damn near a week until we changed up an got chicken from churches.

Cara got up early Thursday morning an woke me up by kissing all over my body. I missed my baby because I'm busy, busy, busy but it will all make up for the lost time.

After we were done with our morning of love making we both took a sit-down bubble bath an chilled. I'm laughing and playing with her while I help her sit down in the circle bath tub. I poured a glass of Hennessy with two ice cubes in my glass.

"Baby, RonRon is blowing up major now." Cara said. "Yeah that's his field, him and D.H.C. They will be the only ones I'm going to work with for now an Success basically don't need my help because they have a DJ making their music they just need my studio to use the booth and the system which they staff there will let them in every time to do their thing." I responded.

"They are really good I heard the cd in the cd player." She said.

"We are going down to Miami this weekend to do a video shoot." I said while sipping on my Hennessy.

"Wow honey that will be all you guys need to blow up." She replied.

We both fell into a world of fantasy once we started talking about the rich and the famous.

"Even though we are good on cash I'm just waiting on the industry can take full control of my income so we can stop the hustling.

"Yes, baby that will be wonderful plus I'm still trying to find you a good lawyer." She replied.

Bring that subject up brought Los back on the mind. I still can't believe he is a snitch ass mutherfucker. Now that Tom is out of the picture I wonder what he is up to now.

After the talk me and Cara took it from the bubble bath to outside in the back on out patio and set on our lawn chair on the side of the pool.

She let me feel when the baby is kicking which is a funny feeling. We stayed home all day until night then we went to sleep early.

I got up early the next day and I let Cara sleep until she awakens on her own. I decided to do breakfast this morning. I put some grits and sausage patties on the stove. The aroma circulated through the air onto the bedroom waking Cara.

"Baby, you must have felt my hunger because I'm thinking what we were going to eat this morning." She said, while standing in the hallway of the kitchen.

I laugh and gives her a kiss. "Good morning baby, how are you feeling?" I asked.

"Fine honey just a little tired from yesterday, I don't know why." She answers.

After we finish eating breakfast she went into the living room to watch T.V. I went into the music room an work some more on they beat I started. Eric called me up.

"Hello. I answer on the second rang.

"What's up 50ty, I got twenty-five grands for you pimp. He said.

"Cool playa just hold it down an continue stacking because I want all us to meet up in Miami Tomorrow if possible, because they have a photo shoot up there and a after party they will be going to New York, Cara made reservation at a nice hotel there taking up most of the rooms so if you have anybody that want to come down there with you and Rodney feel free to bring them homey I believe this will be one of the biggest shows ever for them." I said.

"Yeah, I talk to derrick him and Jermaine is already in Miami waiting on us to get there Tomorrow." He said.

I didn't know that Jermaine and Derrick went to Miami already. That made me want to move with rush on getting down there to be with them. They are down there giving out RonRon, and D.H.C fliers to let Miami know that we are coming to their town this weekend for them to be ready for us.

RonRon called me and told me that he wants to do a couple shows down there, which a couple of club managers called to set up shows for them. He set off for Miami today with Tera by plane. I told them we will leave in the morning.

We were pumped up and ready to go. I had to play it smart. We caught flight to Tallahassee, then we rode with Eric and Rodney to Miami but their SUV.

I'm in a day dream in reminiscing as we drove through Tampa and St. Pete on 275.

"Baby, there's your home." Cara said with a beautiful voice.

I smiled at her then I looked back outside the window at the Burg.

Glad we drove down because I'm strapped with my forty-five and my 30/30 an I know Eric them is strap as well.

Pulling up to the Hamilton Hotel in Dade county, there is two limos in front of the building. We parked an grabbed our bags then walked pass the limo that is in front of the building into the entrance. It is too dark to look inside the lime through the tent. Everybody is in the lobby we gave each other hugs an daps.

"50ty what's going on homey?" Hakeem yelled when he saw me an gives me a one arm hug.

"I didn't know you and Anthony came down here." I replied with excitement.

"They wanted to surprise you bro." Jermaine said. Well they did surprise me.

I miss both of them. I brought a copy of the beats I made. I wanted them to listen to. It is sixteen of us down in Miami. Me, Jermaine, Derrick, RonRon, Eric, Rodney, Mike, Wil, Anthony, Hakeem, Cara, Tera, and four of our staff members from N.Y. We got eleven rooms. We all couldn't meet up in one room so we plan to meet in the lobby.

I call the video crew guys to let them know that we were here. They wanted us to come to south beach early in the morning to show us where we will be performing at. The limo's that's in the front of the hotel is their limos for us to get around in Miami. But I let all them enjoy themselves an me and Cara got access to Eric SUV.

Me, Cara, Tera and RonRon, took a ride around Miami just to view the areas ourselves in the SUV., I drove. It is late once we rode on south beach there is a couple people's out but not many.

South beach be crowded through the summer twenty-four hours a day but not really through the year unless spring break comes. But the view is nice to see buildings on one side and water on the other.

It's amazing on how the scene going to look tomorrow.

We went back to the room an peak out the limo's still out in front of the hotel.

"Baby I can't wait until tomorrow, I know you are going to open things up." Tera said to RonRon.

I parked in the parking lot and we chilled for a while.

"I'm going to do my thing even though it's just for practice tomorrow." He replied.

"Yeah they will have the crowd far back from the scene just for you guys to be comfortable." Cara said.

I rolled up all the windows it is late and they want us to get up early in the morning. We took it on to our rooms.

The next morning RonRon called me and told me that they had some green over in their room, that's what I need a wakeup call. I knew Cara is going to take forever to look her best so I made a lot of noise so she would get up and start getting dress while I went an hit RonRon blunt.

When I walked into RonRon room they had four blunts burning an Derrick gives me a sack and a cigar. "That's for you solo cuz." He said.

We are higher than a mother fucker going to South beach.

There are orange cones on the side walk leading up to the beach. We followed the limo RonRon and D.H.C is in up on the grass onto the beach where there were guys with cameras and lights around them. Three guys walked up to the limo RonRon and D.H.C. is in. I got out of the SUV an walked up to the limo an met up with the three guys. "Are you guys ready?' One of the guys asked. "Fo sho." RonRon answers as he got out of the limo with his Perry Ellis suit on. "Well let's do this then." The guy responded.

They had me and RonRon roll up the set, he is performing on the passenger side while I drove. Basically, he is talking about how his life changed for the better, now that he is set, he is about what ever. They kept the camera's rolling on him and me. On the beach they had staff members open the door for us while he got out still rapping. Females is in the crowd with dudes that is all hired to be there to dance. We went to a table on the beach an sit down while two hoes came up to us an pored some Hennessy in our glass then they placed the bottle on the table, they both is in a T-back swim suit. Toward the end of the shoot we went back to our ride the same staff open the door for us opened it again so we can ride off. "Cut". They yelled.

"Wow, RonRon you might don't have to do this again Tomorrow kid." One of the agents said.

They put the show on the big screen that they had set up on the beach. We all set around the T.V. and watch it. The agent kept saying Good, good, great all the way until the end of the video.

Everybody clapped even me RonRon did his thing. He is smiling an saying thank you to the peoples.

"Perfect you guys don't have to worry about doing this again because this is a done deal." The photo shoot guy said shaking our hands.

We stayed on the beach for a while talking to different people's and D.H.C and RonRon is signing autographs. There is a lot of different record labels on the set that want to sign RonRon, he took all their numbers just to keep everything at a study pace.

After a whole day of chilling at the beach we decided to leave an take it back to the room for tonight show. Me, RonRon, Anthony, and Keem rode back in the SUV an blazed it up. RonRon is going to chill tonight and D.H.C is going to perform at club Coconuts. D.H.C is out for a long time tonight and I kept trying to call their phone and I didn't get no answer which is strange but I didn't say anything about it.

"Where is Mike and Wil?" RonRon asked. While we were chilling in the lobby.

"I haven't saw them since the video on South Beach." Tera replied.

"It's cool maybe they no people's here, we will see them tonight at their show." I said.

Me and Cara went to the room an chilled for the remaining three hours we have left before the show.

RonRon, Anthony, Hakeem and Eric rode around in the limo until it is time to go to the club. Me and Cara took a nap.

The eight grand we spent on the video we will get back tonight. Inside Coconuts there were bitches and niggas everywhere. They had two rap artists open before D.H.C. which I spotted Mike in V.I.P. the artist is good but I knew D.H.C. is going to tear this mother fucker up tonight.

When they came out to do their thing me and RonRon watch from the stairs of the V.I.P. while Derrick, Jermaine, Eric, and Rodney is in the crowd on the floor. Anthony, Cara, Tera, and Hakeem are watching from the V.I.P.

Mike spit his verse first and the crowd is going crazy the staff and bouncers couldn't barley hold them back. Then Wil started rapping doing his verse.

"50ty I'll be right back homey." RonRon said while walking to the V.I.P. stairs. He stood there until Wil stop rapping then the lights went off an a loud explosion happen then the lights came back on an RonRon is on stage with D.H.C. rapping. Everybody started going crazy even Tera and Cara up in the V.I.P. I had a chill of excitement flow through my body as well. I walked down the stairs a little bit to watch them do their thing live.

The show is going great until RonRon yelled. "Hold up, hold the fuck up, stop the music." The music stopped and it is silence. "What's happing nigga I saw you throw that Ice at me playa. He stressed to someone the crowd. "Who threw ice?" Mike asked. "Physical Madness pussy ass.

After he said that around twelve or more niggas jump on the stage and attacked RonRon

I quickly jump down the stairs and spotted D.H.C. exit the back door. I grab to beer bottles of a table and went to swing everybody that is around the stage trying to get at RonRon. Jermaine and Derrick snatch two of them off of RonRon and they all started fighting. Eric, and Rodney is handling the ones they are fighting. I couldn't get to RonRon so I started swinging on the niggas that tried to jump on my peoples on the floor. I kept looking at them punching RonRon. Jermaine somehow jump on the stage and started throwing niggas off of the stage then Eric big ass got up an help him handle them that is jumping on RonRon. I had a tight grip on the bottles that I had in my hands.

The police came out of nowhere, with the S.W.A.T. team. They started spraying pepper spray in the air and it covered the entire club. I knew everybody that I'd hit with those bottles had gone down. I grabbed Jermaine and Derrick and followed our staff out of the back of the club where D.H.C. had gone. They weren't anywhere in sight. Jermaine and Derrick were going to get into the limo until I stopped them and made them ride with us in the SUV. I was worried about RonRon, but I couldn't stay with him because of my situation. My staff, Eric and Rodney stayed behind with him. Cara, Tera, Anthony and Hakeem were still in the V.I.P.

On our way to the room I called D.H.C. back-to-back but got no answer. I called RonRon phone and the A.M.R. answered.

"Yo, where is RonRon?" I asked.

"He is on his way to the Dade County Hospital right now," the guy responded.

"Is he hurt?" I asked.

"No. He'll be alright. He's just going there to get checked out, that's all. His wife and another lady went with him," he replied.

I was relieved that everything was okay.

"Them motherfuckers were in the club in a pack," Jermaine said. He had a big knot over his right eye.

"They set us up tonight. They had that planned. I don't trust nobody up here now," I said.

We rode up to the hospital. The staff told me that they knew where the other limo driver had taken D.H.C. I told Jermaine and Derrick to stay at the hospital with RonRon while I found out if D.H.C. were alright.

We pulled up to a studio that said Grand City Studio. The other limo that D.H.C rode in was parked in front of the building.

"Stay in the car, 50ty," one of the staff members said. They both got out of the car and went inside the studio. I guess they took me for a dumb ass. I waited until they got inside then I jumped out and hurried across the street to a store.

I brought a blunt and a Lottery ticket. While I stood at the register, I spotted an all-black Pontiac pull beside the limo. Seconds later gunshots were fired. They shot up the limo with multiple shots then sped off.

The clerk panic as I just stood there watching the whole thing go down. I saw Wil and Mike come to the door and peaked outside. If that wasn't a set up then what the fuck could it be? I stayed there continuing to look out the glass door from the store.

Our staff opened up the back door to see if I was in there and when they saw that I wasn't I noticed the stress that covered their faces.

"Were you in that car?" the clerk asked. I looked at him. "

"No." I walked up from around the counter.

"Those bullets were meant to have a name on them," he remarked.

"I thought so myself," I replied.

Five police cars pulled up with two policemen in each car. I waited until they got out of their cruisers then I walked out of the store, crossed the street, and went to the studio.

"Where is D.H.C?' I asked. I behaved as if everything was cool and played it off. They all stared at me in shock. I remained calm.

"50ty, man, I thought you were in the car. Damn, I'm glad you weren't," one of the staffs said.

"What the hell happened?" I looked at the car, pretending to be puzzled. "Who shot the car up?" I asked. No one answered.

The police questioned me, but I had no information. While the police were there, I called Jermaine and Derrick, telling them to catch flight back home because it wasn't safe anymore. I let them know that I was fine. I wanted them to bring Tera with them as well as Anthony and Hakeem.

After I finished my conversation and disconnected, I inquired about D.H.C. again. I was told that they hadn't seen them.

"50ty, let's go back to the room. We need to get from around here, playa," someone suggested. They really must have thought I was stuck on stupid, but they'd find out who's the fool soon enough.

"Let me get a ride please," I said.

We got into the other limo and left the area. I sat all the way in the back facing the front so I would be able to watch them. Little did they know, I was strapped too. I just didn't want to have my guard down and fuck up so I kept my eye on them as they kept theirs on me.

Two more of the staff entered the limo with us and sat in the back seat with me. I knew then it was going to be something, but I remained calm. I didn't trust any of those guys from the beginning and they'd tried to kill me. They were giving me crazy looks as if I didn't notice.

"Yo driver, stop at McDonalds. I'm starving back here," I said. They continued to play innocent and pulled over at the McDonalds. They were discussing the drive-by like it was nothing.

I guess they wanted to scare somebody by just shooting up the back seat of a limo where I happened to be sitting, I thought.

"I want to sit down and eat on the inside, fellas," I told them. The limo parked in a parking space. "Do you guys want something?" I asked.

"I'll take something," one of them said, getting out of the car with me. I knew that it was in order to keep an eye on me. They didn't know what the fuck they were up against.

I remained behaving like I was clueless to the act they were putting on.

"Order me a number one with a Coke," I told the guy that was standing in line with me. I gave him a twenty. "Get whatever you guys want. I got to pee." His eyes followed me all the way to the restroom. I knew I had to be quick getting in touch with Rodney and Eric. I told them the scoop and I made sure I told them the street that I was on so they could come to McDonalds ASAP.

All I had to do was hang around until they arrived. I examined my .45 that I had in my jacket and placed a bullet in the chamber just to be prepared to ride or die. I really did have to pee too.

One of the staff members came into the rest room acting like he had to pee. His timing was good because I was flushing the toilet. I smiled at him as I walked by and washed me hands then went back into the lobby. The two guys that had been in the limo and the driver were at the table eating.

I went to join them as if we were the best of friends. They actually thought I wasn't on point, but they were the ones not on point. They ate like hogs. I just sat there and ate my fries and sipped on my Coke. I kept my eyes on them and my surrounding. I engaged in conversation to keep everybody in check. Ten minutes passed and I spotted a black Mercedes pull in the parking lot. It caught my attention because one of the staff members looked at the car strangely.

I only glanced at the car to throw them off. The limo drives really gave his self away when he nodded his head at the staff members while looking outside. I guess he thought I wasn't paying that any attention either. Those guys were so lame.

"50ty, are you ready?" the driver asked. "I got shit to do."

They all got up at the same time.

"I didn't finish my food, but since you're in a hurry I don't want to keep you waiting any longer, pimp," I said. I wore a calm look and a smile.

I spotted a SUV pull in the parking lot. Their lame asses didn't notice it. We walked toward the limo which was parked by the Mercedes. Four doors of the Mercedes opened at the same time. I looked at my watch and saw that it was three forty-one. I looked back and smiled when I saw Eric and Rodney get out of the truck with guns in their coats. They started walking behind the staff members.

When I saw the guy standing next to the Mercedes and the limo holding his gun under his shirt, I dropped my bag of food like it was an accident. There was quite a distance between me and those guys in the Mercedes. I kneeled like I was going to pick the bag up, but I placed my hand in my coat and pulled out the .45. I stood up quickly, shooting the guy by the Mercedes in the head. I ran between two parked cars in parking lot as they returned fire.

Eric and Rodney surprised the staff members and the limo driver, shooting all three in the back, killing the driver instantly. I quickly finished off the other two. We then had a shoot-out with the guys in the Mercedes. People began screaming and running.

The Mercedes sped out of the parking lot leaving a lot of smoke in the air. We vanished like ninjas in the smoke. While we rushed out of the area I called Tera to see how RonRon was doing. She informed me that he would be released in an hour.

I called the hospital to talk to RonRon and told him when he got released to go straight to L.A. He was pissed off with D.H.C. but didn't have time to think about them niggas.

I quickly made it to the hotel and grabbed all our stuff while Eric stayed outside watching.

Eric and Rodney wanted to head out, but I knew I couldn't get over it if I left it alone. I had to face Physical Madness straight up. At that time the police were the least of my problems.

Just as RonRon and I did with Sweetman, we went straight to Physical Madness's studio to face his ass. We parked on the side of the studio, got out and went inside of the building, surprising them.

Eric and I went straight to the back where we found D.H.C. with the three guys from the club. Rodney stood at the door with a Mac 11 in his hand

I told the D.J. to stay put in front of his mixer and computer. Eric stood in view of Rodney to make sure he was alright while I handled my business.

I walked up to Mike and swung with all of my might, hitting him in the face. We both fell to the floor. I landed on top of him.

"That's for leaving us at the club and letting RonRon get jumped like that." I got up quickly and backhanded Wil with all my might, knocking him into the wall. "Y'all motherfuckers better be glad RonRon is not here because your niggas would end up dead and forgotten about. Plus y'all started too soon trying to take over shit. I don't know if it's the youngness or the dumbness in you small timer motherfuckers." I went in Wil's pocket pulling out well over 15 grands, all in hundreds. I threw it to Eric and he put it in his pocket. When I went to go in Mike's pocket, he jerked back a little, refusing me. I swung, hitting him in the forehead with my gun, knocking him back down to the floor. This time, I started kicking the shit out of him.

"Now pussy ass nigga, go in your own pocket and give me everything you possess even your jewelry," I ordered, kicking him again in his ribs. He was in pain as he took off his jewelry and placed it on the floor beside him. He slowly went in his pocket and took out his cash and put it on the floor, too.

I picked him up by his neck, slinging him against the wall. I clicked my gun back, bringing the bullet into the chamber. One of the three dudes from the club was getting ready to say something, but Eric stole him with the handle of his gun, knocking him out cold. The other two just stared at me in fear.

"Speak when you motherfuckers are being spoken to," Eric said.

"Rodney, bring the D.J. over here and lock the door," I said. The D.J. was scared as hell. "What's wrong nigga? It's a lil too late to panic. Call up Physical Madness and if you say you don't know the number then there will be a serious blood bath in here."

Rodney clicked the Mac back. Just as I'd figured, the DJ dialed him up. He put him on the speaker phone.

"What up nigga?" he answered.

"What's going on with you, playa? Where are you?" I asked.

"Who is this?" he asked.

I looked at Mike and aimed my gun at him urging him to finish the conversation.

"This Mike from D.H.C., homey," Mike said.

"Where are you at, pimping?" Wil asked in a calm voice.

"I'm on my way to my girl's house, playa, in Fort Lauderdale. Why? What's going on?" he asked.

"Nothing, man. I just wanted to know if I could see you tonight because I'm going back to New York in the morning, kid," Wil said.

"No doubt, but I'm out right now, pimp. Just leave your number in the studio and I'll call you sometime this week. I'll bring you back down here to visit and kick it with some bitches," Physical said. The guy that Eric knocked out was waking up. He moaned as if in pain.

"What the fuck was that noise?" Physical asked. I aimed my gun at the man while Eric covered his mouth.

"That was me, dawg. I was yawning," The D.J. lied.

I instructed for Mike to tell him that he would holla at him when they got back to New York.

After hanging up with Physical Madness, Eric and Rodney tied everybody except the D.J. up.

"Your name is Kenny, right?" He nodded. "Well Kenny, you're coming with us," I said.

I glared at D.H.C. "You're cut from the contract. Y'all know RonRon will shut your career down by telling the world the truth. Y'all niggas lucky that you're still alive." We headed out with the DJ.

"The last time we had a nigga kidnapped they was tied up. Why is he so special?" Eric asked. The DJ and I sat in the back seat. I just laughed. The way my life had turned out, the things that happened made me not give a fuck anymore.

"I want you to show me where this nigga's bitch lives in Fort Lauderdale and I will let you go unharmed," I told Kenny the D.J.

"Please," he begged. "I don't have nothing to do with none of this crazy shit. From what I saw and heard, they did something fucked up to you guys. I knew it was wrong when they shot up your limo in front of the studio. They told me and D.H.C. that it was an accident, but we didn't know what was going on," he said.

So D.H.C. didn't know about them trying to kill me. Well, they just fucked up trying to find a better way of leaving Misery-n-Pain Records. Oh well, farewell. I just listened as Kenny continued talking. Physical Madness was on my mind. I knew he probably hired them motherfuckers in that Mercedes to knock me off. Now, payback would be a bitch.

We drove out of Miami and went to Fort Lauderdale.

"Damn Physical traveled for a minute to get a piece of pussy," Rodney said.

"Yeah, he wasn't planning on coming back to Miami no time soon," I replied.

We went past his girlfriend's house and he hadn't pulled up yet. We just circled the block to check out our surroundings. By time we went around the block once, Physical pulled on the block.

"There he goes right there," Kenny said.

"Drive slow, Eric," I instructed.

"Are you going to kill him?" Kenny asked. "

Stop the truck, E," I said. Hearing that, Kenny looked at me in fear.

"The only punishment you're going to get is getting the fuck out right here and finding your own way back to Miami. Let me have your phone before you leave," I told Kenny.

Without a word he gave me his phone, got out of the SUV, and took off running. I almost laughed, but I had things to tend to.

Eric quickly rushed up to the house where Physical was parked. Physical was getting ready to get out of the car. He was in the passenger's side.

Eric stayed in the car while Rodney and I got out and rushed both of them.

"Payback's a bitch, aint it man?" I whispered. Physical Madness turned around, saw me and tried to run. I shot one time, hitting him in the back, dropping him. I ran up to him. "Blood for blood motherfucker." I shot three more times. One bullet hit him in his neck and the other struck him in the head. The driver just stood still, in shock. Rodney looked at me. I gave him the go-ahead. Rodney shot one single time hitting the driver in the temple. He dropped instantly.

Damn I'd never seen anything like that before. We ran and hopped back in the SUV. Eric sped off. We heard Physical Madness's girlfriend screaming for help while we exited the block.

We left Fort Lauderdale, headed to St. Pete., without looking back.

"You saw how that dude dropped after I shot him?" Rodney asked.

"He never saw that coming." I answered.

I called D.H.C. on Kenny's cell phone.

"Yo," Mike answered.

"I thought you were a wise man. A dumb ass makes dumb decision such as what you niggas did," I said.

"Yo, fuck you niggas. You better not come back to New York kid, real talk. We going to hit you niggas up," Mike yelled. Wil was saying something too but I couldn't really hear him over Mike's yelling. I just hung up.

I rolled up a blunt and we blazed on our way home.

"Nice razor phone Kenny had," I said, laughing as I let the back window down and tossed it out on Alligator Alley. Alligator Alley was nothing but a long road surrounded by swamp and plain fields. "Damn that's the second cell phone I threw out the window," I said laughing. They joined in.

"Fuck it," Eric said.

"That's real," I responded.

CHAPTER 25

Back in "the Burg" we got another room at the Hilton on St. Pete Beach. I called Tera to let them know I was in St. Pete. Cara was already there with Jermaine, Anthony and Hakeem. When she found out I was back, she rushed to the Hilton. She knocked on the door just as I was getting ready to take a shower. I opened the door and gave her a kiss then I went to take a shower. I wasn't in there for long when she came into the bathroom and pulled the shower curtain back. She was butt naked.

I laughed at her pregnant belly and she smiled. "Mind if I join you, baby?

"No need to even ask," I answered, stepping back and making room for her under the cascading water.

We stayed in St. Pete for a month. I remained low key as always. RonRon and Tera stayed at his grandma house. The neighbors and his friends were happy to see him. They saw how much he'd changed in the game. He had a lil homey that hustled for him that kept breaking him off money.

I told RonRon about the situation with Physical Madness and what D.H.C. said would happen when I returned to New York. He called his Uncle Blitty. Blitty told him that he would find out what was going on.

One day we all met at Campbell's Park and chilled. RonRon had his friends with him and when they saw me it was almost like they wanted to kneel before me. I just laughed at them all and gave them a one-armed hug. They played basketball while I sat on the bench and talk to Tera and Cara.

Anthony and Hakeem flew back to L.A. early. Derrick was ready to return to Bainbridge so Rodney, Eric and I got prepared to head back.

Back in Bainbridge we dropped Derrick off then went to Eric and Rodney's crib to relax. I called Cara while they were at the airport in Tampa getting ready to go back to Los Angeles. I told her I'd see her the next night and to have a safe flight.

Our plan was to leave early the next morning, get to California, and prepare for the show the following day. I decided to just sleep over their house instead of getting a room. I'm tired and Rodney and Eric are exhausted as well. We called it a night early and crashed.

The next morning Derrick knocked on my door at a quarter after three. Rodney and Eric were catching a twelve o'clock flight so it is just Derrick and I catching the five o'clock flight.

"Damn cuz did you get any sleep last night?" Derrick asked because I was wide awake.

"Only a couple of hours. I'll make up for it on the plane and when I get to L.A.," I said.

Cara had reserved rooms at the Hilton where she waited for us to arrive. Derrick went straight to his room, but Cara was hungry and wanted to eat. I suggested that we go to Red Lobster and sit down to eat.

We talked as we ate. Cara informed me that she'd hired another lawyer. I was proud of her because she always kept on top of things.

After paying the bill, we sat and talked for a while inside of the restaurant because it was raining hard. When the rain slacked up a bit, we headed back to the hotel. On the way Cara got a call. It was eleven o'clock. Rodney and Eric should be heading to the airport for their flight. My thoughts were interrupted when Cara gasped.

"Oh my God! Oh my God! Terrill turn around. Turn around now," she cried. I quickly made a U-turn without asking any questions, alarmed by her tone of voice. I didn't panic because it was raining heavily again. I focused on the road, barely able to see the street in front of me. I just continued to drive and listen to her half of the conversation with Anthony. "Oh my God!" she cried again. She placed her hands over her mouth then looked at me. "My aunt just got into a serious accident," She finally informed me and began to cry hysterically. I remained silent as she continued to talk with Anthony.

I pulled up to the street she directed me to. The whole area was roped off. My heart started to thump in my chest and I could barely breath. It was hard to remain calm, especially when Cara lost it.

After I stopped the truck, she dropped the phone on the seat, jumped out and ran under the yellow tape, up to the scene of the accident. I picked up the phone.

"Hello?" I said.

"Hey 50ty," Anthony said. I could tell he was crying.

"What happened?" I asked.

"My aunt....and Hakeem got into an accident. I didn't want to tell Cara.... but Hakeem died on the scene...and they flew my aunt to the hospital," he said, and began crying even harder.

I looked at Cara. She was screaming out loud, kneeling over a white sheet which had to be Hakeem's body. The tears came then, in puddles and dropped down my face.

I heard Anthony crying and Cara screaming out of control. I wanted to just leave again and never return. But I knew that I couldn't.

"I'm so sorry, Anthony," I choked out. "Stay by your aunt's side. She needs you there. Be strong."

I hung up and got out of the truck. The rain drenched me as I walked up to the yellow tape. I stopped near a black police officer.

"Is that your wife and was that your son?" he asked.

I stared at him for a second. "Yes, that's my wife. He wasn't my son but I loved him like a father would love his son," I replied. The officer bowed his head. "My wife is six months pregnant." I said quietly.

He looked at me then lifted the tape. "Then she really needs you by her side," he said and let me pass through the tape.

As I walked toward Cara and Hakeem another officer tried to stop me, but the first cop called him off.

"Why? Why? Why did it have to be Hakeem and not me? Why?" she wailed. She was crying so hard and in so much anguish that it tore at my heart. After a while, I touched her on the shoulder.

"Cara, please. I need you to be strong for me and for our baby," I told her.

She turned around and fell against my chest. I placed my arms around her and she cried some more. I felt as everything was my fault. The pain I felt inside made me wonder why it wasn't me in Hakeem's place. Hakeem was a good kid and he was young. It just seemed so unfair. I cried along with Cara then I nudged her.

"Come on baby. Let's go. There's nothing you can do here and your aunt needs you," I said holding her close to me as we walked back to the Hummer.

The roads were slippery from the rain so I understood how someone could lose control of the wheel. I drove really slowly to the hospital, careful not to get into an accident myself. It wasn't long before we were back at the hospital where Ronnie died.

RonRon and I sat in the lobby while the others were in the room with Aunt Laura.

"Hey homey, how are you?" RonRon asked.

"Man, why is it constantly tragedy and pain?" I responded.

He stared at the ground then stared at the ceiling. "I can't believe Hakeem is gone, dawg."

Tera returned to the lobby with her face covered in tears.

"Hey 50ty," she said, giving me a hug.

"How are you, Tera?" I asked

"I'm alright," she said sadly.

"What's going on in there, baby?" RonRon asked.

"They took her into surgery. She's fighting for her life," she said, beginning to cry. RonRon got up and gave her a hug.

I stood and went into the hospital room where Cara was with her family. I gave Anthony a hug and told him to stay strong. I hugged Cara and returned to the lobby.

"50ty, Rodney and Eric are at the Hilton," he said.

"Cool, I'm going to head there now. Tell Cara to call Derrick's phone if she needs me," I replied.

At the hotel, we all chilled in Derrick's room. We sat in complete silence smoking blunt after blunt. Derrick had brought a fifth of Hennessy. I drank mine straight. I had about six cups and smoked every blunt that was passed my way.

My body was paralyzed.

"I love y'all guys. I put my life on the line for y'all, and I'm going to ride for y'all," I said. Everything was spinning like a tornado.

"What do you mean you will ride for us?" Eric asked.

"That nigga is fucked up, man," Jermaine joked.

"But they said when you're drunk, you tell the truth," Rodney said, laughing.

"That's no joke, but what I'm saying is reality. It doesn't 't has anything to do with me being fucked up or not being fucked up," I responded.

"So, what do you mean you are going to ride for us?" Jermaine asked.

What I'm saying is, I feel like everything that we are going through is my fault. If we didn't have the money we wouldn't have the power to do the shit that we have done to cause shit, feel me? And everything is starting to catch up with us. I will have to face the consequence, feel me?" I tried to explain. They continued to crack jokes and laugh at me because I was drunk, especially when I tried to get up and fell back down. I finally gave up and staggered to my room where I fell on the bed and went to sleep.

I woke up the next morning with one of the biggest headaches of all time. I threw up the entire morning. Tera brought me some Advil and breakfast. I ate, took the pills, and went back to sleep. Three hours passed and I woke up again feeling better. I looked at the time and saw it was seven hours before RonRon's show. I was hungry so I ordered a pizza. I turned on the television and called RonRon.

"50ty, what's going on? Have you thrown up your guts yet?" he joked. "My baby told me that you look like hell, homey. The fellas told me how you were acting last night, talking about how you are going to ride for us if shit pop off. Nigga, I told you from the beginning, if you go down I'm going down. Ain't shit going to change that, playa. So, stay focus nigga and let's maintain," he said.

"Yea. I was stressing, homey, but I'm cool now. I'll see you in the club tonight, no doubt." I replied.

RonRon was a soldier and I knew he would be there until the end. Just knowing that was enough to make me stay strong and focus on maintaining.

I contacted Cara at the hospital and inquired about her aunt's condition.

"She is very upset. They had to give her some drugs to relax her after she found out what happened to Hakeem," she said.

"I see."

"Have fun at the show tonight baby, and please be careful," she told me.

"I will, baby."

After talking to Cara, I took a shower. I pulled out a brand-new G-Unit outfit that I hadn't worn yet. Cara brought it at the mall when we first moved to L.A. After getting dressed, I called the lawyer and we agreed to meet in V.I.P. upstairs at the club that night.

When it was time to go I walked out to my brother's Hummer. A police car was parked out front, facing me. I thought officers were going to rush me, but they got out of the car and went to a house nearby. I breathed a sigh of relief. It was ten o'clock p.m. I quickly headed to the club.

When I arrived, the club was jam packed already. I was glad that I had my V.I.P. pass to get past the long line. There were local rappers, opening for RonRon, on the stage doing their thing when I entered the building. The rappers caught my attention to the fullest, because they had their own singer and band mixing their tracks. The crowd was already getting hype.

I went up to the V.I.P. section and spotted the lawyer standing near the stairs. I had a flashback and thought about Tom. I continued walking up the stairs, passing him. He was dancing to the music. I just laughed and walked on into V.I.P. and headed for the bar.

I didn't know if it was because I stood six-four or because of my jewelry and clothes, but all eyes were on me from the time I stepped foot in the club.

I saw Anthony sitting on the couch next to Rodney and that made me feel good. I walked over to them after getting a cup of Hennessy.

"Oh, shit Anthony, lil homey, what's going on playa?" I greeted.

"RonRon made me come. He said I needed to get out tonight and watch him do his thing and that it would give him confidence while he's onstage," he said.

I notice the bright look on Anthony's face showing that he was happy to be out with us. That was a good thing.

"Do you want something to drink?" I asked.

"Yeah, I can take a drink." I went back to the bar and got him a cup of Hennessy too.

Those boys that were on the stage did their thing then another group came up. RonRon would come on last because he was the star for the night.

Two of the club's staff members came to our table.

"Which one of you guys are 50ty?" one of them asked. I didn't have to say anything because after he asked everybody stared my way.

"What's up?" I asked.

"RonRon is up next and he wants you to come onstage with him on his first song," he relayed.

"Alright. Thank you for the information," I replied.

I left the V.I.P. and went to locate RonRon. He was in the back of the club getting ready.

"Hey, 50ty. I need you on the stage for my first song, playa," he said. Two females were putting make up on him so that his skin would light up on the stage.

I sat down and they did the same to me. When they were done, I stood in front of the wide mirror and examined myself. We were ready to go out there. They gave us a wireless microphone.

"You guys are up next," a bouncer informed. I nodded my head at him.

"50ty, I just need you to back me up on my first song," RonRon said.

"I got you, playa." The ladies that were backstage with us gave us three energy drinks a piece.

The thing about RonRon and I was that we were never scared. I was blitzed off the Hennessy, already pumped and ready to do the damn thing. The beats I made in Long Island blasted over the loud speakers. I walked out onto the stage and yelled:

Yea, motherfuckers throw y'all bird's in the air.

Aint no stopping this playa right here.

I pointed at RonRon then spit a freestyle to the beat catching everybody off guard. RonRon was even shocked but tried to play it off. He got really hyped and spit his verse. He was on fire, cranking the whole club. The crowd sang his verse with him as they swayed to and from. It made him proud that they knew his song. He damn near performed his whole album on stage.

When the show was over I was tired as hell and my voice was almost gone from screaming backup. My body was tense too.

"Damn 50ty, you caught me off guard with that. I didn't know you knew how to rap," RonRon said, giving me a one-armed hug.

"You guys were outstanding out there," someone from backstage said, showing love. For a moment I felt like a star which made me feel good about going out there and rapping.

I know the lawyer saw me onstage, but from the looks of it I believed he would have been a waste of my time. I never said a word to him and I never returned to V.I.P. The club was still jumping, but we left out the side door and went to get something to eat.

RonRon was having a block party on his street too. I told him that I needed to go back to New York to check on my equipment.

"I'm going back with you, pimp, because I want to run up on D.H.C.," he said.

"No doubt. We'll leave in the morning because the block party is going down tonight."

RonRon had the whole block for the night. His neighbors had been well paid, so we planned to take full advantage of it. Jermaine and

RonRon's Hummers blocked off the left end of the street. We had two barbecue grills out in the front yard with huge ice coolers full of sodas and beer. Tera had a bar in the living room where RonRon sold liquor.

Three Cadillac's and four Acura pull up on the set at the same time. The people in them got out of their cars. They'd gotten the spots where they were going to chill at all night. I knew that once the club closed, everybody would arrive at the block party.

I remembered RonRon's birthday party last year and it caused me to make everybody put on their bulletproof vests. I planned to keep an eye on everybody as much as possible.

I stayed near the house because I knew L.A. niggas got wild with that gangbanger shit. They met up on the block. I started to think that maybe the party was a bad idea. I kept my 45mm on me at all times. I knew everybody else was packing, too.

The aroma of barbecue floated in the air. Jermaine hooked the meat up on one of the grills while Eric did his thing on the other one. By time the club closed, everybody was at the block party and the food was ready to be served.

RonRon made over fifty grands at the club and he gave me thirty of it.

"Now we're on another level," he said proudly. We did find our way out of the game.

Bosco, if you were here with us, homey, I thought. I know this isn't what you meant when you said to invest in something, but I bet this is way better than what you had planned.

"50ty, 50ty!" Jermaine yelled getting my attention. He pointed into the street. I spotted around thirty niggas wearing all blue walking up the side walk. I placed my hand on my gun just to feel it there. I walked over and stood next to Eric. Rodney and RonRon stood by the grill near Jermaine.

The gang walked across the street from RonRon's crib to where some females were chilling. RonRon sent one of his men over and he gave me the phone.

"Hello." I answered

"Hey baby," Cara greeted. "How is the party going?" she asked.

"It's going smooth ma. How is your aunt doing?" I asked.

She took a deep breath. "She's okay. She's sitting up and walking around a bit. She only broke her wrist." She explained what happened the night of the accident. "She said she was driving up the highway when another car pulled in front of her, almost hitting them. It made her swerve out of her lane into the other lane, in front of a gas truck. The gas truck blew its horn, almost hitting her. She swerved back into her lane. The road as you know, were slippery. When she swerved back into her lane the car in front of her hit its brakes for no reason, making her hit her own breaks. It caused her car to hydro slide and spin in a circle. It went back into the lane with the gas truck, causing the truck to jackknife. The tail end of the truck slide hitting her bumper, knocking her car over. As she flipped, she blanked out. That's all she remembered. I was all ears.

"Did she and Hakeem have on their seatbelts?" I asked.

"She said she had on hers, but she had just picked Hakeem up and he hadn't put on his," she said. I could tell that she was trying not to cry.

"Okay. I understand, ma. I'm sorry that it happened like that," I consoled. "I'm going to New York in the morning to check out the studio and the crib and I'll be back in a couple days," I told her. We talked for a while longer then I got off the phone.

People started gathering on the block in packs. It was jam pack before we knew it. Local rappers and singers were trying to get at me, but RonRon's men held them back. Jermaine and Eric served food to a long line of people. I went inside where RonRon was playing cards with a few people from around the way.

"It's mad crazy outside right now," RonRon said, trying to focus on his hand as they played Spades.

"Yeah motherfucker is jam packed outside."

RonRon's cell phone rang and he told me to answer it because he was tied up in the game.

"What's going on, bro?"

"There are some niggas out here starting shit, playa. I don't know what the deal is. Come check it out," Jermaine said.

I grabbed the Walkie Talkie and instructed the staff to come up to the house. I told Anthony to come inside. I walked to the door to see if I recognized anybody in the crowd starting drama. It was hard to see who all was out there for a distance.

Jermaine and Eric continued serving their food. The crowd causing the drama had everybody's attention.

"Which one of y'all is Ronnie people?" someone from the crowd asked.

"Why?" somebody else in the crowd asked.

"I just want to let y'all niggas know that Hakeem and Ronnie were examples," the dude said.

"What the fuck?" RonRon swore.

"What that supposed to mean?" the hidden person yelled.

"The niggas missing in action," the dude bragged.

I eased off the porch and slipped into the crowd.

"So is Sweetman and all them niggas that were at the corner store," I said. I ducked into the crowd and moved closer to them.

"Who said that?"

"Your momma nigga! Go home." Everybody started laughing and some people walked off. That left a gap in his area, exposing him. Another crew rushed him, but he ran and got lost in the crowd. They gave chase. I tried to follow him from a distance, but he vanished. They group that chased him came back and grabbed another dude.

"Nigga I saw you with that clown."

"I didn't do anything," the guy responded.

One of the dudes just scooped the man up and slammed him hard into the streets. Females yelled at them telling them that he didn't have anything to do with that, and to stop kicking him. That didn't do any good.

Feeling rage, I went to pull out my gun. Suddenly, we heard five shots and everybody ducked. I saw two of the dudes drop and everybody started screaming and running. I lot of commotion broke out. Several gunshots were fired and another person got shot in the chest. I quickly disappeared and went back to RonRon's house.

The two dudes in front of RonRon's house were going to be okay. One was hit in the leg and the other was caught in the arm.

We quickly got ready to head for New York. RonRon left his staff to talk to the police as we headed to the airport. We waited for over two hours for our plane.

At a quarter till six, we caught a flight to Long Island. We arrived quickly and caught a cab to my house. Once there, we grabbed our guns and got into my Hummer, heading straight to Brooklyn.

For some reason I felt like New York was going to be against me and RonRon because of the shit D.H.C. put us through. I had to return because of my studio.

At the studio everything looked normal and untouched. It would have been difficult to break into the building because of the cages over the windows and doors.

We all got out of the Hummer. Rodney and Derrick stayed near the truck while Jermaine, RonRon, Eric and I went inside. I was surprised to see that it wasn't broken into.

"50ty, you have a letter on the window outside." RonRon noticed from inside the studio.

I opened the unknown letter and read it.

50ty, this letter is to let you know that Blitty stepped to me when I was at the mall with my mom, man. I'm sorry about what happened to you in Miami. We didn't have anything to do with that there. But anyway, we're not trying to beef with you so tell Blitty that everything is cool. Keep your head up and stay safe, 50ty. Tell RonRon to keep them skills together.

One.

Mike and Wil. (D.H.C.)

"Yeah, yeah, yeah. I forgive them, and I'll holla at them if I see them in the streets. But I won't ever do another track for them and we will never become friends again," I said, smirking as I ripped up the letter.

I called a moving company to have them ship all of my equipment to my house in Long Island. We waited until they arrived and followed them to the house.

Back home, we went into the studio room and freestyles over beats that we'd already created. I let them rap because I was tired. I went into my room to take a nap.

Rodney, Eric and Derrick caught flight back to Bainbridge once they saw there wasn't going to be any drama in N.Y. Jermaine and RonRon spent the night and went back to California the next evening because Jermaine had to work the following day.

CHAPTER 26

A week passed in which all I did was make beats to occupy my time while Cara was still in L.A. with her aunt while she recovered. RonRon informed me of an upcoming show for a soft drink commercial. I would take place at the San Diego Dome. He was going to be paid a lot of money, too. He was excited about the deal because other rapper and singers would be there. That would pave the way for him to be able to feature some of them on his next album. The show would be in a week. I would fly out to San Diego the day before.

I was back in L.A. a day before RonRon's show. Jermaine picked me up from the airport. We went to a barbeque stand that he found in the area and got a couple of rib sandwiches and ate in the truck.

While we listened to Hot 97 on the radio, RonRon's song, featuring Success came on. Jermaine called everybody he knew and told them that RonRon was on the radio. I was happy to hear him. He was going to have an album release party in two months. I wasn't worried about drama because only stars were going to be in attendance.

"Everybody is talking about the upcoming show in San Diego. I know it's going to be jam packed," Jermaine said.

"Yeah it is bro. This will blow RonRon up the charts though, especially with Success being here with him. I haven't seen them in a while, but that's good that they are working with RonRon."

That day Hakeem's funeral would take place. We all gathered at Aunt Laurie's house dressed like stars. Derrick, Eric, and Rodney were with RonRon in his Hummer. Jermaine, me, Cara and Tera were in Jermaine's Hummer. We formed a long line in front of Aunt Laurie's house and followed the limo she rode in.

There were well over twenty-five cars in a line with their lights on. The police held up traffic to let us pass. I noticed most people pulling over to the side of the road giving respect as we rode by them. Cara and Tera couldn't stop crying, Jermaine and I were silent thinking of our mom.

The funeral took place at a Baptist church. From the entrance we all walked up to Hakeem in a line. I saw people holding Aunt Laurie to keep her balanced because it was her first-time seeing Hakeem since the accident.

I held Cara's hand. She started squeezing hard once we walked up to view Hakeem. RonRon held Tera's hand too. Cara was pretty strong while she rubbed his hand for the last time. I removed my platinum necklace and placed it in his casket. My eyes started to get teary. We walked past Aunt Laurie I stopped to give her a hug.

My crew and I sat in the back of the church. The preacher had some moving words to say. Hopefully, he reached someone in the church because I tuned him out.

Cara and Tera got out of the Hummer at the graveyard to see Hakeem for the last time and to say their final goodbyes. It was a sad day.

The next day, two hours before the show, everyone was in San Diego at the dome. Cara, Tera and Anthony left early to meet up with Jermaine and the rest of them.

"You and I is going to roll up there solo, 50ty. I just want us to chill for a bit," RonRon said. He took off his shirt and bulletproof vest and put on his jewelry, T-shirt, and Ralph Lauren shirt over it. He placed his vest on the bed.

"What are you thinking about RonRon? Put on your vest, dawg," I said.

"Nah, pimp. This is me, homey. I'm not hiding anymore. For what? My enemies are useless to me, 50ty. Fuck'em," he said. I didn't respond because when he acted that way, everything went in one ear and out the other.

We left the room and went to grab some green to smoke then we headed to the concert.

As we rode, we listened to RonRon's CD and smoked.

"50ty, I just want to let you know that I really appreciate everything you done for me, homey. For real, dawg. You turned us into made niggas, man, self-made millionaires. It's hard to run up on real niggas like you, dawg. You are a real motherfucker. That's why we are quick to ride with you and for you," he said, all sensitive and shit.

"You're the one that made it this far for both of us, pimp. I want to thank you for staying loyal to the game," I replied.

The stripped was packed. We scrolled the city since we were an hour early. We stopped at a fast-food joint to get something to eat. For some reason, RonRon was on this bold level shit.

"Let's eat on the outside at the table, 50ty and get all the attention," he said.

"What? Are you crazy, RonRon? That's taking it too far there," I warned.

"For the first time, man, I want to do something fun and exciting. You need to relax and have fun nigga. We will enjoy this day, believe me. Nigga come on," he said as he got out the Hummer.

The place was crowded. I grabbed my .45 and placed it in my holster.

"Oh my God! There's RonRon!" somebody screamed. They all went crazy and started rushing him. I pushed him behind me.

"Y'all calm the fuck down," I said.

"Chill 50ty. Relax man. You're acting like a staff member," he laughed. "They're only human. They got love for me." I just stared at him and shook my head.

"Can y'all just back up and let us order our food?" I asked the crowd. They complied. We ordered our food and ate outside at the table with the crowd of peoples. Everything was cool after they'd calmed down.

RonRon signed autographs as soon as he sat down, one after another. They had much love for RonRon. I even felt like a fan of his.

After all that was over, we finally got ready to go back to the dome. When we pulled up to a stop sign, RonRon told me to stop. He jumped out of the Hummer and ran up to a bus stop where two females were sitting waiting on their bus. When they saw it was RonRon they started screaming and jumping up and down, hugging him. He talked to them for a while. I got out of the Hummer and stood beside the truck and watched him. I really felt like a staff member since he'd mentioned it. I laughed.

I looked up the block and spotted a Volvo passing by. They stopped half-way up the road. A dude got out of the Volvo. It pulled up a little and stopped again. The dude that got out of the car made it look like he was going to the house that he'd been dropped off in front of, but he continued walking past the house. He walked toward RonRon while his back was turned.

As the guy got close to RonRon I started heading toward him too. The dude already had his gun in his hand, but I hadn't noticed it until it was too late. My eyes widened once I spotted the gun. I yelled as loud as I could.

"RonRon!!!" When he looked at me and turned around, the guy open fire before I could pull out my own gun. He shot at RonRon a few times before I start shooting at him. He ran toward the Volvo but I was right behind him still shooting. He shot back twice, missing. My last shot hit him in the back, dropping him. I reload my clip instantly and started shooting at the Volvo. It sped off, leaving the area.

I walked up to the wounded guy and rolled him over onto his back.

"I'll give you a chance to live. Who sent you?" I asked him.

"Hott Rodd," he screamed, in pain.

"Who is that? One of Sweetman boys?" I asked?

"Yeah," he cried. I stood up and shot him twice in the head.

In silence, I looked back and saw RonRon lying in a puddle of blood. I start running toward him when I spotted the police turning onto the block. Instead of going to RonRon, I ran off into the darkness.

Breathing hard, chest hurting because of the pounding in my heart, nose bleeding, I couldn't control myself. I was thinking about Bosco. I'd placed RonRon in the same spot. I got scared. I kneeled down in the ally and started mumbling and crying, out of control. I tried not to make any noise. I kept throwing up while I heard sirens in the distance.

I was lost in thought and didn't know my next move. My body was stiff. There was a dog barking like hell in the yard where I'd stopped. The owner came to the back door and saw me there in tears.

"Who are you?" he asked. I raised my finger indicating that he should give me a second to calm down and I would leave. "Are you crying, son?" he asked walking outside and up to me. "Son, by any chance, do I need to call the police or ambulance for you?" he inquired. I wanted to talk so bad, but nothing would come out. He helped me to my feet. "Come in the house, son. Everything will be okay."

When I finally found my voice, I thanked him. "Just let me pull myself together and I'll leave," I told him. I pulled out ten grands in stacks of hundred and placed them on the table.

"Son, I don't need no blood money in my house," he said fearfully.

"It's not blood money, sir. I'm legit." I showed him my manager's I.D.

I knew my time was up. I just needed to catch my breath and pull myself together. The old man never asked me what was wrong because he didn't want to get involved. I had him drop me off at the nearest hospital in San Diego. I found out that RonRon was there, too.

I expected the clerk to tell me that RonRon was dead, but she said he was in critical condition. The doctor said that he might not live through the night.

I sat in the lobby in San Diego waiting for anybody to come get me. Instead of the police arriving, ten guys walked through the double doors of the lobby. One was in a wheelchair. It was Blitty, RonRon's uncle. He looked at me and rolled right past to the room RonRon was in.

The concert was over. I didn't have a cell phone and I left RonRon's cell phone in the truck. Tera would be devastated. Tears continued to drop from my eyes.

I waited for whatever was going to happen to just happen so I could have the pain taken away from me.

I thought about Cara and quickly got up and left the hospital. I didn't have it in me to tell Tera what happened. I caught a cab to Los Angeles. I had the cab driver drop me off at Aunt Laurie's house. The two elders were sitting on the porch as usual.

"Hey there son. How have you been?" one of them asked. I smiled, but the happiness wasn't there and they knew it.

"I know how you feel, son. You just need to stay strong and continue on," the other said. I looked at them strangely.

"Do you know what happened?" I asked.

"Son, that boy is famous around here. Everybody knows what happened. Shit, it's all over the news from San Diego to the news on the street."

That's how Blitty must have found out. I got up to leave but Aunt Laurie came to the door and stopped me.

"Come in, baby," she said, holding the door open. I turned around and went inside.

"This has been going on for many, many years. Before you were even thought of. Before my time. Don't go around feeling down, baby, because this world is hell on earth. All of this is in Revelations. Time is running out," she said.

The tears dropped from my eyes and I couldn't stop them. She got up, walked over to me and gave me a hug. We both cried together.

"I love you like family so don't think that you are alone, baby," she said.

I got up.

"I love you too, Auntie," I said. She smiled and I smiled back. She walked me to the door.

"I'm going to go back to the hospital where everybody is. Y'all take care of Auntie," I told the elders after shaking their hands.

They stared behind me as I left on foot. For some reason, they must have known that I wasn't ever going to return.

I got a cab from the corner store and had him take me back to San Diego Hospital. I didn't say one word to the cab driver, but I did over pay him more than the necessary fare.

I stood at the entrance of the hospital and looked around me. It would be for the last time as a free man.

RonRon must have had the same feeling because he decided not to wear his vest and he was acting really strange. Shit didn't last forever and it wasn't hard to see that.

When I made it to the second floor, the elevator opened. Cara was standing there in tears. Rodney and Jermaine were there also. I got off the elevator and gave Cara a hug.

"Be strong for me and the baby," she told me. I looked at her, feeling so much guilt.

"I'm sorry."

I gave Jermaine a one-armed hug because he'd known RonRon just as long as I had. I walked passed them into RonRon's room to see him, probably for the last time. When I looked at him lying there with tubes running from his mouth, I felt weak again.

"If anybody could be blamed for this, I wonder who it could be?" Blitty said, rolling into the room.

I turned around and stared into Blitty eyes. "Well, you weren't around to prevent this from happening," I said in sorrow.

"True, true, but you were. We know who a leader is and who should have been a follower," he replied.

I felt Blitty because I should have made RonRon put on that vest. I lead them all down the wrong path. I looked at Tera who was on the other side of RonRon holding his hand.

"The reason why you're still living is because it seems as if I'm the only one blaming you," Blitty said.

I looked back at Blitty. "Well you're right. I shouldn't be breathing, Blitty, because I do take full responsibility for all my people's actions," I replied.

Jermaine walked into the room after hearing that. So, did Derrick, Rodney and Eric.

"Blitty, you've known Terrill and me since we were young and that's my brother, man. It's just me and him now. He created a family and RonRon was a part of our family too," Jermaine said.

"And we will die for both of them," Derrick responded.

"Okay. That's all good to know. Y'all soldiers. But understand this: aint nobody scared. Believe that. Don't go around thinking you can defeat the world because you are in for a rude awakening, "Blitty said, bitterly.

I walked out of the room and into the hallway. Blitty followed me.

"I forgive you, 50ty. But everybody has their set time. The game doesn't last forever, playa. I just want to know who did this?" he asked.

I gave him all the information on Hott Rodd and his clique. But, like Aunt Laurie said, it wouldn't change anything.

Blitty rolled back into the room and Cara came out crying.

"I love you, baby. I will always be there for you," she said. I noticed the police were coming toward us. I rejected the thought of running.

"Baby, I love you too. But do whatever you need to do to stay strong. You know where the cash at in Long Island. Just concentrate on your aunt and Anthony," I told her. She started to cry more and gave me a tight hug.

"Mr. Terrill Holiday, we're here to arrest you for the murder of Thomas Harrell and also other murders that occurred in Atlanta and Los Angeles," an officer informed me.

I stared at my feet, not knowing if RonRon was going to survive or die. I looked back at Cara who was bawling like a baby. I had to see RonRon for the last time.

"I'm not resisting arrest. Just let me say goodbye to my friend," I said, getting choked up. Surprisingly, the officers didn't object. Everybody was silent as I said goodbye.

They handcuff me and walked me out of the hospital. Outside, they had the area surrounded with police. They even had the helicopter out there.

I put my head down while they walked me to the police car.

Jermaine and the rest of them stood at the entrance of the hospital because the police wouldn't let them past. I sat in the car making my mind blank. Two detectives came. One got in the front seat and the other opened the back door of the car.

"Are you the one that did all that killing around here?" the detective in the front seat asked. I didn't answer. "It's okay. You don't have to answer. We will see you back in L.A. I feel sorry for your friend, RonRon. He will be arrested too, if he makes it through this," he said.

They got out of the police cruiser and got into their undercover car and vanished. The officer got into the cruiser and got ready to take me to L.A. I looked at the fellas and waved goodbye. Cara blew me a kiss as we rolled off.

They put me in an empty room with a long table with chairs around it. I was chilly, but not worried about that. RonRon and Cara were on my mind. I'd already cried enough tears for the day. I was stuck. I had to get my mind off money and place it on survival.

The two detectives that were at the hospital entered the cold room.

"Hey Terrill. Nice to see you again," he said standing at the door. I just stared at him.

"So, what happened back there?" he asked politely. I didn't answer him.

"What will it take to hear the truth from you, Terrill?" the other inquired.

I remained quiet and just stared at the ground.

"I'm not going to stress you, young man. I'll leave that for my partner to take care of," he said and walked out of the room.

Those motherfuckers really had to be on some coco puffs or some shit. Did they really think I was going to talk?

I just couldn't stop thinking about my life and about how I screwed it up trying to be a better man. While I was thinking, a Clint Eastwood looking guy walked into the room.

They had my back against the wall, but I wasn't a snitch. They kept me in the room for a long time before the paddy wagon came to hall my ass off to the county jail. It was my first time going to jail and it might be my last time being free.

I had to strip naked in front of two sheriffs, bend over and cough. They checked my mouth for any weapons, like razors, etc. After that I just chilled inside the holding cell until they called my name to go to the back to my bunk. They placed me back in maximum security. H2545 was the I.D. number they told me to remember.

I had plenty of time to call Cara or whoever else, but I didn't want to cause any more pain at that point. I'd just wait until court was over in the morning.

I ignored the inmates and kept to myself. I stayed in my bunk and slept until the next morning. I woke up the next day, realizing that it wasn't a joke. I sat up and waited until they called my number for me to show up in the courtroom.

It was loud as hell on the D-Block. The police were worse than the ones in the street. They were everywhere. They had me place my wrists through the cell so they could shackle my wrists then my feet.

Inside the courtroom, the judge was on a T.V. screen. He denied my bond and denied me being released on R & R, deeming me a threat to society.

Epilogue

Months passed. RonRon was still comatose and in critical condition. They fed him through a tube. I talked to my brother, but I hadn't talked to anybody else and I refused to allow Cara visitation. I told Jermaine to let her know that I was sorry, but I couldn't see anyone until everything died down.

The Crips were really packed in the jail I was in, but I didn't let them get to me even though I got into many fights. It wasn't bad as I thought it would have been in the county, but I still kept a low profile. I refused the lawyers that Cara set up for me because I knew they would have been a waste of money. A lawyer fighting for me was a losing battle.

On my first day of trial, I knew I would have to face Cara. If I could have refused it, I would. But I had no control over that.

My feet were shackled as I entered the courtroom from the side door, escorted by a sheriff. I looked over my shoulder into the rows of people and saw Cara holding a little baby girl. I looked back at the judge.

"Terrill Holiday, please come to the stand." I shuffled up to the podium as best as I could.

"Mr. Holiday, can you place your right hand up? Do you promise to tell the truth, and nothing but the truth?" The judge asked.

"I do." I replied.

They state went over every crime that I'd committed in my life, from the misdemeanors to the felonies.

"Mr. Holiday, why don't you have an attorney present to help you in this case?" the judge asked.

I shrugged my shoulders. "I don't know," I said lowly.

"Are you Terrill Holiday?

"Yes."

"What is the highest-grade level you completed?"

"I graduated."

"So, there for you can read and write and if you had a lawyer, would you be able to understand him? You should be looking into hiring one. If you are found guilty of all these charges, you can face life or be ordered to serve a death sentence. How do you plead?"

"No contest."

"We will set this up for another trial date in three months. Terrill, look into hiring a good lawyer, sir, because your life depends on it."

The judge let me get ten minutes with my family.

"Hey baby," Cara said giving me a hug and a kiss. "This is your daughter, Tori. She is a year and a couple days old." Tears started to form in my eyes when I picked her up. Love flowed through both of our bodies and souls. I could feel that she knew I was her daddy.

I told Cara that I would start accepting her letters and I would write her soon. I told her when she came to visit not to bring Tori. I didn't want to see her while I was in the county because I couldn't touch her.

Cara and Tera were crying. I gave all of them a hug because my time was up.

"We miss you, 50ty." They called behind me.

I turned around in told them to maintain and I missed them too. I walked back into the room to be escorted to my cell.

Back in my cell they gave me all of my letters. I placed them on my bunk and slowly read each one of them. I read the ones Tera wrote telling me about RonRon's condition. I read Cara's from when she was in the hospital having my baby. I read Derrick's letter from Bainbridge. He told me how him, Eric and Rodney still maintained their hustling status. He promised they'd send me money every month so I wouldn't ever need commissary.

I smiled for the first time once I found out that life started to pick up for everybody. That's all I wanted. Jermaine had written to tell me that Anthony got a job with him and they were doing fine.

Cara wrote me damn near every day telling me how much she missed me. She said she was sorry for everything that happened. She felt that if we wouldn't have gone to California none of it would have happened. I responded to her letter and told her that everything was alright. It all started before her time and not to take blame for my actions. I told her to move on and find somebody that would be there for her and my daughter.

Through the last three months before my trail date, I accepted all invitations from her and the rest of the crew. I had a lawyer that Cara hired for me. I talked to him and gave him all the information that I thought he should know. I let him know that Carlos was my main problem.

The day before my court date Cara and Tera came to visit me.

"Carlos is supposed to be at court tomorrow," Tera said.

"Yeah, I already know that," I replied.

"We will be there to support you, baby," Cara said.

We talked for the remaining time I had then I was escorted back into my cell where I went to sleep.

The next day I was back in court with the same judge. I spotted Carlos sitting at the table in front of the jury. We waited until it was our turn. The judge was sentencing people to prison left and right.

"The next case is Terrill Holiday. Please step up to the stand."

As I approached, a man walked up to the judge with a bag and handed it to him. The judge thanked him and the man went back to his seat which was next to Carlos, to testify against me.

"Mr. Holiday, we have proof of all the murders you committed, from St. Petersburg, Florida, to Atlanta, to California. We have other murders that lead to you, as well. We hereby sentence you to life without the possibility of parole."

I was floored. Tom had been right. He hadn't set me up after all. Carlos had eyes in my crew. I looked back at them. Who could it be? Tera was walking out of the courtroom in a hurry. She looked back at me in panic. That look told me all I needed to know.

Damn Tera! Out of everybody in the crew, I should have known. That was Reco's girl and they both knew Carlos really well. She was barely around and now I knew why. She'd set me up.

I looked back at Carlos. He gave me a nasty look and smiled. I clicked before I knew it.

"Fuck you, you snitch ass motherfucker!" I yelled. I tried to charge him, but the sheriff behind me stopped me before I could make a move. They pulled me out of the courtroom. I was cursing Carlos out the entire time until the doors closed.

It was pure luck that Derrick, Rodney and Eric weren't there because Tera snitched them out, too. The police were looking for them. They didn't have anything on Jermaine.

The first chance I got, I called Cara.

"Hey, baby."

"Cara, where is Tera?" I asked her.

"I don't know. I tried calling her. I haven't seen her since your court date," she answered.

I told her how Tera snitched me out. Cara couldn't believe what I was telling her. I told her to spread the news to my brother and the rest of the crew.

Everything went downhill from that point forward. I fought for everybody. Tera hadn't been around to see any of the drama that had taken place so she couldn't say who killed who. She only went by what RonRon told her and he wasn't there to testify. She just basically made a fool out of herself.

Tera married RonRon to get close to me. She took pictures of everything that we had, from the guns, to the drugs, to the money. Cara lost the house and everything in it. I filed for a divorce so she could move on with her life and not hang on to me.

Two weeks after they sent me to prison, RonRon, my ace, my partner in crime, my boy, died from his injuries. Everybody except for Derrick, Rodney, Eric and Tera attended his funeral.

Loyalty was only a word to most. Carlos got a lesser sentence for turning in me and my clique. I was already prepared to face everything. I planned to take the heat off my homeboys and ride alone. They knew that I couldn't have committed all those murders alone, so I said RonRon was the other person with me. Somehow, I felt that RonRon would approve.

When the attention got off them, Derrick, Eric, and Rodney would be on a manhunt for Tera. Hadn't she heard that "Snitches get stitches?" Somebody better tells her.

The End

CHARATER LIST

All the names appear are not made up of real peoples.

Terrill the protagonist of Fast Cash, He made a-way for the crew to live a wonderful but powerful life. He had chosen only a hand few peoples to follow him down his road of luxury

Jermaine the brother of Terrill Jermaine unlike his brother didn't believe in hustling, he kept a job and knew that his brother will always need him so he sticks by his side through the entire ride.

RonRon Was the first to make Terrill a million-dollar man. RonRon stuck by Terrill side to not only help him come up but to also protect him from the surrounding world of haters. Every hustler needs a RonRon in the crew, a soldier to the finish with loyalty and respect for the game.

Derrick Terrill cousin. Bosco strengthen the crew size with a few helpers from his crew in Bainbridge, Eric and Rodney. They became Terrill dealers and soulja's ready for what every Derrick made way.

Bosco A friend of the family who been locked up for a while inspires Terrill about a strong come up to get out the game and becoming the man to the small timers.

Rodney Eric brother and Derrick partner. Rodney known Derrick for a while now and whatever Derrick got into, Rodney always were involved.

Eric Rodney brother and Derrick partner. Eric got to become Terrill partner as well as Rodney in a matter of no time they took Terrill in as family too and made him very important.

Reco Derrick supplier, who met Terrill and both conduct business together with Carlos in Atlanta Gia. The product Terrill was needing Reco didn't have enough to support him so the two-tag team to holla at Los when both were ready to cop.

Carlos Atlanta City police officer, Los been dealing drugs for years to Reco. With trust Los let Terrill inside his organization because of the trust he has for Reco so finally he became Terrill supplier.

Cara One of Derrick, Rodney and Eric friends introduce to Terrill and became his girlfriend in a matter of time. Cara sticks be Terrill side stronger than his home boys, gain Terrill trust and soul. The two made a perfect match.

Tera Cara best friend and also Derrick, Rodney and Eric friend. At one time Reco's girlfriend got introduce to RonRon and they hooked up. She felt RonRon 100% and stick by his side through their come up.

G-Rod Is the person who made Terrill who he was and what he became. "Rich".

Sasha G-Rod mom.

Aunt Laurie Cara auntie in California she kept Terrill focus and surviving the heat of Cali streets. Laurie introduce them to her Landlord and the found a place in Cali to live.

Ronnie Cara cousin who were shot in the leg at a corner store and lost both of leg.

Anthony Cara cousin who refuse to let the ones who shot Ronnie get away. Anthony became good friends with the crew and gain more respect from them.

Hakeem Cara and Anthony younger cousin. He and Anthony stay hanging out together even though he smokes his weed he keeps it from Cara and his Aunt Laurie. Hakeem also gain the respect from the crew.

Tom Terrill lawyer that help him find out why Jermaine and Derrick was in jail back in Bainbridge GA.

Tom and Frank Good friends of Laurite sit and talk on her porch everyday all-day nothing changes with these two old Koon's. When Terrill got introduce to them, they became his friends.

DHC New York local rappers that Terrill found near his studio and let them inside to make good music to promote his work more. DHC and RonRon became good friends, and they made music together.

Ashley and Jasmine Two girls Terrill met at the club during the police search in California.

Physical Madness a local rapper in the NYC area that beef worth RonRon and DHC.

Sweetman Became enemies of Terrill and his gain in L.A. And he is the reason of the shooting of Ronnie.

Blitty is the cousin of RonRon and a big-time gangster in St. Petersburg Fla.

Kenny Physical Madness' DJ and also DHC.

Oriel Laurie and Terrill landlord in L.A.

Success local New York singers and the first to get sign by Terrill.

www.ingramcontent.com/pod-product-compliance
Lightning Source LLC
Chambersburg PA
CBHW051209170526
45166CB00005B/1823